The Ultimate Finance Book

Roger Mason

The Teach Yourself series has been trusted around the world for over 75 years. This book is designed to help people at all levels and around the world to further their careers. Learn, from one book, what the experts learn in a lifetime.

Roger Mason is a Chartered Certified Accountant and has many years' practical experience as a Financial Director. He now lectures on financial and business topics. In addition, he has edited a financial publication and written many books.

The Ultimate Finance Book

Master Profit Statements, Understand Bookkeeping and Accounting, Prepare Budgets and Forecasts

Roger Mason

Teach Yourself®

First published in Great Britain in 2015 by Hodder & Stoughton. An Hachette UK company.

First published in US in 2015 by The McGraw-Hill Companies, Inc.

This edition published in 2018 by John Murray Learning.

Copyright © Roger Mason 2015, 2018

Based on original material from *Finance for Non-Financial Managers In A Week; Bookkeeping and Accounting In A Week; Understanding and Interpreting Accounts In A Week; Successful Budgeting and Forecasting In A Week.*

Previously published as *Accounting & Finance in 4 Weeks*

Database right Hodder & Stoughton (makers)

The *Teach Yourself* name is a registered trademark of Hachette UK.

British Library Cataloguing in Publication Data: a catalogue record for this title is available from the British Library.

Library of Congress Catalog Card Number: on file.

Paperback: 978 1 473 68381 5

eBook: 978 1 473 68382 2

Audiobook: 978 1 473 68384 6

1

Typeset by Cenveo® Publisher Services.

Printed and bound in Great Britain by CPI Group (UK) Ltd., Croydon, CRO 4YY.

John Murray Learning policy is to use papers that are natural, renewable and recyclable products and made from wood grown in sustainable forests. The logging and manufacturing processes are expected to conform to the environmental regulations of the country of origin.

Carmelite House
50 Victoria Embankment
London EC4Y 0DZ

www.hodder.co.uk

Also available
in ebook

Contents

PART 1

Your Finance for Non-Financial Managers Masterclass

Introduction

Depending on how far you are willing to stretch the definition, there are well over two million non-financial managers in the UK, with considerably more in other countries. Many of them would like to know more about finance, and the knowledge would help them do their jobs and progress in their careers.

A basic understanding of finance is very relevant to our personal lives. It is also important to virtually all managers and supervisors, both junior and senior. This has always been so and its significance has considerably increased in recent years.

Some managers have been financially trained but many more wish to increase their level of understanding. Doing so will enable them to become more effective and improve their scope for development and promotion.

CHAPTER 1

An introduction to the profit statement

Nearly all private sector businesses are conducted in the hope of making a profit, though of course not all succeed in doing so. Profits and losses, which perhaps should be called surpluses and deficits, are also important to large parts of the public sector and to such bodies as charities and membership organizations. There is of course much more to it, but many managers would say that the point of bookkeeping and accounting is to find out the amount of the profit or loss.

The Profit Statement is important and an introduction to it is a very good way of starting this Part. The more advanced published accounts will be studied in Chapter 3, but first we will study an internal document produced for the managers.

We will work through:

- a simple example
- a trading company
- a manufacturing company
- some further concepts explained
- preparing a full example.

A simple example

The heading 'Profit Statement' may be optimistic because it implies that a profit has been made. In some cases it would be more appropriate to call it a Loss Statement.

Profit Statement is the name often given to an internal document setting out the trading activity and results. It is sometimes called the Profit and Loss Account or Income Statement and these are the titles used in the more formal published accounts.

Understanding the principles of the Profit Statement is the first step towards using it to improve future performance. This is covered later in this Part but as a first step we will consider a simple example.

Julia Brown writes a book. Her agreement does not provide for royalties, just a fee of £5,000 payable on delivery of the manuscript to the publisher. The costs of the enterprise are small and she pays them in cash as she goes. After receipt of the £5,000 her Profit Statement may well look like the following:

	£	£
Income		5,000
Less Costs:		
Typing costs	600	
Stationery	100	
Travel	200	
Postage	30	
Telephone	40	
Miscellaneous	120	
		1,090
Net Profit before Tax		3,910

The profit (or loss) is the difference between money received and all the money paid out. Julia Brown may need the Profit Statement for her bank and for Her Majesty's Revenue and Customs (HMRC). She may use the information herself. For example, if she has spent 391 hours working on the book her time has been rewarded at the rate of £10 per hour.

A trading company

Numerous very small businesses do prepare simple Profit Statements in the manner of the previous example. However, there is another step when things are bought and sold.

It is essential that the costs shown in the Profit Statement relate only to goods sold during the period. All Profit Statements cover a defined period with a specified starting date and a specified closing date. For published accounts this period is often a year but for internal documents it can be whatever period is considered most useful.

Many businesses produce quarterly Profit Statements, but it may be desirable to produce them monthly or even weekly. Some intensively managed retailers, such as Tesco and Asda, produce key profit information on a daily basis. They withdraw items and change displays according to the results shown.

A distorted result will be given if costs include articles purchased (and paid for) but still in stock at the end of the period. This is overcome by counting stock at the beginning and end of the period. The cost of sales is calculated by adding purchases to the opening stock, then subtracting the closing stock.

If there has been any theft or other form of stock shrinkage, the cost of sales will be increased accordingly.

Sometimes the calculation as far as Gross Profit is shown in a separate Trading Account. However, the following simple example shows everything in one Profit Statement.

A Borough Council Leisure Centre operates a bar and prepares monthly Profit Statements. Sales in the month of July were £30,000 and purchases in the same month were £20,000.

Stock of food and drink at 30 June was £10,000 and at 31 July it was £9,000. Wages were £4,000, insurance was £1,500, and the total of all other overheads was £3,000.

The Profit Statement for July was as follows:

	£	£
Sales		30,000
Stock at 30 June	10,000	
Purchases	20,000	
	30,000	
Less stock at 31 July	9,000	
		21,000
Gross Profit		9,000
Less Overheads:		
Wages	4,000	
Insurance	1,500	
All other	3,000	
		8,500
Net Profit		500

A manufacturing company

It is only a small step to set out the Profit Statement of a manufacturing company. It is essential that the cost of manufacturing must exactly relate to the goods sold. The cost of these goods, no more and no less, must be brought into the Profit Statement.

Probably, stocktakes will be necessary at the beginning and end of the period. However, according to circumstances, this may not be necessary. If internal controls are good a calculated stock figure may sometimes be used, though the results are never quite so accurate or dependable. It is most likely to be done when the results are produced very quickly.

The following example shows the principles. Sometimes the manufacturing costs are shown in a separate Manufacturing Account but in this straightforward example they are included in the Profit Statement.

Chiltern Manufacturing Company Ltd manufactures and sells household goods. Sales in the year to 31 December 2017 were

£750,000. Purchases of raw materials and components in the year were £300,000. Stock at 31 December 2016 was £280,000 and at 31 December 2017 it was £320,000.

Wages of production staff were £200,000, power costs were £60,000 and other production costs were £80,000. Salaries of salesmen, administration staff and management totalled £70,000 and other overheads totalled £85,000.

The Profit Statement for the year to 31 December 2017 is as follows:

	£	£
Sales		750,000
Stock at 31.12.16	280,000	
Purchases	300,000	
	580,000	
Less stock at 31.12.17	320,000	
	260,000	
Production wages	200,000	
Power costs	60,000	
Other production costs	80,000	
Cost of Manufacturing		600,000
		150,000
Less Overheads:		
Salaries	70,000	
Other overheads	85,000	
		155,000
Net Loss before Tax		(5,000)

(Note that the brackets indicate a minus figure.)

Key points so far

- There are definite starting and finishing dates.
- Total Sales appears at the top.
- Profit or Loss appears at the bottom.
- Only expenditure on goods actually sold is included.

Some further concepts explained

All the examples so far have been extremely simple but unfortunately real life is often more complicated. It is necessary to be familiar with certain further principles that are likely to be incorporated into many Profit Statements.

Accruals (costs not yet entered)

Examples so far have assumed that all costs are paid out as they are incurred, but this is unrealistic. Invoices are submitted after the event and some will not have been entered into the books when they are closed off.

This problem is overcome by adding in an allowance for these costs. The uninvoiced costs are called accruals.

Let us take as an example a company whose electricity bill is around £18,000 per quarter. Let us further assume that accounts are made up to 31 December and that the last electricity bill was up to 30 November. The accountant will accrue £6,000 for electricity used but not billed.

If electricity invoices in the period total £60,000 the added £6,000 will result in £66,000 being shown in the Profit Statement.

Prepayments (costs entered in advance)

A prepayment is the exact opposite of an accrual. Costs may have been entered into the books for items where the benefit has not yet been received. An example is an invoice for production materials delivered after stocktaking.

Consider an insurance premium of £12,000 paid on 1 December for 12 months' cover in advance. If the Profit Statement is made up to 31 December the costs will have been overstated by $\frac{11}{12}$ x £12,000 = £11,000. The accountant will reduce the costs accordingly. These reductions are called prepayments.

Bad debt reserves and sales ledger reserves

Many businesses sell on credit, and at the end of the period of the Profit Statement money will be owed by customers.

14

Unfortunately not all of this money will necessarily be received. Among the possible reasons are:

- bad debts
- an agreement that customers may deduct a settlement discount if payment is made by a certain date
- the customers may claim that there were shortages, or that they received faulty goods; perhaps goods were supplied on a sale-or-return basis.

The prudent accountant will make reserves to cover these eventualities, either a bad debt reserve or sales ledger reserve. Sales (and profit) will be reduced by an appropriate amount.

Time will tell whether the reserves have been fixed at a level that was too high, too low, or just right. If the reserves were too cautious there will be an extra profit to bring into a later Profit Statement. If the reserves were not cautious enough there will be a further cost (and loss) to bring into a later Profit Statement.

Depreciation

Fixed assets are those that will have a useful and productive life longer than the period of the Profit Statement. Examples are factory machinery, computers, motor vehicles and so on.

It would obviously be wrong to charge all the costs of fixed assets to the Profit Statement in the year of purchase. The problem is overcome by charging only a proportion in each year of the expected useful life of the asset.

There are different methods of doing this calculation but the simplest, and most common, is the straight-line method. For example, let us consider an item of equipment costing £300,000 with an expected useful life of five years. The Profit Statement for each year would be charged with £60,000.

This is one of many examples of how profit accounting may differ from the equivalent position in cash. It is quite possible to be profitable and still run out of cash. This will be examined later.

Prudence and the matching of costs to income

Earlier it was explained that costs must be fairly matched to sales. This is so that the costs of the goods actually sold, and only those costs, are brought into the Profit Statement. This is very important, and sometimes very difficult to achieve.

Consider a major building project lasting four years and for which the contractor will be paid £60,000,000. Costs over the four years are expected to be £55,000,000 and the anticipated profit is £5,000,000. Almost certainly the contractor will receive various stage payments over the four years.

This poses a multitude of accounting problems and there is more than one accounting treatment. The aim must be to bring in both revenue and costs strictly as they are earned and incurred. Accounting standards provide firm rules for the published accounts.

The full £60,000,000 will not be credited until the work is complete. In fact there will probably be a retention and it will be necessary to make a reserve for retention work. The final cost and profit may not be known for some years.

Conventions of prudent accounting should ensure that profits are only recognized when they have clearly been earned. Losses on the other hand should be recognized as soon as they can be realistically foreseen. Failure to act on this convention has led to scandals and nasty surprises for investors, the collapse of Enron being just one example.

Before leaving this section, tick off the following boxes to confirm that you understand the principles.

- Accruals are costs incurred, but not yet in the books. ❑
- Prepayments are costs in the books, but not yet incurred. ❑
- Profit is reduced by expected bad debts. ❑
- Depreciation is a book entry to reduce the value of fixed assets. ❑
- Profit accounting may differ from cash accounting. ❑
- Profit Statements should be prudent. ❑
- Costs must be matched to income. ❑

Preparing a full example

Here is a slightly more advanced example incorporating the points covered so far.

J. T. Perkins and Son Ltd manufactures and sells pottery. Sales in the year to 31 December 2015 were £800,000. At 31 December 2015 the company expects to issue a credit note for £10,000 for faulty goods that have been delivered. It also believes that £30,000 owing to it will turn out to be a total bad debt. No such expectations existed at 31 December 2014.

Invoices received for parts and raw materials delivered during the year totalled £240,000, but a £20,000 invoice is awaited for a delivery received on 22 December.

Stock at 31 December 2014 was £308,000. Stock at 31 December 2015 was £302,000.

Manufacturing wages were £150,000 and other manufacturing costs were £60,000. Plant and machinery used for manufacturing originally cost £900,000 and is being depreciated at the rate of 10 per cent per year.

Overheads paid have been:

Salaries	*£80,000*
Rent	*£70,000*
Insurance	*£60,000*
Other	*£50,000*

Insurance includes a premium of £7,000 for a year in advance paid on 31 December 2015.

J. T. Perkins and Son Ltd

Profit Statement for the year to 31 December 2015

	£	£
Sales		790,000
Stock at 31.12.14	308,000	
Add purchases	260,000	
	568,000	
Less stock at 31.12.15	302,000	
	266,000	
Wages	150,000	
Depreciation of plant and machinery	90,000	
Other manufacturing costs	60,000	
Cost of Sales		566,000
Gross Profit		224,000
Less Overheads:		
Salaries	80,000	
Rent	70,000	
Insurance	53,000	
Other	50,000	
Reserve for bad debts	30,000	
		283,000
Net Loss before Tax		(59,000)

Summary

In this chapter we have been introduced to the basic principles of the following:

- Simple Profit Statements
- Trading companies
- Manufacturing companies
- Accruals and prepayments
- Bad debt reserves and sales ledger reserves
- Depreciation
- Prudence and the matching of costs to income
- An example illustrating most of the principles

Next, we will take a look at Balance Sheets.

Fact-check (answers at the back)

1. To what is the term 'Profit Statement' given?
   a) A published Profit and Loss Account ❏
   b) An internal document setting out the trading activity and results ❏
   c) A statement for the tax authorities ❏
   d) A statement for the shareholders ❏

2. In a Profit Statement, where is the figure for income usually placed?
   a) At the top ❏
   b) At the bottom ❏
   c) On the left ❏
   d) On the right ❏

3. In a Profit Statement of a trading company, to what must the figure for Cost of Sales relate?
   a) Goods stored in the period ❏
   b) Goods purchased in the period ❏
   c) Goods paid for in the period ❏
   d) Goods sold in the period ❏

4. If goods for sale are stolen, how will the Cost of Sales in the Profit Statement be affected?
   a) It will increase ❏
   b) It will decrease ❏
   c) It will not be affected ❏
   d) It will be estimated ❏

5. Which stock figures appear in the Profit Statement of a manufacturing company?
   a) None ❏
   b) Figures for the beginning and end of the period ❏
   c) The figure for the beginning of the period ❏
   d) The figure for the end of the period ❏

6. The telephone bill is usually about £3,000 per quarter. The last invoice received was for the quarter to 31 May. What should be the accrual for the three months to 30 June?
   a) £3,000 ❏
   b) Nothing ❏
   c) £1,000 ❏
   d) £2,000 ❏

7. On 29 December rent of £6,000 was paid in advance for the quarter to the following 31 March. What should be the prepayment for the three months to 31 December?
   a) Nothing ❏
   b) £6,000 ❏
   c) £1,000 ❏
   d) £3,000 ❏

8. The Profit Statement for the month of December included a bad debt reserve of £10,000 in respect of money owed by Smith Ltd. On 17 January Smith Ltd paid in full. What is the effect on the Profit Statement for January?

a) There is no effect ❑
b) A contribution to profit of £5,000 ❑
c) A contribution to profit of £20,000 ❑
d) A contribution to profit of £10,000 ❑

9. A company buys a car for £40,000 and using the straight-line method depreciates it over four years. What is the depreciation charge in the Profit Statement in the second year?

a) £40,000 ❑
b) Nothing ❑
c) £10,000 ❑
d) The square root of £40,000 ❑

10. Which of the following should be reflected in a Profit Statement?

a) Prudence ❑
b) Optimism ❑
c) Pessimism ❑
d) Happiness ❑

CHAPTER 2

An introduction to the balance sheet

The main constituents of a set of accounts are the Profit and Loss Account and the Balance Sheet, which in the published accounts may be called the Statement of Financial Position. The Balance Sheet is extremely important and fulfils a completely different function from the Profit Statement. If someone wants answers to questions such as 'What are the assets?' or 'Is the Company safe?' it is a very good place to start.

A Balance Sheet gives details of the assets and liabilities of the business, and this detailed information is often very valuable to the users of accounts. It also reveals the 'net worth' of the business, though perhaps it would be more accurate to say that it does so according to sometimes controversial accounting rules. When a business is sold it is rare for the sum realized to be the same as the 'net worth' according to the Balance Sheet.

In this chapter we will study the Balance Sheet and cover:

- what is the Balance Sheet?
- two accounting rules explained
- a simple example
- some further concepts explained
- test your knowledge of Balance Sheets.

What is the Balance Sheet?

The clue is in the name. The Balance Sheet is a listing of all the balances in the accounting system, and what is more it must balance. The debit balances must equal the credit balances, or put another way the assets must equal the liabilities. If they do not, a mistake has been made.

A freeze-frame picture

Unlike the Profit Statement, the Balance Sheet does not cover a trading period. It is a snapshot of the financial position at a precise moment and the date is always given as part of the heading. It is usually produced to coincide with the last day of the trading period.

To complete the photographic analogy, the Balance Sheet is like a freeze-frame picture of the finances of an enterprise. If the picture were to be taken a day earlier or a day later, different financial details would be revealed.

Format of the Balance Sheet

A long time ago it was the custom to set out the figures side by side. The assets (debit balances) went on the right-hand side and the liabilities (credit balances) went on the left-hand side. The two columns, of course, added up to the same figure.

You will not see a Balance Sheet displayed in this way because Balance Sheets are now shown in a vertical format. The whole thing adds down to the net worth of the business, which is shown at the bottom. There are still two figures which must be the same and which prove that the Balance Sheet balances.

Grouping of figures

Of course not every individual balance is listed in the Balance Sheet. If they were, the Balance Sheet of Marks and Spencer PLC would cover hundreds of pages. For example, a company may have six different bank accounts, all overdrawn by £100,000. The total of all these overdrafts would be shown as just one figure of £600,000.

Two accounting rules explained

In order to improve your understanding of Balance Sheets you must be familiar with the following two fundamental accounting rules.

- For every debit there must be a credit.
- Balance Sheet assets are debit balances and Balance Sheet liabilities are credit balances.

Debit and credit balances

If a moment of levity could be excused, the first rule of double-entry bookkeeping is said to be that debit is nearest the window and credit is nearest the door and I was certainly told this on my first morning as a trainee. It is of course only true if you sit with your left shoulder nearest the glass and in any case computers have probably made the joke obsolete. The real first rule of double-entry bookkeeping is that for every debit there must be a credit. Accountancy students are traditionally told this on their very first day. This means that an accounting entry always involves one account being debited and another account being credited. Scientists sometimes help themselves to remember this by thinking of the law of physics: 'every action has an equal and opposite reaction'.

For example, let us consider what happens when a £20,000 car is purchased. The Motor Vehicles account (which is an asset) is debited with £20,000. The bank account is credited with £20,000. At this stage you might be confused by which entries are debits and which are credits. This is explained in the next section.

Assets and liabilities

Assets in the Balance Sheet are the debit balances in the bookkeeping system. Liabilities in the Balance Sheet are credit balances in the bookkeeping system. This is probably exactly the opposite of what you would expect.

In the Profit Statement, sales and income are the credit balances: costs are the debit balances. The net total of all the balances is the profit or loss.

This one figure goes into the Balance Sheet as a single item. A profit is a credit which is listed with the liabilities. This too is probably exactly the opposite of what you would expect.

The explanation is that the profit belongs to someone outside the business. If the Balance Sheet is for a company, the profit belongs to the shareholders. It may one day be paid to them in the form of a dividend or by return of capital on the winding up of the company.

A simple example

John Brown commences business as a gardener on 1 July 2015, using the name Cotswold Gardeners. On his first day he pays £6,000 capital into the business. He buys a motor van for £5,000 and a motor mower for £500. They are immediately second-hand so he depreciates them by 20 per cent.

By the end of the gardening season on 31 October he has invoiced his customers £7,000 and been paid in full. His costs have been £2,000, of which he has paid £1,700 and still owes £300.

During the four months he has taken £4,000 out of the business for his living expenses.

Look at the following Balance Sheet and, with a pencil, make sure that you understand how each of the figures is calculated. The figure for profit is after deducting £1,100 depreciation. You should particularly notice that:

● The Balance Sheet is headed and dated, and it balances.
● The creditor of £300 is money owing by the business. It is an accrual, which is one of the things that we studied in the previous chapter.
● The business is separate from John Brown's personal affairs. This is why the payment of £4,000 living expenses to John Brown takes money out of the business and affects the Balance Sheet.

John Brown Trading as Cotswold Gardeners
Balance Sheet at 31 October 2015

	£	£
Fixed Assets		
Motor vehicle	4,000	
Motor mower	400	
		4,400
Current Assets		
Bank account	1,800	
Less Current Liabilities		
Creditor	300	
		1,500
		5,900
Capital employed		
Capital paid in at 1/7/15	6,000	
Add profit since 1/7/15	3,900	
	9,900	
Less drawings since 1/7/15	4,000	
		5,900

Some further concepts explained

Balance Sheets that will be audited and published are laid out according to certain rules and we will look at these in Chapter 3. In this chapter, we are concerned with Balance Sheets prepared just for management use. It will be very helpful if you are completely familiar with the following concepts.

Fixed assets and depreciation

Fixed assets are grouped together in the Balance Sheet and one total is given for the net value of all of them. Examples of fixed assets are:
- freehold property
- plant and machinery
- computers
- motor vehicles.

They are assets that will have a value to the business over a long period, usually understood to be any time longer than a year.

They do usually lose their value, either with the passage of time (e.g. a lease), with use (e.g. a piece of machinery that wears out) or due to obsolescence (e.g. computers). Therefore, as we saw in Chapter 1, they are written off over a number of years. Depreciation is a book entry and no cash is involved. The entry is:

- debit depreciation (thus reducing profit)
- credit the asset (thus reducing the value of the asset).

Current assets

Different types of current asset are listed separately in the Balance Sheet with one total being shown for the sum of them all. They are assets with a value available entirely in the short term, usually understood to be a period less than a year.

This is either because they are what the business sells, or because they are money or can quickly be turned into money. Examples of current assets are:

- stock
- money owing by customers (debtors)
- money in the bank
- short-term investments.

Current liabilities

These too are listed separately in the Balance Sheet with one total given for the sum of them all. They are liabilities which the business could be called upon to pay off in the short term, usually within a year. Examples are a bank overdraft and money owing to suppliers (creditors).

Definitions of debtors and creditors

- A debtor is a person owing money to the business (e.g. a customer for goods delivered).
- A creditor is a person to whom the business owes money (e.g. an unpaid electricity bill).

Working capital

This is the difference between current assets and current liabilities. In the simple example given earlier it is £1,500.

It is extremely important, as we will see later. A business without sufficient working capital cannot pay its debts as they fall due. In this situation it might have to stop trading, even if it is profitable.

Possible alternatives might include raising more capital, taking out a long-term loan, or selling some fixed assets.

Prudent reserves

When something happens that causes an asset to lose value, it is written off. For example, if some stock is stolen, the value of stock in the Balance Sheet is reduced.

The same thing must happen if a prudent view is that an asset has lost some of its value. This happens, for example, if some of the stock is obsolete and unlikely to sell for full value. Normally the Balance Sheet will just show the reduced value, which will be explained with notes.

The creation of a stock reserve reduces the profit. If it is subsequently found that the reserve was not necessary, the asset is restored to its full value and the profit is correspondingly increased in a later period.

It is often necessary to create a bad debt reserve to cover money that may not be collectable from customers.

Test your knowledge of Balance Sheets

A Balance Sheet for Patel Brothers is given below. For the sake of brevity, taxation and the explanatory notes have been omitted.

Now test your knowledge of Balance Sheets by answering the following questions. The answers are given at the end of this chapter, immediately before the end-of-chapter Fact-check.

1 Is the capital employed of £448,000 an asset or a liability?
2 Suggest two possible additional types of current asset.
3 What is the working capital?

4 What would the working capital be if stock valued at £10,000 was sold for £18,000 (payable after 30 days) and if an extra piece of machinery was purchased for £30,000?

5 Assume that a customer had paid a debt of £3,000 written off as bad at 31 October 2015.

   a What would the profit for the year have been?

   b What would Trade Debtors at 31 October 2015 be?

Patel Brothers
Balance Sheet at 31 October 2015

	£	£
Fixed Assets		
Freehold premises	200,000	
Fixtures and fittings	30,000	
Plant and machinery	50,000	
		280,000
Current Assets		
Stock	130,000	
Trade debtors	190,000	
Other debtors	16,000	
	336,000	
Less Current Liabilities		
Trade creditors	70,000	
Bank overdraft	48,000	
	118,000	
		218,000
Bank Loan repayable on 31/12/18		(50,000)
		448,000
Capital employed		
Capital at 31/10/14	350,000	
Add profit for year	300,000	
	650,000	
Less drawings for year	202,000	
		448,000

Summary

In this chapter we have been introduced to the basic principles of the following:

- What is the Balance Sheet?
- Format of the Balance Sheet
- Elementary rules of double-entry bookkeeping
- An example of a simple Balance Sheet
- Fixed assets and depreciation
- Current assets and current liabilities
- Debtors and creditors
- Working capital
- Prudent reserves

Finally, we have examined another Balance Sheet and tested our understanding of it.

Next, we will try to understand published accounts.

Test your knowledge of Balance Sheets – Answers

1. Liability
2. Short-term investments, bank accounts, cash
3. £218,000
4. £196,000
5.
   a) £303,000
   b) £190,000 (no change)

Fact-check (answers at the back)

1. Which words complete the following: 'The total of the debit balances must equal'?
   a) the total of the assets ❑
   b) the total of the liabilities ❑
   c) the total of the credit balances ❑
   d) the income ❑

2. The figures in the Balance Sheet reflect the position at which point in the trading period?
   a) The beginning ❑
   b) The end ❑
   c) The average ❑
   d) One week before the end ❑

3. What is not shown in a Balance Sheet?
   a) Net worth of the business ❑
   b) Fixed assets ❑
   c) Current liabilities ❑
   d) Salaries ❑

4. What are Balance Sheet liabilities? ❑
   a) Certain credit balances ❑
   b) Certain debit balances ❑
   c) Loss for the period ❑
   d) Overheads ❑

5. Where in the Balance Sheet is a bank overdraft shown?
   a) Fixed assets ❑
   b) Current assets ❑
   c) Current liabilities ❑
   d) Capital employed ❑

6. Plant and machinery cost £400,000 and depreciation to date has been £100,000. What will be shown in the Balance Sheet?
   a) £300,000 in the fixed assets ❑
   b) £300,000 in the current assets ❑
   c) £400,000 in the fixed assets ❑
   d) £100,000 in the current liabilities ❑

7. What is the period during which an asset can reasonably be expected to be turned into cash in order for it to be classed as a current asset?
   a) One month ❑
   b) Six months ❑
   c) One year ❑
   d) Two years ❑

8. What is a creditor?
   a) A director ❑
   b) A person or business to whom the business owes money ❑
   c) A person or business who owes money to the business ❑
   d) An employee who behaves in a creditable way ❑

9. What is working capital?
   a) The difference between all the assets and all the liabilities ❑
   b) All the assets ❑
   c) The employees ❑
   d) The difference between current assets and current liabilities ❑

33

10. What is the effect of a stock reserve?

a) It reduces the profit ❏
b) It increases the profit ❏
c) It increases the current liabilities ❏
d) It reduces the fixed assets ❏

CHAPTER 3

Understanding published accounts

In this chapter, we will be studying published accounts and it will be helpful if you obtain a set of accounts. The accounts will be particularly useful if they are for a company well known to you, such as your employer. Advice on how to get hold of published accounts is given in the first section of this chapter.

A study of published accounts cannot help but be interesting and useful. One of the reasons is that it will help you understand your investments and help you decide whether to buy or sell. You may think that you do not have investments but you very probably do, perhaps through the medium of a pension fund or a share-based ISA. Another possible reason is to help judge the security of your employer or prospective employer. Published accounts, of course, have many other uses and, short of fraud, much information must be disclosed and cannot be hidden.

This chapter's programme is perhaps the most demanding. It looks at:

- availability of published accounts
- what is included
- the Profit and Loss Account and Balance Sheet
- the remainder of the Annual Report and Accounts.

Availability of published accounts

Accounts are published for one or both of the following reasons:

- because it is required by law
- as a public relations exercise.

All but a tiny number of registered UK companies are required by law to produce accounts annually, although, subject to strict limits the period can be changed. In many cases an audit is required. A private company must file accounts at Companies House within nine months of the balance sheet date and a public company must do so within six months of the balance sheet date. An extension of the filing period may be allowed in rare and exceptional cases. The law and accounting standards stipulate the minimum content and standard of the accounts.

Certain bodies other than companies are also required to produce accounts. Examples are building societies, charities and local authorities. Our work in this chapter deals exclusively with the accounts of companies.

Companies House

The address for companies registered in England and Wales is *Companies House, Crown Way, Cardiff CF14 3UZ*. There is an office in Edinburgh for companies registered in Scotland and an office in Belfast for companies registered in Northern Ireland. The telephone number for all three offices is *0303 1234 500* and the website for all three offices is www.gov.uk/government/organisations/companies-house. There are over 3,750,000 companies on the active register and the accounts of all but a handful of them may be inspected.

How to obtain published accounts

A listed public company will probably be willing to make accounts available. A request should be made to the Company Secretary's department.

Alternatively, you can get the accounts of any company, even the corner shop, by applying to Companies House. You can also get a copy of the company's annual return, articles and other documents. You will need to give the company's exact registered name or its registered number, preferably both. You can telephone and have the document posted to you or do it through the website. There is a charge of £3 per document if it is posted. You can pay with a credit or debit card. It may be useful and particularly interesting if you look at the accounts of your employer or another company that you know well.

Late filing

Unfortunately, a small minority of companies file their accounts late or even not at all. This is an offence for which the directors can be punished and the company incur a penalty, but it does happen. It is often companies with problems that file late.

What is included

The content of the Annual Report and Accounts is governed by the law and accounting standards, though directors do still have some discretion. Listed companies are required to use international accounting standards, whereas other companies can use international accounting standards or UK accounting standards. However, once international standards have been used a company can only go back to UK standards in exceptional circumstances. Which set of accounting standards is used makes a difference, both to the presentation and to the figures.

If you are looking at the Report and Accounts of a listed company you will see the following:

- Independent Auditors' Report
- Balance Sheet (it might be called Statement of Financial Position)
- Statement of Comprehensive Income or it might be called Income Statement (this corresponds with the Profit and Loss Account)

- Statement of Changes in Equity
- Statement of Cash Flows
- notes to the financial statements
- Chairman's Statement
- Directors' Report
- Business Review
- Directors' Remuneration Report.

If the company is using UK standards, the financial information will comprise:

- Balance Sheet
- Profit and Loss Account
- Statement of Total Recognized Gains and Losses
- probably a Cash Flow Statement
- notes to the financial statements.

Reports will be filed with this financial information.

Space here is limited and there is so much detail that there is really no substitute for diving in and having a look at the Report and Accounts of your chosen company. Try not to get bogged down and I wish you the best of luck. Assuming that you are not looking at the Report and Accounts of a small or medium-sized company and assuming that the company uses UK accounting standards, can you locate the following?

- the pre-tax profit (Profit and Loss Account)
- details of the fixed assets (Balance Sheet and supporting notes)
- the amount of any exports (the notes)
- is it an unqualified audit report? (the Audit Report)
- details of any political or charitable donation (the Directors' Report)
- was there a cash outflow in the period? (the Cash Flow Statement)
- details of the share capital (Balance Sheet and supporting notes)
- the amount of the capital employed (the Balance Sheet).

Profit and Loss Account and Balance Sheet

These are the core of the accounts and we have already looked at some of the principles in the first two chapters. The Profit and Loss Account will give the figures for the previous period as well as the current period. Figures in the Balance Sheet will be given as at the previous Balance Sheet date as well as for the present one.

Now we will have a look at what will be shown in the published Profit and Loss Account and Balance Sheet of a company and once again UK accounting standards are assumed. Some of the information may be given in notes with a suitable cross-reference.

Profit and Loss Account

Most people consider that the key figure is the one for Profit before Tax. You may think that taxation is fair, or at any rate inevitable, and that Profit before Tax is the best measure of the company's success. The bottom part of the Profit and Loss Account will look rather like this. Fictitious figures have been inserted.

Profit before Tax	£10,000,000
Less Tax on Profit	£3,200,000
Profit for the Year	£6,800,000
Less Dividends Paid and Proposed	£4,000,000
Retained Profit for the Year	£2,800,000
Retained Profit brought forward	£7,000,000
Retained Profit carried forward	£9,800,000

In this example Her Majesty's Government is taking £3,200,000 of the profit and £4,000,000 is being distributed to shareholders. The company started the current period with undistributed profits of £7,000,000 and it is prudently adding £2,800,000 to this figure. Undistributed profits are now £9,800,000 and this figure will appear in the Balance Sheet.

The Profit and Loss Account will give the turnover, which is the total invoiced sales in the period. This is very important and it is useful to work out the relationship between the profit and the turnover.

Balance Sheet

Fixed assets are normally the first item appearing in the Balance Sheet. Usually you will see just one figure for the net amount of the fixed assets and a cross-reference to a note. This note will:

● break down the assets by type
● give cumulative expenditure for each type
● give cumulative depreciation for each type
● give net asset value for each type
● state the depreciation policy for each type.

The fixed assets are usually one of the most interesting sections of the accounts. This is because it is rare for the assets to be worth exactly the figure shown.

Depreciation, according to accounting rules, rarely reflects the real-life situation, especially in times of inflation. One wonders what would be the book value of St Paul's Cathedral if the Church of England had followed depreciation rules at the time of Sir Christopher Wren.

In practice, companies sometimes revalue property assets though not usually other assets. Asset strippers specialize in buying undervalued companies then selling the fixed assets for more than book value. This is one of the reasons why the details, which will be in the notes, are so important.

Current assets and current liabilities

First the current assets will be listed by type and a total of the current assets will be given. Then the current liabilities will be listed by type and the total of the current liabilities will be given.

The difference between the two figures will be stated and this is the *net current assets* or the *working capital*. A problem is usually indicated if the current assets are smaller than the current liabilities or only slightly larger.

The assets and liabilities will be cross-referenced to notes giving appropriate details such as the following:

- a breakdown of stocks into finished goods and work in progress
- a split of debtors between trade debtors (customers) and other debtors
- details of the different types of creditor.

Capital and reserves

In Chapter 2 we examined the net worth of an organization shown at the bottom of its Balance Sheet. This section is the net worth of the company.

If the company were to be solvent and wound up, ignoring the costs of the winding up and in the unlikely event of all the assets and liabilities realizing exact book value, the total of this section is the amount that would be distributed to shareholders.

A note will give details of the different types of share capital if there are more than one. It will also give the figures for the different types of reserves, and the retained figure in the Profit and Loss Account.

The remainder of the Annual Report and Accounts

Notes to the Accounts

There are always notes to the Profit and Loss Account and Balance Sheet. Their purpose is to give further details, and they are in the form of notes to prevent the accounts getting horribly detailed and complicated. Many of the notes give a breakdown of such figures as stock and debtors.

The notes also state the accounting policies and conventions used in the preparation of the accounts. These are extremely important because these policies can greatly affect the figures. An example of such a policy would be to value stocks at the lower of cost and net realizable value. Any change to this policy could greatly affect the profit figure.

The Directors' Report

The directors are required by law to provide certain information. This includes, for example, the amount of directors' remuneration and details of any political or charitable contributions. This information is disclosed in the Directors' Report.

Cash Flow Statement

There are sometimes disputes about the figures in the Profit and Loss Account and Balance Sheet. This is one reason why cash is so important. Cash is much more a matter of fact rather than of opinion. It is either there or it is not there.

Where the cash came from (banks, shareholders, customers) is also a matter of fact. So too is where the cash went to (dividends, wages, suppliers, etc.). The Cash Flow Statement gives all this information.

The Auditor's Report

The law requires company accounts to be audited by a person or firm holding one of the approved qualifications.

Subject to certain conditions and exceptions no audit is required for a non-charitable company if it qualifies (on a group basis) as a small company. It must meet two out of three conditions in the current and preceding financial period. One of the conditions is that turnover must not exceed £10,200,000. The auditors will state whether in their opinion the accounts give a true and fair view. They do not certify the accuracy of the figures, a point which is often misunderstood.

If the auditors have reservations, they will give reasons for their concern.

Serious qualifications are rare, partly because it is in the interests of directors that they be avoided. Technical, and less serious, qualifications are more common. It is a matter of judgement how seriously each one is regarded.

Consolidated Accounts

A large group may have a hundred or more companies. It would obviously give an incomplete picture if each of these companies gave information just about its own activities. This is especially true when companies in a group trade with each other.

This is why the holding company must include consolidated accounts as well as its own figures. The effect of inter-group trading is eliminated and the Consolidated Balance Sheet gives the group's position in relation to the outside world. This does not, however, remove the obligation for every group company to prepare and file its own accounts. Such accounts must include the name, in the opinion of the directors, of the ultimate holding company.

Summary

In this chapter we have:

- examined the obligation to publish accounts and seen where copies can be obtained
- seen what is included in the Annual Report and Accounts
- tested our knowledge
- conducted an outline study of the Annual Report and Accounts.

Now, we will go on to look at accounting ratios and investment decisions.

Fact-check (answers at the back)

1. Where is the Companies House for companies registered in Scotland located?
   a) London ❏
   b) Cardiff ❏
   c) Edinburgh ❏
   d) Glasgow ❏

2. Which bodies do not have to make published accounts generally available?
   a) Building societies ❏
   b) Registered charities ❏
   c) Local authorities ❏
   d) General partnerships ❏

3. How much does Companies House charge for sending a copy of a company's accounts by post?
   a) £3 ❏
   b) £4 ❏
   c) £5 ❏
   d) £20 ❏

4. To what extent must listed companies use international accounting standards?
   a) Always ❏
   b) Usually ❏
   c) Always unless special permission is obtained ❏
   d) Never ❏

5. What is the turnover limit (subject to conditions) for the filing of abbreviated accounts for small companies at Companies House?
   a) £1,000,000 ❏
   b) £5,000,000 ❏
   c) £10,200,000 ❏
   d) £7,500,000 ❏

6. Which document explains the change in the amount of cash?
   a) The Balance Sheet ❏
   b) The Statement of Cash Flows ❏
   c) The Directors' Report ❏
   d) The Independent Auditors' Report ❏

7. Which document gives details of any charitable donations?
   a) The Profit and Loss Account ❏
   b) The Directors' Report ❏
   c) The Balance Sheet ❏
   d) The Cash Flow Statement ❏

8. What does the auditor do?
   a) Give an opinion ❏
   b) Certify the figures ❏
   c) Prepare the accounts ❏
   d) Comment on whether the directors are being fairly paid ❏

9. How many companies in the UK send accounts to Companies House?
   a) More then 50,000 ❏
   b) More than 1,000,000 ❏
   c) More than 2,000,000 ❏
   d) More than 2,500,000 ❏

10. Must a Business Review be provided in the Report and Accounts of a listed company?
    a) Yes, always ❏
    b) Usually ❏
    c) Sometimes ❏
    d) No ❏

CHAPTER 4

Accounting ratios and investment decisions

So far we have studied accounts and what they mean. Now we will devote a chapter to the active use of financial information. First we will take a look at ratios in the accounts, and then move on to investment decisions. This chapter is far from the easiest but, provided that you have mastered the basics, it should be one of the most interesting and rewarding.

The programme for this chapter covers:

- accounting ratios
- four key questions
- testing our understanding of accounting ratios
- investment decisions.

Accounting ratios

There are many useful ratios that can be taken from accounts. The following are among the most important but there are many others. It is a good idea to have a set of accounts with you as you work through this section. Pick out relevant figures, work out the ratios, and try to draw conclusions.

Profit to turnover

For example:

Annual turnover	**£10,000,000**
Annual profit before tax	**£1,000,000**
Profit to turnover	**10%**

This uses Profit before Tax but it may be more useful to use Profit after Tax. Perhaps you want to define profit as excluding the charge for bank interest. You should select the definition most relevant to your circumstances.
The ratio may be expressed in different ways (e.g. 1 to 10 instead of 10%).

Return on capital employed

For example:

Capital employed	**£5,000,000**
Annual profit after tax	**£1,000,000**
Return on capital employed	**20%**

Again the profit may be expressed before or after tax.
Capital employed is the net amount invested in the business by the owners and is taken from the Balance Sheet. Many people consider this the most important ratio of all. It is useful to compare the result with a return that can be obtained outside the business. If a building society is paying a higher rate, perhaps the business should be closed down and the money put in the building society.
Note that there are two ways of improving the return. In the example, the return on capital employed would be 25 per cent

if the profit was increased to £1,250,000. It would also be 25 per cent if the capital employed was reduced to £4,000,000.

Stock turn

For example:

Annual turnover	**£10,000,000**
Annual cost of sales (60%)	**£6,000,000**
Stock value	**£1,500,000**
Stock turn	**4**

As the name implies, this measures the number of times that total stock is used (turned over) in the course of a year. The higher the stock turn the more efficiently the business is being run, though adequate safety margins must of course be maintained.

It is important that the terms are completely understood and that there are no abnormal factors. Normally the definition of stock includes all finished goods, work in progress and raw materials.

The stock value will usually be taken from the closing Balance Sheet but you need to consider if it is a typical figure. If the business is seasonal, such as a manufacturer of fireworks, it may not be. A better result may be obtained if the average of several stock figures throughout the year can be used.

Number of days' credit granted

For example:

Annual turnover including VAT	**£10,000,000**
Trade debtors	**£1,500,000**
Number of days' credit	**55**

The calculation is $\dfrac{1,500,000}{10,000,000} \times 365 = 55$ days

Obviously the lower the number of days the more efficiently the business is being run. The figure for trade debtors normally comes from the closing Balance Sheet and care should be taken that it is a figure typical of the whole year.

If £1,500,000 of the £10,000,000 turnover came in the final month, the number of days' credit is really 31 instead of 55. Care should also be taken that the VAT-inclusive debtors figure is compared with the VAT-inclusive turnover figure. VAT is normally excluded from the Profit and Loss Account.

Number of days' credit taken

The principle of the calculation is exactly the same. In this case the figure for closing trade creditors is compared with that for the annual purchases.

Gearing

The purpose of this ratio is to compare the finance provided by the banks and other borrowing with the finance invested by shareholders. It is a ratio much used by banks, who may not like to see a ratio of 1 to 1 (or some other such proportion) exceeded.The ratio is sometimes expressed as a proportion, as in 1 to 1. Sometimes it is expressed as a percentage: 1 to 1 is 50 per cent because borrowing is 50 per cent of the total. Gearing is said to be high when borrowing is high in relation to shareholders' funds. This can be dangerous but shareholders' returns will be high if the company does well. This is what is meant by being highly geared.

For example:

Loans	**£6,000,000**
Shareholders' funds	**£3,000,000**
Gearing	**200%**

Dividend per share

This is the total dividends for the year divided by the number of shares in issue. Any preference shares are normally disregarded.

For example:

Total dividends	**£2,000,000**
Number of issued shares	**10,000,000**
Dividend per share	**20p**

Price/earnings ratio

This is one of the most helpful of the investment ratios and it can be used to compare different companies. The higher the number the more expensive the shares. It is often useful to do the calculation based on anticipated future earnings rather than declared historical earnings, although of course you can never be certain what future earnings will be.

The calculation is the current quoted price per share divided by earnings per share.

For example:

Profit after tax	£5,000,000
Number of issued shares	10,000,000
Earnings per share	50p
Current share price	£7.50
Price/earnings ratio	15

For all the ratios, if you have access to frequently produced management accounts the ratios will be more useful.

Before leaving accounting ratios please take warning from a true story. Some years ago one of the accountancy bodies asked examination candidates to work with ratios and draw conclusions from a Balance Sheet given in the examination paper.

Many of the students said that the company was desperately short of working capital and predicted imminent trouble. They were badly mistaken because the Balance Sheet had been taken from the latest published accounts of Marks and Spencer PLC. The students had not spotted the possibilities that the sales were for cash, the purchases were on credit and the business was very well managed.

Four key questions

There are many traps in using financial information and interpreting accounting ratios. You are advised to approach the job with caution and always to keep in mind four key questions.

Am I comparing like with like?

Financial analysts pay great attention to the notes in accounts and to the stated accounting policies. One of the reasons for this is that changes in accounting policies can affect the figures and hence the comparisons.

Consider a company that writes off research and development costs as overheads as soon as they are incurred. Then suppose that it changes policy and decides to capitalize the research and development, holding it in the Balance Sheet as having a long-term value. A case can be made for either treatment but the change makes it difficult to compare ratios for different years.

Is there an explanation?

Do not forget that there may be a special reason for an odd-looking ratio.

For example, greetings card manufacturers commonly deliver Christmas cards in August with an arrangement that payment is due on 1 January. The 30 June Balance Sheet may show that customers are taking an average of 55 days' credit. The 31 December Balance Sheet may show that customers are taking an average of 120 days' credit.

This does not mean that the position has deteriorated dreadfully and the company is in trouble. The change in the period of credit is an accepted feature of the trade and happens every year. It is of course important, particularly as extra working capital has to be found at the end of each year.

What am I comparing it with?

A ratio by itself has only limited value. It needs to be compared with something. Useful comparisons may be with the company budget, last year's ratio, or competitors' ratios.

Do I believe the figures?

You may be working with audited and published figures. On the other hand, you may only have unchecked data rushed from the accountant's desk. This sort of information may be more valuable because it is up to date. But beware of errors. Even if you are not a financial expert, if it feels wrong, perhaps it is wrong.

Test your understanding of accounting ratios

The Balance Sheet of Bristol Adhesives Ltd follows. The following information is available for the year to 31 October 2015.

Turnover was	*£6,600,000*
Profit before Tax was	*£66,000*
The bank overdraft limit is	*£800,000*
Cost of sales was	*50%*

1 What was the ratio of Profit to Turnover?
2 What was the Return on Capital Employed?
3 What was the Stock Turn?
4 What was the number of days' credit granted? (Ignore possible VAT implications.)
5
  a What is the working capital?
  b Does this give cause for concern?

Answers are given at the end of the chapter, just before the Fact-check.

Bristol Adhesives Ltd

Balance Sheet at 31 October 2015

	£	£
Fixed Assets		2,000,000
Current Assets		
Stock	1,800,000	
Trade debtors	700,000	
Other debtors	300,000	
	2,800,000	
Less Current Liabilities		
Trade creditors	1,400,000	
Bank overdraft	800,000	
Other creditors	400,000	
	2,600,000	
Net Current Assets		200,000
		2,200,000
Capital and Reserves		
Called-up share capital		1,500,000
Profit and Loss Account		700,000
		2,200,000

Investment decisions

Some investment decisions are easy to make. Perhaps a government safety regulation makes an item of capital expenditure compulsory. Or perhaps an essential piece of machinery breaks down and just has to be replaced.

Many other investment decisions are not nearly so clear cut and hinge on whether the proposed expenditure will generate sufficient future cash savings to justify itself. There are many very sophisticated techniques for aiding this decision, but now we will look at three techniques that are commonly used.

Payback

This has the merit of being extremely simple to calculate and understand. It is a simple measure of the period of time taken for the savings made to equal the capital expenditure. For example:

A new machine will cost £100,000. It will save £40,000 running expenses in the first year and £30,000 per year after that.

The payback period would be three years because this is the time taken for the saving on costs to equal the original expenditure. Hopefully this only took you a few seconds to work out and it is very useful information to have.

The disadvantage of the payback technique is that no account is given to the value of holding money. The £30,000 saved in year 3 is given equal value to £30,000 of the £100,000 paid out on day 1. In fact, inflation and loss of interest mean that, in reality, it is less valuable.

Return on investment

This takes the average of the money saved over the life of the asset and expresses it as a percentage of the original sum invested. For example:

A new machine will cost £100,000 and have a life of eight years. It will save £40,000 running expenses in the first year, and £30,000 in each of the remaining seven years.

The return on investment is $\dfrac{250,000 \times 100}{100,000 \times 8} = 31.25\%$ p.a.

Return on investment, like payback, takes no account of the time factor. A pound in eight years' time is given equal value to a pound today.

Discounted cash flow

This technique takes account of the fact that money paid or received in the future is not as valuable as money paid or received now. For this reason it is considered superior to payback and to return on investment. However, it is not as simple to calculate and understand.

There are variations to the discounted cash flow technique but the principles are illustrated by the following example.

The purchase of two competing pieces of machinery is under consideration. Machine A costs £100,000 and will save £60,000 in year 1 and £55,000 in year 2. Machine B costs £90,000 and will save £55,000 in both year 1 and year 2. The savings are taken to occur at the end of each year and the company believes that the money saved will earn 10 per cent p.a. in bank interest.

The calculations are:

	Machine A	Machine B
Expenditure now	£100,000	£90,000
Less year 1 savings (discounted)	£54,600	£50,050
	£45,400	£39,950
Less year 2 savings (discounted)	£45,650	£45,650
Savings at Net Present Value	£250	£5,700

The example has of course been unrealistically simplified. However, it shows that after bringing the future values back to Net Present Value, Machine B is the better purchase.

Summary

In this chapter, we have looked at how financial information is actively used and specifically at:

- useful accounting ratios
- four possible reasons for caution
- our understanding of accounting ratios
- financial techniques aiding investment decisions.

Next, we shall go on to increase our understanding of cash and the management of working capital.

Test your understanding of accounting ratios – Answers

1. 66,000/6,600,000 = 1%
2. 66,000/2,200,000 = 3%
3. 3,300,000/1,800,000 = 1.8
4. 700,000/6,600,000 x 365 = 39 days
5.
    a) £200,000
    b) Yes (cause for further enquiry anyway)

Fact-check (answers at the back)

The following information is taken from a Profit and Loss Account, Balance Sheet and other sources. Please use it to answer the first seven questions.

Turnover for year (excluding VAT)	£100,000,000
Turnover for year (including VAT)	£120,000,000
Profit after tax for year	£6,000,000
Capital employed (shareholders' funds)	£40,000,000
Loans	£50,000,000
Cost of sales for year	£50,000,000
Stock	£10,000,000
Trade debtors	£20,000,000
Dividends paid and proposed	£4,000,000
Number of shares in issue	10,000,000
Current share price	£6.00

1. What is the ratio for profit to turnover (excluding VAT)?
a) 10% ❑
b) 5% ❑
c) 6% ❑
d) 20% ❑

2. What is the return on capital employed?
a) 10% ❑
b) 12% ❑
c) 15% ❑
d) 20% ❑

3. What is the stock turn?
a) 4 ❑
b) 5 ❑
c) 6 ❑
d) 7 ❑

4. What are the number of days' credit taken by customers?
a) 55 days ❑
b) 60 days ❑
c) 61 days ❑
d) 64 days ❑

5. What is the gearing?
a) 50% ❑
b) 80% ❑
c) 100% ❑
d) 125% ❑

6. What is the dividend per share?
a) 20p ❑
b) 40p ❑
c) 60p ❑
d) 80p ❑

7. What is the price/earnings ratio?
   a) 10.0 ❏
   b) 10.5 ❏
   c) 11.0 ❏
   d) 11.5 ❏

8. A new machine will cost £500,000 and will save £200,000 running expenses for each of five years. What is the payback period?
   a) 24 months ❏
   b) 30 months ❏
   c) 36 months ❏
   d) 60 months ❏

9. A new computer system will cost £80,000 and have a life of four years and it will then be scrapped. It will save £50,000 per year. What is the return on investment?
   a) 60.0% ❏
   b) 62.5% ❏
   c) 65.0% ❏
   d) 67.5% ❏

10. Which of the following (in the opinion of many people) makes discounted cash flow superior to return on investment? The other three statements are not true.
    a) It is easier to calculate ❏
    b) It is a legal requirement ❏
    c) It is recommended by the European Union ❏
    d) It takes account of the changing value of money ❏

CHAPTER 5

Cash and the management of working capital

It is a bad mistake to underestimate the importance of cash and it is another bad mistake to confuse cash and profit. They can be very different and the reasons are explained in this chapter. It is sometimes said that 'Cash is King'. The origins of the saying are not beyond doubt but the words are often attributed to Jim Slater. He was the financier of Slater Walker fame who, in his words, became a minus millionaire, but went on to recover much of his fortune.

In this chapter we look at the importance and management of cash. We also look at the management of working capital and the place of cash within it.

The programme for this chapter covers:

- the distinctions between profit and cash
- what is cash?
- the Cash-Flow Forecast
- the management of working capital.

The distinctions between profit and cash

Cash is completely different from profit, a fact that is not always properly appreciated. It is possible, and indeed quite common, for a business to be profitable but short of cash. Among the differences are the following:

● Money may be collected from customers more slowly (or more quickly) than money is paid to suppliers.
● Capital expenditure (unless financed by hire purchase or similar means) has an immediate impact on cash. The effect on profit, by means of depreciation, is spread over a number of years.
● Taxation, dividends and other payments to owners are an appropriation of profit. Cash is taken out of the business, which may be more or less than the profit.
● An expanding business will have to spend money on materials, items for sale, wages, etc. before it completes the extra sales and gets paid. Purchases and expenses come first. Sales and profit come later.

It is worth illustrating the problems of an expanding business with a hypothetical but realistic example.

Company A manufactures pens. It has a regular monthly turnover of £20,000. The cost of the pens is £10,000 (50%). Other monthly costs are £8,000 and its monthly profit is £2,000.

At 31 December, Company A has £3,000 in the bank and is owed £40,000 by customers to whom it allows two months' credit.

It owes £15,000 to suppliers who are paid within 30 days. Monthly costs of £3,000 are payable in cash.

The company secures an additional order for £60,000. The extra pens will take two months to make and will be delivered on 28 February. The customer will then have 60 days to pay.

The cost of the additional pens will be £30,000 (50%) and there will be extra expenses of £14,000 in the two months. The new order will contribute a very satisfactory £16,000 extra profit.

By 30 April, Company A will have made £24,000 profit. This is the regular £2,000 a month plus the £16,000 from the additional order.

Now let us assume that the new customer pays on 1 May, just one day late. Despite the extra profit, on 30 April the £3,000 bank balance will have turned into a £33,000 overdraft. The calculation is as follows:

Balance at 31 December	£3,000
Add receipts in four months	£80,000
	£83,000
Less payments to creditors in four months	£90,000
	(£7,000)
Less cash expenses in four months	£26,000
Overdraft at 30 April	(£33,000)

What is cash?

Cash includes the notes and coins in the petty cash box. It also includes money in bank current accounts, and money in various short-term investment accounts that can quickly be turned into available cash.

It is common for a Balance Sheet to show only a tiny amount for cash. This is because the business has an overdraft and only such things as the petty cash are included.

Practical management usage of the term cash includes a negative figure for an overdraft. A Cash-Flow Forecast can often result in a series of forecast overdrafts.

The Cash-Flow Forecast

It is extremely important that cash receipts and payments are effectively planned and anticipated. This has not been done in nearly all businesses that fail. A good manager will plan that sufficient resources are available but that not too many resources are tied up.

This can be done in isolation but it is better done as part of the overall budgeting process. Budgets are examined in Chapter 7.

The preparation of a detailed Cash-Flow Forecast will yield many benefits. Calculating and writing down the figures may suggest ideas as to how they can be improved. For example, the figures for cash payments from trade debtors will be based on an estimate of the average number of days' credit that will be taken. This will pose the question of whether or not payments can be speeded up.

When the Cash-Flow Forecast is finished it will be necessary to consider if the results are acceptable. Even if resources are available the results might not be satisfactory, and improvements will have to be worked out.

If sufficient resources are not available, either changes must be made or extra resources arranged. Perhaps an additional bank overdraft can be negotiated. Either way, a well-planned document will help managers to take action in good time.

The principles of a Cash-Flow Forecast are best illustrated with an example and a good one is given in the following table.

Variations in the layout are possible but a constant feature should be the running cash or overdraft balance.

Do not overlook contingencies and do not overlook the possibility of a peak figure within a period. For example, Ace Toys Ltd are forecast to have £17,000 on 31 March and £5,000 on 30 April. Both forecasts could be exactly right and the company still need a £15,000 overdraft on 15 April.

Ace Toys Ltd – Cash-Flow Forecast for half year

	January £000	February £000	March £000	April £000	May £000	June £000
Receipts						
UK customers	50	55	55	55	60	80
Export customers	20	20	20	20	25	20
All other	5	5	8	2	12	6
	75	80	83	77	97	106
Payments						
Purchase ledger suppliers	30	33	29	40	44	38
Wages (net)	14	13	13	17	13	13
PAYE and National Insurance	4	4	4	4	5	4
Corporation tax	–	–	30	–	–	–
Capital expenditure	7	4	25	20	2	2
All other	8	9	9	8	6	11
	63	63	110	89	70	68
Excess of Receipts over Payments	12	17	(27)	(12)	27	38
Add Opening Bank Balance	15	27	44	17	5	32
Closing Bank Balance	27	44	17	5	32	70

It will help fix the principles in your mind if you now prepare your own personal Cash-Flow forecast. Set it out in accordance with the format illustrated below.

The figures will be smaller but the principles are identical. Most people have never done this and the results may well be revealing. The opening bank balance in month 1 should be the latest figure on your personal bank statement.

	Month 1	Month 2	Month 3
	£	£	£
Receipts			
Salary			
Interest			
Dividends			
Other (specify)			
Payments			
Mortgage or rent			
Telephone			
Gas and electricity			
Food			
Car expenses			
Other (specify)			
Excess of Receipts over Payments			
Add Opening Bank Balance			
Closing Bank Balance			

The management of working capital

Is it important?

The effective management of working capital can be critical to the survival of the business and it is hard to think of anything more important than that. Many businesses that fail are profitable at the time of their failure, and failure often comes as a surprise to the managers. The reason for the failure is a shortage of working capital.

Furthermore, effective management of working capital is likely to improve profitability significantly. Turn back to Chapter 4's section on return on capital employed. You will remember that the percentage return increases as capital employed is reduced. Effective management of working capital can reduce the capital employed. It increases profits as well as enabling managers to sleep soundly without worries.

The four largest elements affecting working capital are usually debtors, stock, creditors and cash. Success in managing the first three affect cash, which can be reinvested in the business or distributed. We will consider the three elements in turn.

Debtors

British business is plagued by slow payment of invoices and it is a problem in many other countries, too. Most businesses, and the government, would like to see an improvement. A statutory right to interest has been in place for a number of years but nothing seems to make much difference. An improvement can significantly affect working capital.

It is a great problem for managers, who sometimes are frightened of upsetting customers and feel that there is little that they can do. This is completely the wrong attitude.

Customer relations must always be considered, but a great deal can be done. Some practical steps for credit control are summarized below:

- Have the right attitude; ask early and ask often
- Make sure that payment terms are agreed in advance
- Do not underestimate the strength of your position
- Give credit control realistic status and priority
- Have well-thought out credit policies
- Concentrate on the biggest and most worrying debts first
- Be efficient; send out invoices and statements promptly
- Deal with queries quickly and efficiently
- Make full use of the telephone, your best aid
- Use legal action if necessary.

This may sound obvious, but it usually works. To sum up: be efficient, ask and be tough if necessary.

Stock

The aim should be to keep stock as low as is realistically feasible, and to achieve as high a rate of stock turnover as is realistically feasible. In practice, it is usually necessary to compromise between the wish to have stock as low as possible, and the need to keep production and sales going with a reasonable margin of safety.

Exactly how the compromise is struck will vary from case to case. Purchasing and production control are highly skilled functions and great effort may be expended on getting it right.

You may be familiar with the phrase 'just in time deliveries'. This is the technique of arranging deliveries of supplies frequently and in small quantities. In fact, just in time to keep production going. It is particularly successful in Japan where, for example, car manufacturers keep some parts for production measured only in hours.

It is not easy to achieve and suppliers would probably like to make large deliveries at irregular intervals. It may pay to approach the problem with an attitude of partnership with key suppliers, and to reward them with fair prices and continuity of business.

Finished goods should be sold, delivered and invoiced as quickly as possible.

Creditors

It is not ethical advice, but there is an obvious advantage in paying suppliers slowly. This is why slow payment is such a problem and, as has already been stated, the control of debtors is so important. Slow payment is often imposed by large and strong companies on small and weak suppliers.

Slow payment does not affect the net balance of working capital, but it does mean that both cash and creditors are higher than would otherwise be the case. Apart from moral considerations, there are some definite disadvantages in a policy of slow payment:

- Suppliers will try to compensate with higher prices or lower service.
- Best long-term results are often obtained by fostering mutual loyalty with key suppliers; it pays to consider their interests.
- If payments are already slow, there will be less scope for taking longer to pay in response to a crisis.

For these reasons it is probably not wise to adopt a consistent policy of slow payment, at least with important suppliers. It is better to be hard but fair, and to ensure that this fair play is rewarded with keen prices, good service and perhaps prompt payment discounts.

There may be scope for timing deliveries to take advantage of payment terms. For example if the terms are 'net monthly account', a 30 June delivery will be due for payment on 31 July. A 1 July delivery will be due for payment on 31 August.

Summary

In this chapter we have:

- studied the distinctions between profit and cash
- examined an example illustrating the differences
- learned what is meant by the term 'cash'
- looked at Cash-Flow Forecasts
- studied the importance of working capital and looked closely at debtors, stock and creditors.

Next, we will continue by taking a look at costing.

Fact-check (answers at the back)

1. 'A business may be profitable but short of cash'. How prevalent is this?
   a) It is relatively common ❏
   b) It is relatively uncommon ❏
   c) It is very uncommon ❏
   d) The statement in the question is self-evidently absurd ❏

2. Money is collected from customers more slowly than in the past. What effect will this have on cash in the business?
   a) There will be no effect ❏
   b) It will reduce the cash in the business ❏
   c) It will increase the cash in the business ❏
   d) It will greatly increase the cash in the business ❏

3. How important (in many people's opinion) is it that a cash-flow forecast is regularly prepared?
   a) It is a waste of time ❏
   b) It might be interesting ❏
   c) It could be useful ❏
   d) It is important ❏

4. Which of the following is not included in the definition of cash?
   a) Notes and coin in the petty cash box ❏
   b) Money in bank current accounts ❏
   c) Money owing by customers and due to be paid within three days ❏
   d) Bank overdrafts ❏

5. Which of the following statements is not true?
   a) The cash requirement in the middle of a month may be higher than the cash requirement at the beginning and end of the month ❏
   b) Capital expenditure is a cash outflow ❏
   c) The running cash or overdraft balance should always be a feature of a cash-flow forecast ❏
   d) Cash is the same as retained profit ❏

6. Which of the following will not help keep working capital at a satisfactory level?
   a) Persuading customers to pay quickly ❏
   b) Reducing dividends paid by the company ❏
   c) Changing the policy on depreciating fixed assets ❏
   d) Turning over stock more quickly ❏

7. Payment terms are 'net monthly account'. When is an invoice dated 6 September due for payment?
   a) 6 September ❏
   b) 30 September ❏
   c) 6 October ❏
   d) 31 October ❏

8. Slower payment by customers has which two of the following consequences?
a) Debtors are increased ❏
b) Creditors are increased ❏
c) Cash is increased ❏
d) Cash is reduced ❏

9. What are the two ways to increase the return on capital employed?
a) Increase the profit ❏
b) Increase the fixed assets ❏
c) Reduce the capital employed ❏
d) Negotiate better terms with the bank ❏

10. Who is famous for coining the phrase 'Cash is King'?
a) Gordon Brown ❏
b) Robert Maxwell ❏
c) Jim Slater ❏
d) Richard Branson ❏

CHAPTER 6

Costing

It is probably true to say that most non-financial managers instinctively know that costing is important. Unfortunately it is probably also true to say that most non-financial managers do not know very much about it. This is a pity because it affects so many business decisions. To take just one example, the fact that the fixed costs of running a cruise ship do not vary (or realistically only vary slightly) according to the number of passengers is the reason that large last-minute price reductions are often available. Think of that when you book your holiday.

A basic understanding of the principles of costing is important in business management. The aim is to master these key basic costing principles:

- the value of costing
- the uses of costing
- absorption costing
- break-even charts
- marginal costing and standard costing.

The value of costing

The value of costing can be illustrated with a simple example. Consider a company with three products. Its financial accounts show sales of £1,000,000, total costs of £700,000 and a profit of £300,000. The managers think that this is very good and that no significant changes are necessary. However, the costing details disclose the following:

	Product 1 £000	Product 2 £000	Product 3 £000	Total £000
Sales	600	300	100	1,000
Fixed costs	70	60	50	180
Variable costs	280	160	80	520
Total costs	350	220	130	700
Profit contribution	250	80	(30)	300

This shows that Product 1, as well as having the biggest proportion of sales, is contributing proportionately the most profit. Despite the overall good profit, Product 3 is making a negative contribution.

The obvious reaction might be to discontinue Product 3, but this may well be a mistake: £50,000 of fixed costs would have to be allocated to the other two products and the total profit would be reduced to £280,000.

Product 3 should probably only be discontinued if the fixed costs can be cut, or if the other two products can be expanded to absorb the £50,000 fixed costs.

It is increasingly common for cost accounts to be integrated with financial accounts. If cost accounts are kept separately, they go further than financial accounts. Cost accounts break down costs to individual products and cost centres. Financial accounts are more concerned with historical information.

Much, but not all, of the information comes from the financial accounts. It is important that if cost accounts are kept separately they are reconciled with the financial accounts.

Cost accounts are much more valuable if the information can be made speedily available. Sometimes it is necessary to compromise between speed and accuracy.

The uses of costing

It costs time and money to produce costing information and it is only worth doing if the information is put to good use. The following are some of these uses.

To control costs

Possession of detailed information about costs is of obvious value in the controlling of those costs.

To promote responsibility

Management theorists agree that power and responsibility should go together, although often they do not do so. Timely and accurate costing information will help top management hold all levels of management responsible for the budgets that they control.

Care should be taken that managers are not held responsible for costs that are not within their control. As many readers will know from bitter experience, this does sometimes happen.

To aid business decisions

The case given earlier might be such a decision.

Management must decide what to do about the unprofitable product.

To aid decisions on pricing

We live in competitive times and the old 'cost plus' contracts are now virtually never encountered. What the market will bear is usually the main factor in setting prices. Nevertheless, detailed knowledge concerning costs is an important factor in determining prices. Only in exceptional circumstances will managers agree to price goods at below cost, and they will seek to make an acceptable margin over cost.

Accurate costing is vital when tenders are submitted for major contracts and errors can have significant consequences. It is a long time ago but massive costing errors on the Millennium Dome at Greenwich were a spectacular example of what can go wrong.

Absorption costing

This takes account of all costs and allocates them to individual products or cost centres. Some costs relate directly to a product and this is quite straightforward in principle, although very detailed record-keeping may be necessary. Other costs do not relate to just one product and these must be allocated according to a fair formula. These indirect costs must be *absorbed* by each product.

There is not a single correct method of allocating overhead costs to individual products and it is sometimes right to allocate different costs in different ways. The aim should be to achieve fairness in each individual case.

Among the costs that can be entirely allocated to individual products are direct wages and associated employment costs, materials and bought-in components.

Among the costs that cannot be entirely allocated to individual products are indirect wages (cleaners, maintenance staff, etc.), wages of staff such as salesmen and accountants, and general overheads such as rent and business rates.

Great care must be taken in deciding the best way to allocate the non-direct costs. There are many different ways and the following two are common examples.

Production hours

The overhead costs are apportioned according to the direct production hours charged to each product or cost centre. For example, consider a company with just two products, A having 5,000 hours charged and B having 10,000 hours charged. If the overhead is £60,000, Product A will absorb £20,000 and Product B will absorb £40,000.

Machine hours

The principle is the same but the overhead is allocated according to the number of hours that the machinery has been running.

This is best illustrated with an example. You should try to write down the cost statement before checking the solution.

Fruit Products Ltd manufactures three types of jam. Its overhead costs in January are £18,000 and it allocates them in the proportion of direct labour costs. The following details are available for January:

	Strawberry	Raspberry	Apricot	Total
Jars manufactured	26,000	60,000	87,000	173,000
Direct labour	£2,000	£4,000	£6,000	£12,000
Ingredients	£6,000	£11,000	£17,000	£34,000
Other direct costs	£2,000	£3,000	£6,000	£11,000

The resulting cost statement is shown below:

Fruit Products Ltd – January Cost Statement

	Strawberry	Raspberry	Apricot	Total
Jars produced	26,000	60,000	87,000	173,000
	£	£	£	£
Costs				
Direct labour	2,000	4,000	6,000	12,000
Ingredients	6,000	11,000	17,000	34,000
Other direct costs	2,000	3,000	6,000	11,000
Total Direct Costs	10,000	18,000	29,000	57,000
Overhead allocation	3,000	6,000	9,000	18,000
Total Cost	13,000	24,000	38,000	75,000
Cost per jar	50.0p	40.0p	43.7p	43.4p

You will notice that in the example, direct labour is smaller than the overhead cost that is being allocated. If the overheads had been allocated in a different way, perhaps on floor area utilized, then the result would almost certainly not have been the same.

The trend in modern manufacturing is for direct costs, and particularly direct labour costs, to reduce as a proportion of the total costs. This increases the importance of choosing the fairest method of apportionment.

Break-even charts

In nearly all businesses there is a close correlation between the level of turnover and the profit or loss. The managers should know that if invoiced sales reach a certain figure the business will break even. If invoiced sales are above that figure the business will be in profit.

The break-even point depends on the relationship between the fixed and the variable costs. It is often shown in the form of the following chart:

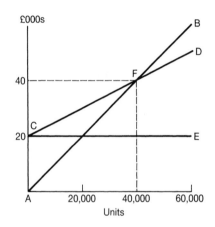

In the example, fixed costs (shown by line C–E) are £20,000. Variable costs are 50 pence per unit and the total costs (shown by line C–D) are the result of adding these to the fixed costs.

The revenue (shown by line A–B) is the result of sales at £1 per unit.

The break-even point is 40,000 units sold at £1 each. This is equal to the total cost of £40,000 (£20,000 fixed and £20,000 variable). It is at point F where the lines cross. Profit or loss can also be read from the chart.

In practice, the relationships are rarely quite so straightforward, as some of the costs may be semi-variable.

Marginal costing and standard costing

Marginal costing

Marginal costing is a useful way of emphasizing the marginal costs of production and services. This information is of great help in making pricing decisions.

If the selling price is less than the variable cost (direct cost), the loss will increase as more units are sold. Managers will only want to do this in very exceptional circumstances, such as a supermarket selling baked beans as a loss leader.

If the selling price is greater than the variable cost, then the margin will absorb part of the fixed cost. After a certain point profits will be made. Marginal costing explains why some goods and services are sold very cheaply. It explains, for example, why airline tickets are sometimes available at extremely low prices for last-minute purchasers.

Once an airline is committed to making a flight, an extremely high part of the cost of that flight can properly be regarded as a fixed cost. The pilot's salary will be the same whether the plane is empty or full. The variable cost is only the complimentary meals and a few other items. It therefore makes sense to make last-minute sales of unsold seats at low prices. As long as the selling price is greater than the variable cost, a contribution is made.

Standard costing

Standard costing involves the setting of targets, or standards, for the different factors affecting costs. Variances from the standard are then studied in detail.

For example:

Standard timber usage per unit of production	4.00 metres
Standard timber price	£2.00 per metre
Actual production	3,500 posts
Actual timber usage	14,140 metres
Actual cost of timber used	£27,714

| Material Price Variance is | £566 favourable (2%) |
| (£28,280 less £27,714) | |

| Material Usage Variance is | £280 adverse (1%) |
| ([14,140 metres less 14,000 metres] x £2) | |

The material price variance happens because the standard cost of the 14,140 metres used was £28,280 (at £2 per metre). The actual cost was £27,714, a favourable variance of £566. On the other hand, 140 metres of timber too much was used, resulting in an adverse material usage variance.

Summary

Costing is a big subject and there is only space to set out some of the basic principles. However, in this chapter we should have:

- formed an understanding of the concept of costing
- formed an understanding of the uses and value of costing
- studied the principles of absorption costing
- examined break-even charts
- answered the basic question 'What is marginal costing?'
- answered the basic question 'What is standard costing?'

Next, we will finish our examination of finance with a look at budgets.

Fact-check (answers at the back)

1. Which of the following is not one of the possible uses of costing information?
   a) To control costs ❏
   b) To ensure that the trial balance balances ❏
   c) To aid business decisions ❏
   d) To aid decisions on pricing ❏

2. What should happen if the cost accounts are kept separately from the financial accounts? There could be at least a tenuous case for all of the following but one of them is particularly important.
   a) They should be kept in the same building ❏
   b) They should be reconciled with the financial accounts ❏
   c) They should be kept by senior managers ❏
   d) They should be locked up ❏

3. Should managers (in the view of the writer and many others) be held responsible for costs that are not within their control?
   a) Always ❏
   b) Usually ❏
   c) Not usually ❏
   d) Of course not ❏

4. Which of the following is a feature of absorption costing?
   a) All costs are allocated to individual products or cost centres ❏
   b) It is very interesting (or sometimes even absorbing) ❏
   c) Fixed costs are disregarded ❏
   d) Variable costs are disregarded ❏

5. Which of the following can be entirely allocated to individual products?
   a) Indirect wages ❏
   b) Rent ❏
   c) Direct wages ❏
   d) The salary of the managing director ❏

6. Which of the following is not a valid way of allocating non-direct costs?
   a) According to the wishes of the government ❏
   b) Pro-rata to production hours ❏
   c) Pro-rata to machine hours ❏
   d) Pro-rata to direct labour costs ❏

7. A business sells watches for £10 each. Fixed costs are £10,000 and indirect costs are £5 per watch. Referring to a break-even chart, if you can prepare one, how many watches must be sold before break-even point is reached?

a) 1,500 ❏
b) 2,000 ❏
c) 2,500 ❏
d) 3,000 ❏

8. Using the information in question 7 above, how many watches must be sold to achieve break-even if the costs are unchanged but the selling price is reduced to £8?

a) 2,500 ❏
b) 3,000 ❏
c) 3,334 ❏
d) 3,667 ❏

9. Which of the following would be true in the event of the variable cost being greater than the selling price?

a) The more units sold the more the loss would increase ❏
b) Variable costs would have to be reallocated ❏
c) The more units sold the more the loss would reduce ❏
d) The directors would have to resign (just joking) ❏

10. Standard material cost per unit of production £5
Actual production 3,000 units
Actual material cost £15,500
What is the material usage variance?

a) £1,000 unfavourable ❏
b) £500 unfavourable ❏
c) £500 favourable ❏
d) £1,000 favourable ❏

CHAPTER 7

Budgets

Budgeting is probably the element of finance that has most impact on the time of non-financial managers and for this reason most of them have at least some knowledge of the subject. Of course, some non-financial managers resent this time commitment and see budgeting as an unproductive chore. It can be, but this should not be the case if it is handled well and budget relationships are understood.

In this chapter we will look at:

- budgeting in different types of organization
- the profit budget
- the sales budget
- revenue expenditure budgets
- the capital expenditure budget
- cash and the Balance Sheet
- after the budget has been approved.

Budgeting in different types of organization

In very large organizations, hundreds of managers may be involved in the budgeting process, and the complete budget will probably be a very thick document. This would be true of, say, a National Health Service Trust and in the private sector of companies such as Shell.

This involvement takes a lot of management time but, if the budgeting is done well, it is likely to be time well spent. This is because the budget will probably be a realistic one, and because after approval the managers should feel committed to it.

When the budget has been approved, individual managers are responsible for their section of it. The responsibility is like a pyramid. At the base of the pyramid are the most junior managers, supervising a comparatively small section, perhaps involving expenditure only. These junior managers should, however, have some knowledge of the overall budget and objectives.

In the middle may be more senior managers and divisional directors, each with a wider area of responsibility for achieving the complete budget objectives. If everyone else meets their targets they will have an easy job.

Budgets should be designed to meet the needs of a particular organization and its managers. For example, a large school could well have an expenditure budget of about £4,000,000. There will be little income and the budgeting emphasis will be on capital expenditure and revenue expenditure. The main aims will be informed choice and value for money.

The rest of this chapter's work is devoted to the budget of a large company because this best illustrates the main principles. However, a smaller organization should budget using the same methods. There will be fewer managers involved, and less paper, but the same procedures should be followed.

In Chapter 1, we considered Julia Brown's book, and in Chapter 2 we considered John Brown's gardening business. Even their budgets follow the same principles. John Brown's van and motor mower constitute his capital expenditure budget. In their case the budgets will probably be on just one or two pieces of paper.

The profit budget

There are usually several budgets and they all impact on each other. The profit budget is arguably the most important and this is considered first.

There are two basic approaches to budgeting in a large organization, both having advantages and disadvantages.

- The so-called 'bottom up' method. Proposals are taken from the lower management levels. These are collated into an overall budget that may or may not be acceptable. If it is not, then top management calls for revisions.
- The so-called 'top down' method. Top management issues budget targets. Lower levels of management must then submit proposals that achieve these targets.

In practice, there is often less difference between the two methods than might be supposed. It is important that at some stage there is a full and frank exchange of views. Everyone should be encouraged to put forward any constructive point of view, and everyone should commit themselves to listening with an open mind. Needless to say, top management will, and should, have the final decisions.

It is a common mistake for managers to be too insular and to overlook what changes competitors are making.

All the budgets are important but in a commercial organization the overall profit budget is likely to be considered the most important. A summarized six-month profit budget for a large organization is given below.

Kingston Staplers Ltd – Profit Budget for half year

	January	February	March	April	May	June	Total half year
	£000	£000	£000	£000	£000	£000	£000
Sales							
UK	1,500	1,400	1,450	1,700	1,600	1,800	9,450
Export	200	220	180	190	400	340	1,530
	1,700	1,620	1,630	1,890	2,000	2,140	10,980
Less cost of sales	1,020	970	990	1,150	1,230	1,320	6,680
Gross Profit	680	650	640	740	770	820	4,300
Overheads							
Sales Department	200	220	230	210	210	220	1,290
Finance Department	190	200	180	190	220	210	1,190
Administration Department	230	240	250	250	250	260	1,480
Total overheads	620	660	660	650	680	690	3,960
Net Profit/(Loss)	60	(10)	(20)	90	90	130	340

Please particularly note the following points:

- Most budgets are for a year but this is not a requirement. They can be for six months or for any other useful period.
- This budget gives monthly figures, which is the most common division, but again this is not fixed. The divisions can be weekly, quarterly, or some other period.
- The figures are summarized in thousands of pounds.
- This is suitable for a summary budget of a large organization. The budgets leading up to these summarized figures will be more detailed. January's budget for postage might, for example, be £2,850.
- As we will see, various subsidiary budgets and calculations feed figures through to this summary budget.

The sales budget

This should be in sufficient detail for management to know the sources of revenue. The figures will be broken down into different products and different sales regions. Each regional sales manager will have responsibility for a part of the sales budget. A section of the sales budget might look like the following:

Scottish Region Sales Budget

	Jan £	Feb £	March £
Product A	16,000	12,000	17,000
Product B	13,000	13,000	13,000
Product C	40,000	45,000	50,000
	69,000	70,000	80,000

Before the sales budget is done it would be normal for top management to issue budget assumptions concerning prices, competition, and other key matters.

The sales budget will be for orders taken. There will usually be a timing difference before orders become invoiced sales.

Revenue expenditure budgets

Still using the example of Kingston Staplers Ltd, the cost of sales will consist of direct wages, items bought for resale, raw materials and so on. The Sales, Finance, and Administration Departments will make up the overhead budget. In practice, this overhead budget is likely to be divided into three, with a different manager responsible for each section.

As with all the other budgets, each manager should submit a detailed budget for the section for which he or she is responsible.

As with the sales budget, top management should give initial guidance on expected performance and policy assumptions. For example, a manager might be told to assume a company-wide average pay rise of 5 per cent on 1 April.

The capital expenditure budget

This is extremely significant in some companies, less so in others. It will list all the planned capital expenditure showing the date when the expenditure will be made, and the date that the expenditure will be completed and the asset introduced to the business. Major contracts may be payable in instalments and the timing is important to the cash budget.

A sum for miscellaneous items is usually necessary. For example, major projects might be listed separately and then £15,000 per month added for all projects individually less than £5,000.

Within the capital expenditure budget, timing is very important. Expenditure affects cash and interest straightaway. Depreciation usually starts only on completion.

Cash and the Balance Sheet

When the profit budgets are complete, it is important that a cash budget is prepared. This is a Cash-Flow Forecast, which was examined in detail in Chapter 5. You might like to spend a few minutes referring back to this.

In practice, the profit budget and cash budget are linked and a chicken and egg problem has to be resolved. The profit budget cannot be completed until the interest figure is available. This in turn depends on the cash budget. The cash budget depends partly on the profit budget.

Dilemmas like this are quite common in budgeting. It is usual to put in an estimated figure for interest and then adjust everything later if necessary. This can be very time-consuming, and budgeting is much simpler if it is computerized. Several hours' work can be reduced to minutes and management is much freer to test budgets with useful 'what if' questions.

You will recall that one of Chapter 2's accounting rules stated that every debit has a credit. It follows that every figure in the budgets has a forecastable consequence in a future Balance Sheet. It is normal to conclude the budgets by preparing a month-by-month forecast Balance Sheet and bankers are likely to ask for this. It may be that some aspect of the Balance Sheet is unacceptable and a partial re-budget is necessary.

In practice, top management is likely to review and alter some aspects of the budgets several times.

After the budget has been approved

After the budget has been approved comes . . . quite possibly nothing at all. This is a pity but it does not mean that the budgeting exercise has been a complete waste of time. The participants will have thought logically about the organization, its finances and its future. Some of the detail will remain in their minds and influence their future actions.

Nevertheless, the budgets will be much more valuable if they are used in an active way. Regular performance reports should be issued by the accountants. These should be in the same format as the budgets, and should give comparable budget and actual figures. Variances should also be given.

All levels of management should regularly review these figures and explain the variances. Significant variances will pose the question of whether corrective action needs to be taken.

Finally, budgets do not necessarily have to be done just once a year. They may be updated, reviewed, or even scrapped and redone as circumstances dictate.

Summary

Finance affects the jobs of virtually all non-financial managers and during this Part you should have significantly increased your knowledge of the subject. Many elements of finance have been examined and much ground has been covered.
The following summarizes the subjects studied:

Profit Statements (Chapter 1)

- A simple example
- A trading company and a manufacturing company
- Further concepts
- A full example

Balance Sheets (Chapter 2)

- What is a Balance Sheet?
- Accounting rules and a simple example
- Further concepts
- Test your knowledge

Published accounts (Chapter 3)

- Availability of published accounts
- Profit and Loss Account and Balance Sheet
- Other items included in published accounts

Fact-check (answers at the back)

1. In a very large company individual junior managers each have responsibility for a relatively small cost centre. Which phrase best describes their cost centres' place in the overall company budget?
   a) In the centre of the circle ❑
   b) At the edge of the rectangle ❑
   c) At the base of the pyramid ❑
   d) Pulsating in the pentagon ❑

2. A large company has a full set of budgets. Which of the following statements should be true?
   a) They should all be independent of each other ❑
   b) Some should impact on each other ❑
   c) The capital expenditure budget should not affect the other budgets ❑
   d) They should all impact on each other ❑

3. Which of the following is a feature of the so-called 'top down' method of budgeting?
   a) Top management issues budget targets ❑
   b) Lower management issues budget proposals without prior guidance ❑
   c) There are frequent meetings
   d) Only revenue budgets are required ❑

4. Must budgets cover a period of a year?
   a) No – and they usually cover a period of six months ❑
   b) No – but they often do ❑
   c) No – and they never do ❑
   d) Yes ❑

5. In a big company in what way is it normal for the sales budget to be broken down?
   a) By region ❑
   b) By period ❑
   c) By product ❑
   d) By all of the above ❑

6. When does capital expenditure usually start to affect cash and interest?
   a) When the orders are placed ❑
   b) When the capital items are brought into use ❑
   c) When payment is made ❑
   d) When depreciation starts ❑

7. How important is the cash budget likely to be?
   a) Important ❑
   b) Not very important ❑
   c) Not at all important ❑
   d) A complete waste of time ❑

8. Can the capital expenditure budget be altered without the balance sheet budget being affected?
   a) Yes ❑
   b) Sometimes ❑
   c) Not usually ❑
   d) No ❑

9. What should happen after the budgets have been approved?

a) Nothing ❏

b) They should be kept available for inspection when required ❏

c) Top managers should look at them from time to time ❏

d) All levels of management should regularly review actual and budget figures and explain the variances ❏

10. What are the advantages in involving all levels of management in budget preparation?

a) The budget is more likely to be realistic ❏

b) Managers are more likely to feel committed to it ❏

c) It may be good for morale ❏

d) All of the above ❏

7 × 7

1 Seven things to do today

- If your business sells goods, make sure you are holding the right amount of stock. Too much and working capital is being tied up unnecessarily; too little and you risk losing sales.
- Make sure you know the cash position and plan accordingly.
- Check which customers have not paid on time and chase them for the money.
- Check the business's progress against the budgets and take any necessary action.
- Keep an eye on the accounting ratios.
- If you do not understand any of the financial figures, ask to have them explained to you. Your colleagues will probably respect you for asking.
- Make sure you understand the differences between profit and cash. They are almost never the same.

2 Seven things to do soon

- The seven things to do today are still good ideas. So do them all again.
- Make friends with your customers, your suppliers and your bank manager.
- Try not to get bogged down in meetings. Make them effective and try to have fewer of them.
- Try to get much of your business borrowing in the form of long-term loans, rather than in overdrafts repayable on demand.
- Check that your anti-virus software is up to date.
- Check that your suppliers are still giving you a good deal. There may be better alternatives.

● Think about the saying (relating to a profit and loss account) that if you take care of the top line the bottom line will look after itself. Then discard it, because it is not true.

3 Seven key ideas

● Remember that the principles of finance are the same whether you work in a mighty corporation or a small business. The difference is in the size of the figures.

● Do not underestimate yourself. You are the expert in what you do.

● It is easy and common to drown in financial detail. Keep your eye on what is important and do not make that mistake.

● Take credit control seriously. If you are being paid late, you are being cheated.

● Prevention is better than cure.

● The information in the accounts is always out of date.

● Be sceptical about expert advice. Experts will probably give you good advice, but do not overlook the possibility that they may be mistaken. For centuries experts said that the world was flat, but Christopher Columbus proved them wrong.

4 Seven trends for tomorrow

● The population of many Western countries is ageing. This will create both opportunities and problems for businesses.

● More and more people are seeking a satisfactory work–life balance. This has important implications (both problems and opportunities) for employers.

● In recent years there have been significant increases in self-employment, business start-ups and the number of small businesses. This is likely to continue.

● There will continue to be takeovers and amalgamations among the world's biggest corporations.

● More people will work from home for at least part of the time.

- Fraudsters will continue to find ingenious ways to separate businesses and citizens from their money.
- Politicians will continue to promise a business-friendly environment and a reduction in bureaucracy. Whether they will deliver these things is another matter.

5 Seven things to remember

- When preparing a cash forecast, remember that the need for cash might peak in the middle of a period.
- Allow for contingencies when preparing budgets and forecasts.
- Allow for seasonal factors when working with accounts, budgets and forecasts.
- Don't spend too much time getting the figures exactly right. Sometimes nearly right figures produced quickly are more useful than exactly right figures produced slowly.
- Thank your staff for their contribution and discuss the figures with them as appropriate.
- Don't allow fixed costs to be too high.
- Remember the consequences of inflation. Inflation may be low today, but it has been high in the past and may well be high in the future.

6 Seven great quotes

- 'When I have to read economic documents I have to have a box of matches and start moving them into position to simplify and illustrate the points to myself.' – Sir Alec Douglas-Home (1903–95), British prime minister
- 'A bank is a place that will lend you money if you can prove that you don't need it.' – Bob Hope (1903–2003), American comedian
- 'In the long run we are all dead.' – John Maynard Keynes (1883–1946), English economist
- 'Money is like a sixth sense without which you cannot make a complete use of the other five.' – W. Somerset Maugham (1874–1965) in *Of Human Bondage*

- 'Annual income twenty pounds, annual expenditure nineteen [pounds] nineteen [shillings] and six [pence], result happiness. Annual income twenty pounds, annual expenditure twenty pounds ought and six, result misery.' – Charles Dickens (1812–70) in *David Copperfield*

- 'In this world nothing can be said to be certain, except death and taxes.' – Benjamin Franklin (1706–90), American statesman, scientist and author

- 'It is well enough that people of the nation do not understand our banking and monetary system, for if they did, I believe there would be a revolution before tomorrow morning.' – Henry Ford (1863–1947), American industrialist

7 Six great sayings and a story

- 'Give a man a fish and he will eat for a day. Teach a man to fish and he will eat for a lifetime. Teach a man how to create an artificial shortage of fish and he will eat steak.' – Jay Leno

- 'The chief business of the American people is business.' – Calvin Coolidge (President of the USA, 1923–9)

- 'Choose a job that you like and you will never have to work a day in your life.' – Confucius

- 'Turnover is vanity. Profit is sanity.' – Anon.

- 'Corporation: an ingenious device for obtaining profit without individual responsibility.' – Ambrose Bierce in *The Devil's Dictionary*

- 'I have found no greater satisfaction than achieving success through honest dealing and strict adherence to the view that, for you to gain, those you deal with should gain as well.' – Alan Greenspan

- 'Two non-financial managers were walking through a wood and were suddenly confronted by an angry bear. Seeing his companion putting on running shoes, one said, "That's no use. You can't outrun the bear in those". "I don't have to," came the reply. "I just have to outrun you."'

PART 2
Your Bookkeeping and
Accounting Masterclass

Introduction

Millions of sets of accounting records are kept in Britain and around the world. They range from the accounts of major companies employing tens or hundreds of thousands of people to the cashbook of small local bodies such as a stamp collectors' club or tennis club. An understanding of the principles of bookkeeping and accounts is of great importance, and not just to people employed in accounts offices.

It is probably true to say that such knowledge is more important now than ever before. Of course, it is not only at work that some knowledge of bookkeeping and accounting is useful. Many good-natured people struggle with the books of clubs and such bodies as parent–teachers' organizations. Often they do a good job, but sometimes they do not.

Most bookkeeping and accounting is now done with computers. This has enormous advantages but it may result in people using them without understanding what they are doing. The accounting packages do (or at least should) follow the old-established and time-honoured principles explained in this Part.

Chapter 14 will be more meaningful to you if you have a company's annual reports and accounts to hand. It would be helpful if you could obtain this in advance.

CHAPTER 8

The basic principles of bookkeeping

We start by looking at the foundations of book-keeping. As with so many things, our end results will be far better if we lay the foundations correctly. As Julie Andrews famously sang in *The Sound of Music*, 'Let's start at the very beginning, a very good place to start.'

Millions of sets of accounting records are kept in a huge range of contexts. At one extreme, scores of qualified accountants toil to prepare the published accounts of a major company. At the other extreme, the treasurer of a local tennis club or PTA reports on the finances to the members.

All the records, from the mightiest to the most humble, should be kept according to the basic principles of bookkeeping. These are timeless and the same for all organizations.

We will look at:

- single-entry bookkeeping
- the concept of double-entry bookkeeping
- the basic rules and disciplines of double-entry bookkeeping.

Single-entry bookkeeping

As the name suggests, single-entry bookkeeping involves writing down each transaction just once. It is, in fact, the simple listing of income and expenditure. Numerous small organizations – such as your local tennis club, for example – will keep their records in this way.

Every time the treasurer writes a cheque, he or she records in a book the date, the amount and the payee. Every time something is paid into the bank, the details are entered elsewhere in the book. Cash paid out or received is entered in a similar way.

If the treasurer has been careful, he or she can use these records to prepare an accurate receipts and payments account. It is necessary, however, to prove the figures as far as possible. Cash actually in the cash box should equal the cash received less the cash paid out, after allowing for the starting balance, of course. The balance on the bank statement should equal money banked less cheques written, after allowing for the opening balance and items that have not yet reached the statement.

Records kept in this way have severe limitations, including the following.

- An item written down wrongly may not be noticed as a mistake.
- Money owing to the organization or by the organization is not shown. The tennis club accounts will not show subscriptions not paid by members, or the amount owing to a painter for painting the clubhouse.
- Long-term assets are not shown: for example, £1,000 spent on tennis nets last year is not shown in the current year's accounts.

Double-entry bookkeeping

The concept and principles of double-entry bookkeeping were first written down in 1494 by an Italian monk named Luca Pacioli. His work has stood the test of time – the same principles are still valid today.

At the heart of double-entry bookkeeping is the idea that every transaction involves the giving of a benefit and the receiving of a benefit. Consequently, every transaction is written into the books twice, once as a credit and once as a debit.

It follows from this that the bookkeeping system must balance, which is an enormous advantage for control purposes. The total of the debits must equal the total of the credits.

A set of double-entry books enables a complete view to be taken, unlike a single-entry system. For example, consider a businessperson writing out a cheque for £100 wages. In a single-entry system the only information recorded is that £100 wages has been paid. A double-entry system also records that £100 has been taken from the bank account and that the bank account balance is reduced accordingly. This is extremely important information.

The basic rules and disciplines of double-entry bookkeeping

A manual ledger or account is ruled for posting on two sides. Here are the basic rules:

1 Debit on the left, credit on the right

Computerized records are not likely to be printed in this traditional way. You are more likely to get a printout showing columns of figures. Some of these figures represent credits and some represent debits. They could be rewritten in the traditional format, though, and the debits would go on the left.

2 For every debit there must be a credit

This rule is infallible. There are no exceptions. Let us return to the businessperson writing out a cheque for £100 wages. The entries are:

Wages account   £100.00 debit
Bank account   £100.00 credit

The entries may be numerous and complicated, but the rule still holds. If it is not followed, the trial balance will not balance. A mistake has been made which must be found and corrected. Let us take the businessperson purchasing £100 stationery which carries 20 per cent recoverable VAT. The entries are:

Stationery account   £100.00 debit
VAT account   £20.00 debit
Bank account   £120.00 credit

Scientists sometimes help themselves to remember the rule by thinking of the law of physics 'For every action there is an equal and opposite reaction.'

3 Debit receives the benefit, credit gives the benefit

This may be hard to grasp and it is probably the opposite of what you would instinctively expect. After all, your bank statement is credited when it receives money paid in. Nevertheless, double-entry bookkeeping does work in this way. An account is debited when it receives a benefit and it is credited when it gives a benefit.

Consider again the businessperson writing out a cheque for £100 wages. The worker receives the money and it is the wages account that is debited. The bank account gives the benefit and, as a result, has less money in it. Consequently, the bank account is credited.

It may help you to remember the rule if you think that a bank overdraft is represented by a credit balance in the bookkeeping system.

For another example we will take a sale of £200 to Smith and Sons. If it is a cash sale, the entry is:

Bank account   £200.00 debit
Sales account   £200.00 credit

Money has been paid into the bank and the bank account is debited. If it is a sale on credit, the entry is:

Smith and Sons   £200.00 debit
Sales account   £200.00 credit

When Smith and Sons actually pay, the entry is:

Bank account   £200.00 debit
Smith and Sons   £200.00 credit

The best way of understanding the basic principles is to work through examples, and two are given here. In the first case the correct entries follow immediately. In the second example just the account headings are given. You should fill in the entries before checking the correct postings, which are given at the end of this chapter.

1 Samantha Jones runs a ladies' dress shop

On one day the following events occur:

- She banks cash takings of £460.
- She makes a credit sale of £100 to Mrs Clarke.
- She purchases dresses from London Dress Supplies for £1,000. This is on credit.
- She pays wages of £110.
- Mrs Clarke pays £80 owing from a previous sale. This is banked.

The layout of the accounts has been simplified because only the principles of posting are being illustrated. In real life each entry would be dated and the balance of each account would be shown. Note that the total of all the debits equals the total of all the credits, i.e. £1,750 in each case.

Bank account

Debit		£		Credit	£
Sales account		460	Wages account		110
Mrs Clarke account		80			

Sales account

Debit		£		Credit	£
			Bank account		100
			Mrs Clarke account		460

Mrs Clarke account

Debit		£		Credit	£
Sales account		100	Bank account		80

Stock account

Debit		£		Credit	£
London Dress Supplies account		1,000			

London Dress Supplies account

Debit		£		Credit	£
			Stock account		1,000

Wages account

Debit		£		Credit	£
Bank account		110			

2 Peter Jenkins starts a manufacturing business

- He pays £50,000 into the bank as his capital for the business.
- He buys plant and machinery for £20,000 from King Brothers Ltd. This is on credit.
- He buys raw materials from Patel Brothers for £10,000. This is on credit.
- He buys raw materials for £6,000 for cash.
- He pays his lawyer £2,000 for negotiating a lease.

Now test your understanding by filling in the entries on the following blank accounts table. You can check the answers at the end of this chapter.

Accounts table

Bank account

Debit		Credit
£		£

Capital account

Debit		Credit
£		£

Plant and machinery account

Debit		Credit
£		£

King Brothers Ltd account

Debit		Credit
£		£

Patel Brothers Ltd account

Debit		Credit
£		£

Raw materials account

Debit		Credit
£		£

Legal and professional account

Debit		Credit
£		£

Summary

In this chapter we have learned the basic principles of bookkeeping, and laid the foundations of our understanding. We have:

- looked at single-entry records and seen the drawbacks
- established what is meant by double-entry and seen the advantages
- seen that the giving and receiving of a benefit is at the heart of double-entry bookkeeping
- gained an understanding of the basic rules and principles
- worked through two examples.

In the next chapter we will establish the five different types of account. We will also examine the different ledgers and day books.

Test your understanding

Answer

Accounts table

Bank account

Debit			Credit
	£		£
Capital account	50,000	Raw materials account	6,000
		Legal and professional account	2,000

Capital account

Debit			Credit
	£		£
		Bank account	50,000

Plant and Machinery account

Debit			Credit
	£		£
King Brothers Ltd account	20,000		

King Brothers Ltd account

Debit			Credit
	£		£
		Plant and machinery account	20,000

Patel Brothers Ltd account

Debit			Credit
	£		£
		Raw materials account	10,000

Raw Materials account

Debit			Credit
	£		£
Patel Brothers Ltd account	10,000		
Bank account	6,000		

Legal and Professional account

Debit			Credit
	£		£
Bank account	2,000		

Fact-check (answers at the back)

1. Which of the following is a disadvantage of single-entry bookkeeping?
a) An asset purchased last year is not shown in this year's accounts ❏
b) It takes more time than double-entry bookkeeping ❏
c) It is against the law ❏
d) It is not usually explained in accounting textbooks ❏

2. Who first wrote down the principles of double-entry bookkeeping?
a) Salvador Dalí ❏
b) Roy Salvadori ❏
c) Luca Pacioli ❏
d) Silvio Berlusconi ❏

3. Which of the following are features of double-entry bookkeeping?
a) Every transaction is entered twice, once as a credit and once as a debit ❏
b) The bookkeeping system must balance ❏
c) The total of the debits must equal the total of the credits ❏
d) All of the above ❏

4. Complete the following. For every debit there must be a...
a) Debt ❏
b) Credit ❏
c) Loss ❏
d) Problem ❏

5. Where in a manual ledger does debit go?
a) At the top ❏
b) At the bottom ❏
c) On the left ❏
d) On the right ❏

6. What happens in the bookkeeping system when a cheque for £600 is written?
a) Nothing happens until the bank pays the cheque ❏
b) Bank account is debited £600 ❏
c) Bank account is credited £600 ❏
d) Sales are debited £600 ❏

7. What happens in the bookkeeping system when cash takings of £600 are banked?
a) Bank account is debited £600 ❏
b) Sales account is credited £600 ❏
c) Both (a) and (b) above ❏
d) Nothing ❏

8. A sale of £600 is made on credit to Banerjee Brothers Ltd. Which account is debited?
a) Bank account ❏
b) Banerjee Brothers Ltd ❏
c) Sales ❏
d) Stock ❏

9. A sale of £600 is made on credit to Banerjee Brothers Ltd. Which account is credited?
a) Bank account ❏
b) Banerjee Brothers Ltd ❏
c) Sales ❏
d) Stock ❏

10. Which of the following statements is correct?
a) Double-entry bookkeeping is far superior to single-entry bookkeeping ❏
b) Double-entry bookkeeping is slightly superior to single-entry bookkeeping ❏
c) Double-entry bookkeeping is slightly inferior to single-entry bookkeeping ❏
d) Double-entry bookkeeping is much inferior to single-entry bookkeeping ❏

CHAPTER 9

Different types of account and ledger

The rules for posting between accounts follow the rules of double-entry bookkeeping. They do not vary according to the types of account involved. However, different types of account fulfil different purposes. They are treated differently when the profit and loss account and balance sheet are prepared.

We start this chapter by looking at the five different types of account. We then progress to an examination of the nominal ledger, together with the subsidiary ledgers and the books of entry.

The programme is:

- the five different types of account
- the nominal ledger
- the sales ledger
- the sales day book
- the purchase ledger
- the purchases day book.

The five different types of account

It will be helpful for you to have an understanding of the different types of account. This is in order to understand the books and it is very important when accounts are prepared. However, it does not affect the bookkeeping, and postings may freely be made from one type of account to another.

Income accounts

These accounts relate to sales and they increase the profit. The income accounts normally have a credit balance and are eventually credited to the profit and loss account. An example is the sales account into which Samantha Jones credited £460 in the previous chapter's first example.

Expenditure accounts

These accounts are made up of expenditure that reduces profit. The expenditure accounts normally have a debit balance and are eventually debited to the profit and loss account. An example of an expenditure account is the wages account with a £110 balance from the previous chapter's first example.

Asset accounts

These accounts normally have a debit balance and are made up of assets that retain their value. This is distinct from, say, the electricity account, which is an expenditure account. Examples of asset accounts are stock, motor vehicles, and bank accounts with no overdraft. Money owing to the business is in debtor accounts and these are asset accounts. An example is Mrs Clarke's account in the previous chapter's first example. Asset accounts go into the balance sheet, not the profit and loss account.

Liability accounts

These accounts are the debts of the business and they normally have a credit balance. They eventually go into the balance sheet, not the profit and loss account. Examples are the accounts for money owing to suppliers and these accounts are called creditors. A further example is the bank account if there is an overdraft.

Capital accounts

These accounts represent the investment in the business by the owners. If the business is a company, it is the net worth owned by the shareholders. If you refer back to the previous chapter's second example, you will see that Peter Jenkins started his business by paying in £50,000, and that this was credited to a capital account. If the business makes profits, the value of the capital accounts will increase in time.

So long as a business is solvent, the capital accounts will have credit balances. If a business is not solvent, the capital accounts will have debit balances. This is a sign of desperate trouble and often means that the closing of the business is imminent.

Test your understanding

Now test your understanding of the types of account by classifying the following list. The answers are given at the end of this chapter, but write them down before checking.
Write the type of account and whether the balances are normally debit or credit.

	Type of account	Debit or credit?
1 Fixtures and fittings account		
2 Salaries account		
3 Legal and professional expenses account		
4 Revenue reserves account		
5 Share capital account		
6 Trade debtors account		
7 Trade creditors account		
8 Hire purchase creditors account		
9 Shop takings account		
10 Goods sold account		

The nominal ledger

The nominal ledger is the principal ledger. If other ledgers are kept, they reconcile to a control account within the nominal ledger.

In very simple accounting systems only one ledger is maintained (the nominal ledger) and every single account is part of this main ledger. If there are, say, ten customers, each one has an account within the nominal ledger. This option is open to all but it is practical only in the case of small and simple systems. Sheer numbers often necessitate the keeping of subsidiary sales and purchase ledgers. The detailed sales and purchase ledgers each reconcile to their own control account within the nominal ledger. According to circumstances, other subsidiary ledgers may be kept. An example is a listing of the various fixed asset accounts.

The nominal ledger may be very big, perhaps containing thousands of individual accounts. This will certainly be the case for a major company and it is therefore necessary to have a system for coding and grouping the accounts.

In a simple system the accounts will just be listed, probably in alphabetical order. In a more complex system they will be grouped in a logical manner. For example, if there are several bank accounts, they may be listed next to each other. This is convenient and, when the balance sheet is prepared, all the bank accounts will be added to the one total that will appear in it. Similarly, it is usual to group all the overhead expenditure accounts by department.

In all but the very smallest systems it is normal to give each account an identifying number. This is quicker to write out and, if the system is mechanized or computerized, the person posting the entries will post according to the numbers only.

Numbering systems

There are thousands of different accounting numbering systems and you may want to design your own to fit your business and individual circumstances. It is worth looking at the numbering system of your employer or some other organization. Whether or not it is a good system, make sure that you understand the principles of the numbering.

The sales ledger

If your business is so specialized that you have only one customer, you will not need a detailed sales ledger, just one account in the nominal ledger. And you will not need a sales ledger if your sales are entirely for cash.

On the other hand, most businesses that sell on credit will have many customers. For them, an efficient sales ledger outside the nominal ledger is essential.

A manual sales ledger account looks very like a nominal ledger account. It is divided in the middle with debit on the left and credit on the right. There will be one account for each customer and the postings to it are as shown below.

Manual sales ledger	
Debit	Invoices issued
Credit	Credit notes issued
Credit	Cash received
Credit	Invoices written off as bad debts

Normally, the debits on each account will exceed the credits. This means that the account has a debit balance, which is the amount owed to the business by the customer. The total of the balances of all the sales ledger accounts is equal to the total amount owed to the business by the customers. This sum is represented by just one account (usually called the sales ledger control account) in the nominal system.

> *The bookkeeping system is designed to ensure that the accounts in the sales ledger do actually add up to the balance of the control account.*

You will rarely encounter sales ledger accounts ruled in the traditional way described, although some small businesses may still use them. You will probably only be familiar with computer printouts that do not look anything like the ledgers described. It is important to remember, though, that a computer is just an efficient way of doing what could be done manually.

Some of the figures on the computer printout will represent credits and some will represent debits. They are just presented differently from a manual ledger. It is worth proving this to yourself by marking the debits and credits on a computerized sales ledger.

A business needs to send out statements and operate credit control procedures. These are a by-product of the sales ledgers; a computerized system simply speeds up the process. A computerized system may operate on the open item principle. This means that cash payments are allocated to specific invoices, and customer statements only show unpaid invoices. A computerized system may readily give useful management information, such as an ageing of the debts.

The sales day book

It is necessary to have a mechanism for posting sales invoices into the sales ledger and the nominal ledger. This could be done laboriously one by one, but it is better to group them together and cut down the work.

This posting medium is usually called the sales day book, although you might find it called the sales journal or some other name. The following is a typical example of a sales day book. However, the design can vary according to individual preference and business circumstances.

Date	Customer	Invoice no.	Folio no.	Goods total £	VAT £	Invoice total £
1 June	Bigg and Son	1001	B4	100.00	20.00	120.00
4 June	Carter Ltd	1002	C1	200.00	40.00	240.00
12 June	XYZ Ltd	1003	X1	50.00	10.00	60.00
17 June	Martin Bros	1004	M2	100.00	20.00	120.00
26 June	Fishers Ltd	1005	F5	10.00	2.00	12.00
30 June	Dawson Ltd	1006	D2	20.00	4.00	24.00
				480.00	96.00	576.00

Please note the following about the columns:

- *Date* This is the date of each individual invoice.
- *Customer* This is the customer to whom each individual invoice is addressed.
- *Invoice no.* Each invoice must be individually numbered.
- *Folio no.* This is the identifying code to each individual sales ledger account.
- *Goods total* This is the total value of each invoice excluding VAT. Sometimes this is further divided to include different totals for different product groups. The example given shows only total sales.
- *VAT* This is the VAT charged on each individual invoice.
- *Invoice total* This is the total amount of each individual invoice and the amount that the customer has to pay.

The columns may be added and the posting done whenever it is convenient to do so. Monthly posting is frequently encountered and, in practice, there are likely to be more than six invoices. The posting to the nominal ledger would be:

Sales account	£480.00 credit	The sales account will eventually contribute to profit in the profit and loss account.
VAT account	£96.00 credit	This is a liability account. It is money owed by the business to the government.
Sales ledger control account	£576.00 debit	This is an asset account. It is money owing to the business by customers.

Six individual sales ledger accounts are debited with the total amount of the six individual invoices. You will notice that the balances of the sales ledger accounts will add up to the value of the sales ledger control account in the nominal system.

If you have a computerized system, your records will probably not look like this example. The computer will follow exactly these principles and do the same job, but it will do it much more quickly.

The purchase ledger

If you have thoroughly understood the section on the sales ledger, you will have no trouble understanding this section on the purchase ledger. This is because the purchase ledger is a mirror image of the sales ledger. It is used for invoices submitted to the business by suppliers.

The layout is similar to the accounts in the nominal ledger and the sales ledger. Postings to it are as shown below.

Purchase ledger	
Credit	Suppliers' invoices received
Debit	Suppliers' credit notes received
Debit	Cash payments made

Each account will normally have a credit balance and this represents the amount owing to the supplier by the business. The total of all the individual purchase ledger accounts is the same as the amount of the purchase ledger control account in the nominal ledger. Customers will submit statements to you and press you to make regular prompt payments to them.

The purchases day book

We have already seen that the purchase ledger is a mirror image of the sales ledger. You will therefore not be surprised to learn that the purchases day book is a mirror image of the sales day book. Do not be confused if you find it called the purchases journal or some other name, and do not be confused if it is a computerized system with a layout that makes sense to computer experts.

A typical purchases day book looks like the following:

Date	Customer	Invoice no.	Folio no.	Goods total £	VAT £	Invoice total £
1 July	Jones Ltd	3001	J8	100.00	20.00	120.00
9 July	King and Co	3002	K3	300.00	60.00	360.00
13 July	ABC Ltd	3003	A1	50.00	10.00	60.00
20 July	Dodd & Carr	3004	D2	200.00	40.00	240.00
28 July	Sugar Co Ltd	3005	S8	30.00	6.00	36.00
				680.00	136.00	816.00

The purchases day book is the medium through which a batch of suppliers' invoices is posted into the nominal system and into the purchase ledger. It avoids the need to enter them individually into the nominal system. It is usually ruled off and entered monthly but you can do this at any suitable interval.

Test your understanding

Now test your understanding by writing down the three nominal posting entries resulting from the above purchases day book. Also write down the balance of Jones Ltd in the purchase ledger. The answers are given at the end of the chapter.

Summary

In this chapter we have understood the five different types of nominal account and the differences between them. We have had a detailed look at:

- the nominal ledger
- the sales ledger
- the sales day book
- the purchase ledger
- the purchases day book.

Next we will continue our study of different aspects of bookkeeping.

Test your understanding

Answers

Types of account

1	Assets account	normally debit balance
2	Expenditure account	normally debit balance
3	Expenditure account	normally debit balance
4	Capital account	normally credit balance
5	Capital account	normally credit balance
6	Assets account	normally debit balance
7	Liabilities account	normally credit balance
8	Liabilities account	normally credit balance
9	Income account	normally credit balance
10	Income account	normally credit balance

Nominal postings

Purchases account	£680.00 debit
VAT account	£136.00 debit
Purchase ledger control account	£816.00 credit

In practice, the £680.00 would probably be spread over several different purchases account.

Jones Ltd will have a credit balance of £120.00 in the purchase ledger.

Fact-check (answers at the back)

1. Where are income accounts eventually credited?
a) The balance sheet ❏
b) The profit and loss account ❏
c) The fixed assets ❏
d) The directors' report ❏

2. What conclusion would you draw if the capital accounts have an overall debit balance?
a) The bookkeeper has made a mistake ❏
b) There has been a loss in the current year ❏
c) The business is insolvent ❏
d) The shareholders have not paid for their shares ❏

3. Which *two* of the following may be credited to a sales ledger account?
a) Invoices issued ❏
b) Credit notes issued ❏
c) Cash received ❏
d) Cash returned to the customer ❏

4. What does it mean if a sales ledger account has a debit balance?
a) The customer owes money to the business ❏
b) The business owes money to the customer ❏
c) Deliveries have not yet reached the customer ❏
d) Orders are still outstanding ❏

5. What does the sales day book do?
a) It tells you the total sales for each day ❏
b) It is the posting medium for sales invoices ❏
c) It lists the credit balances in the bookkeeping system ❏
d) It lists the debit balances in the bookkeeping system ❏

6. To what must the balances of the sales ledger accounts add up?
a) The total sales ❏
b) The profit ❏
c) The assets ❏
d) The balance of the sales ledger control account ❏

7. What does it mean if a purchase ledger account has a debit balance?
a) The supplier owes money to the business ❏
b) The business owes money to the supplier ❏
c) Deliveries have not yet reached the business ❏
d) A mistake has been made ❏

8. What is the purchases day book a mirror of?
a) The sales day book ❏
b) The purchase ledger ❏
c) The sales ledger ❏
d) None of the above ❏

9. When can the purchases day book be ruled off and entered?
a) Weekly ❏
b) Monthly ❏
c) Yearly ❏
d) Any convenient time ❏

10. What sort of account is stock?
a) Income ❏
b) Expenditure ❏
c) Capital ❏
d) Assets ❏

CHAPTER 10

More aspects of bookkeeping

In the first two chapters we examined the basic foundations of bookkeeping and keeping different types of account and different ledgers. Now we will build on that work by looking at more aspects of bookkeeping. We must do this before we can move on to preparatory work for the accounts. This, and the accounts themselves, can only be done properly if the underlying bookkeeping records are complete, accurate and up to date.

Like buildings, accounts will be dangerous if the foundations are not properly laid. This chapter's programme, therefore, is deep and varied. You will study several more aspects of bookkeeping and attempt two practical examples.

We will look at the following:

- the cash book
- the bank reconciliation
- other reconciliations and checks
- the journal
- petty cash
- the trial balance.

The cash book

Almost any set of accounting records involves the receiving and paying out of money. If there are only a few entries, it may all be recorded in the bank account and cash account in the nominal ledger. However, due to the number of entries, it is usual to maintain a separate cash book. Sometimes bank and cash are combined in one book and sometimes two books are kept. We will assume that two books are kept.

Sometimes the cash book is really a posting medium to the appropriate nominal ledger account. In this respect it is rather like the day books studied in the previous chapter. The cash book will have two sides, one for payments and one for receipts. The payments side would probably look like this.

Date	Cheque no.	Payee	Folio	Amount £
4 May	1234	Simpson and Co.	S3	200.68
9 May	1235	Jones Ltd	J8	33.11
14 May	–	Bank charges	39	10.00
17 May	1236	Wainrights	W1	111.00
19 May	1237	Cubitt Ltd	C9	44.00
				398.79

The total of £398.79 would be credited to the bank account in the nominal ledger.

TIP *Payments out of a bank account are credits.*

Various accounts are debited and these are identified by the folio numbers.

In reality, there may be hundreds of entries. The posting may be made easier by analysing the payment amount over extra columns. For example, if there are three entries for bank charges, only the total of the bank charges need be posted, rather than three individual items.

The following is an example of a full cash book balanced at the month end.

Receipts Date		Folio	Amount £	Date				Folio	Payments Amount £
1 Sept.	Balance	b/d	800.00	1 Sept.	4001	Arkwright		PL3	29.16
4 Sept.	Cross and Co.	SL6	101.10	2 Sept.	4002	Rates		NL4	290.00
9 Sept.	Figg Ltd	SL12	17.11	6 Sept.	4003	Stevens Ltd		PL7	34.12
13 Sept.	Morgan Ltd	SL17	34.19	9 Sept.	4004	Wilson Bros		PL19	47.11
18 Sept.	Peters and Brown	SL3	700.00	12 Sept.	4005	Crabbe and Co.		PL8	39.12
30 Sept.	Trapp Ltd	SL22	1 091.00	17 Sept.	4006	Carter		PL2	200.00
				19 Sept.	4007	Jenkins		PL12	56.99
				23 Sept.	4008	Champion and Co		PL17	450.00
				24 Sept.	4009	Wages		NL4	290.00
				29 Sept.	4010	Barton and Hicks		PL1	300.00
				30 Sept.		Balance		c/d	1,006.90
			2,743.40						2,743.40
1 Oct.	Balance	b/d	1,006.90						

This is a completed cash book for the month of September. You will have noticed that the book has been ruled off and balanced, the first time that you have seen this done. The balancing may be done at any time but once a month is typical.

The balancing is done by adding the columns and writing in the difference on the side that has the smaller of the two figures. This is expressed as the balance carried down. The two columns then add to the same amount. The balancing figure is then transferred to the other column and becomes the opening balance in the next period.

In the example the balance brought down on 1 September is on the receipts side, which means that there is money in the bank and no overdraft. This is still the position when the account is balanced on 30 September.

The four-figure numbers before the names on the payments side are cheque numbers. This is optional and will assist when the bank reconciliation is done.

The bank reconciliation

It is good practice to write up the cash book frequently and to keep it up to date. That way, you will know what the statement balance will be when all items reach the bank. You will have prior knowledge if the account is close to an overdraft or an agreed limit.

> ## Case study
>
> The writer Ernest Hemingway often did not bother to bank cheques that he received, preferring instead to use them as bookmarks. After his death, his house was found to contain dozens of unbanked cheques, some as much as 20 years old. They were presented for payment and many of them were paid. This is an extreme example of one reason why the bank statement balance might not be the same as the cash book balance, and why it is necessary to reconcile the two balances.

Possible reasons for a difference in the two figures are as follows:

- Cheques written in the cash book have not yet been debited to the bank statement.
- Receipts written in the cash book have not yet been credited to the bank statement.
- Items have been debited to the bank statement that have not yet been written in the cash book. Common examples are direct debits, standing orders and bank charges.
- Receipts have been credited to the bank statement that have not yet been written in the cash book. This could, for example, be a credit transfer payment by a customer.

- You have made a mistake – perhaps the wrong amount has been written into the cash book or a paying-in slip has been added incorrectly.
- The bank has made a mistake. This is very unlikely, but it can happen.

Test your understanding

You should now be able to have a go at doing a bank reconciliation. The following is a simplified bank statement for the company whose cash book was given earlier in this chapter. It is for September, corresponding with the period covered by the cash book. As it is a bank statement, receipts are printed on the right, the opposite side to the normal cash book layout.

Date	Detail	Payments £	Receipts £	Balance £
1 Sept.	Opening balance			800.00 cr
6 Sept.	Counter credit		101.10	
6 Sept.	4001	29.16		
6 Sept.	4002	290.00		581.94 cr
11 Sept.	Counter credit		17.11	599.05 cr
12 Sept.	Standing order – rates	105.16		493.89 cr
15 Sept.	Counter credit		34.19	
15 Sept.	4003	34.12		
15 Sept.	4004	47.11		
15 Sept.	Direct debit – water rates	61.82		385.03 cr
20 Sept.	Counter credit		700.00	
20 Sept.	Credit transfer received		349.21	1,434.24 cr
21 Sept.	4005	38.12		1,396.12 cr
30 Sept.	4008	450.00		946.12 cr

You must tick off the entries in the bank statement against those in the cash book and write out the differences. Do not worry about the best layout – just have a go and write it down. The answer is given at the end of the chapter, but have a go before you check.

Other reconciliations and checks

If there is a bank account, you should periodically reconcile it with the cash book or with the appropriate account in the nominal ledger. You should also reconcile or check other accounts periodically. One of these is petty cash and this is considered shortly.

From time to time, you should check that all the sales ledger accounts add up to the sales ledger control account in the nominal ledger. Similarly, all the purchase ledger accounts should add up to the purchase ledger control account in the nominal ledger.

If you have any sort of suspense account, it is important that you analyse what items make up the balance.

A suspense account is, of course, an account where money is placed until a final accounting entry is decided.

I can reliably forecast that all sorts of nonsense will get dumped into the suspense account. I forecast this because it seems to happen to all suspense accounts. You must identify the items and take steps to clear them out. The list of potential reconciliations is a long one and it is good practice to reconcile where possible.

The journal

We have seen earlier that entries are made to the accounting records by means of the following **books of entry**:

- the sales day book
- the purchases day book
- the cash book.

Entries are also made by means of the returns inwards book, the returns outwards book and the petty cash book. The petty cash book is examined later. The books of entry are completed by the journal, which is an important item in bookkeeping and worth explaining in some detail.

The journal is used to record important transactions that are not posted through the medium of any of the above books. You could just post the debits and credits to the right accounts without recording them in a book. Many bookkeepers do just this but it is much better to use a journal. This makes fraud and mistakes less likely, makes it easier to check the books, and, most importantly, gives you a narrative explanation for the entries. Auditors favour the use of a journal.

The journal is ruled to show the date, a reference number for the entry, the identity and amount of the account to be credited, the identity and amount of the account to be debited, and a narrative explanation. An example of a journal entry is as follows:

		Debit	Credit
1 March	Bad debts written off	£1,000.00	
JV99	Curzon & Co		£1,000.00

Petty cash

The word 'petty' means small or trivial, and the purpose of the petty cash system is to allow small and trivial disbursements to be made. This limitation may not always be apparent to colleagues who will try to obtain large sums of money from it. Nevertheless, the purpose is to handle small sums of money.

A typical petty cash book is very wide, has two sides, and has a considerable number of columns for analysis. This makes it difficult to reproduce here, but the following is a simplified example of how the payments side typically looks.

Date	Details of expense	Voucher no.	Total £	Stamps £	Petrol £
2 May	Stamps	1	10.00	10.00	
16 May	Petrol	2	18.48		18.48
29 May	Stamps	3	10.00	10.00	
			38.48	20.00	18.48
May	Balance c/d		11.52		
			50.00		

In practice, there would, of course, be many more entries and a further dozen or so analysis columns to record the different categories of expense (milk, stationery, etc.).

149

Note that the total column is always used and this is the total amount paid out on each voucher. If someone is claiming £10 for stamps and £10 for petrol, £20 would be entered in the total column.

The imprest system

The example above assumes that the imprest system is in use and that the float is £50. The imprest system is loved by auditors and is much superior to other systems.

Under the imprest system the amount of money in the petty cash box, plus the payments made and recorded in the book, should add up to the amount of the float. If they do not, a mistake has been made. In the previous example a cheque for £38.48 would be written and cashed. This would restore the float to £50, which would then be the opening balance for June.

The accounting entries to record the May transactions would be:

Postage account	£20.00 debit
Petrol account	£18.48 debit
Petty cash account	£38.48 credit

The entry for the reimbursement cheque would be:

Petty cash account	£38.48 debit
Bank account	£38.48 credit

After all the entries have been posted, the petty cash account should have a balance of £50 debit in the nominal ledger. It is an asset account and there is £50 cash to support it. A £50 cheque would have been written on Day 1.

The trial balance

The trial balance is not an account and it does not involve posting. It is the listing of all the balances in the ledger.

There are two very good reasons for taking out a trial balance:

1 It is one of the steps towards preparing the profit and loss account and the balance sheet.
2 It is proof that, subject to certain exceptions described below, the books are in order.

It is good practice to take out a trial balance regularly, perhaps once a month. This means that, if there is a mistake to be found, only a month's entries need be checked. Of course, in a computerized bookkeeping system it should be guaranteed that the system balances and that the total of the debit balances equals the total of the credit balances.

> ## Taking out a trial balance
> You will remember that for every debit there must be a credit. It follows that the total of all the debit balances must equal the total of all the credit balances. If they do not do so, then a mistake has been made. Taking out a trial balance will find this out.

There are limitations to the proofs provided by a trial balance. It may balance and yet not disclose the following two types of error:

● a compensating error: this is two mistakes for the same amount, one increasing or reducing the debits and one increasing or reducing the credits
● the right amount posted to the wrong account.

Both these types of error are nasty and you may never realize that a mistake has been made. They each mean that two accounts are wrong.

A difference on the trial balance will disclose one of the following mistakes:

● a wrong addition on an account
● a mistake in writing out the brought forward balances
● one side of an entry not posted (double entry not complete)
● posting of wrong amount
● a missing ledger sheet.

How to conduct a trial balance

You might find the cause of a trial balance difference by means of a random search. However, it is much better to conduct the search in a systematic manner. You *must* locate the cause of the difference if you do the following in a *systematic* way:

1 Check the listing of the balances within the trial balance.
2 Check the addition of the trial balance.
3 Check the listing of the opening balances. These are either the balances brought down or the balances at the time that the last trial balance was agreed.
4 Check the addition of each individual account within the trial balance. Check from the brought forward balances or the balances making up the last trial balance.
5 Tick each individual posting during the period under review. Every debit should have a matching credit and there should be no unticked entries at the end.

If done properly, this must find the difference.

Test your understanding

We will finish this chapter with a simple example of a trial balance, a series of postings and the new trial balance.
The new trial balance is given at the end of the chapter, but prepare it for yourself before checking the answer.

Summarized trial balance

	Debit £	Credit £
Capital account		50,000
Sales account		1,000,000
Sales ledger creditors		20,000
Cost of sales account	500,000	
Stock account	300,000	
Overhead account	190,000	
Bank account	80,000	
	1,070,000	1,070,000

Cash sales of £400,000 are made. Cost of sales is 50 per cent of sales. £300,000 is spent on overheads, half on credit and half for cash. £600,000 fixed assets are purchased for cash.

Summary

In this chapter we examined several more essential aspects of bookkeeping. We have:

● studied the layout and operation of the cash book and the postings from it

● studied bank reconciliations and attempted an example

● considered other reconciliations and checks

● examined the journal

● considered petty cash, especially the imprest system

● examined trial balances and tried working from one trial balance through to another.

Now we will look at how to prepare for the accounts.

Test your understanding

Answers

Bank reconciliation

Cash book balance at 30 September		1,006.90 dr
Add cheques not yet presented:		
4006	200.00	
4007	56.99	
4009	290.00	
4010	300.00	
		846.99
		1,853.89
Add credit on statement not in cash book		349.21
		2,203.10
Less receipt in cash book not on statement		1,091.00
		1,112.10
Less payments on statement not in cash book		
Standing order – rates	105.16	
Direct debit – water rates	61.82	
		166.98
		945.12
Add difference to be investigated (cheque 4005 for £39.12 entered by bank as £38.12)		1.00
As per bank statement balance at 30 September		946.12 dr

This is not easy, so congratulations if you got it right. It does illustrate all the principles effectively.

Trial balance

	Debit £	Credit £
Capital account		50,000
Sales account		1,400,000
Sales ledger creditors		170,000
Cost of sales account	700,000	
Stock account	100,000	
Overhead account	490,000	
Bank account		270,000
Fixed asset accounts	600,000	
	1,890,000	1,890,000

Fact-check (answers at the back)

1. What should happen to the total of the payments recorded in the cash book?
   a) It should be debited to bank account in the nominal ledger ❏
   b) It should be credited to bank account in the nominal ledger ❏
   c) It should be added to the accumulated total of payments made in previous periods ❏
   d) Nothing ❏

2. What happens to the total of payments for stationery recorded in the cash book?
   a) It should be debited to stationery account in the nominal ledger ❏
   b) It should be credited to stationery account in the nominal ledger ❏
   c) It should be added to the accumulated total of payments made for stationery in previous periods ❏
   d) Nothing ❏

3. What happens to the closing balance when the cash book is ruled off at the end of a period?
   a) It is entered on the same side as the opening balance in the next period ❏
   b) It is entered on the opposite side as the opening balance in the next period ❏
   c) It is posted to the bank account in the nominal ledger ❏
   d) Nothing ❏

4. What is the journal used for?
   a) To keep a record of important events ❏
   b) To reconcile different ledgers ❏
   c) To reconcile different accounts ❏
   d) To record important transactions that are not posted through the medium of the other books ❏

5. Which of the following are advantages of using a journal rather than posting directly to the nominal ledger?
   a) Fraud and mistakes are less likely ❏
   b) The narrative explanation may be useful ❏
   c) Auditors like it ❏
   d) All of the above ❏

6. An employee is reimbursed in cash £10 for the purchase of biscuits. In which book will the entry be made?
   a) The cash book ❏
   b) The journal ❏
   c) The petty cash book ❏
   d) The purchases day book ❏

7. Which of the following is a feature of the imprest system for petty cash?
   a) It is impressive ❏
   b) There is a float of a fixed amount ❏
   c) It is not possible to run out of money ❏
   d) Employees will not claim unreasonably large sums ❏

8. What is a trial balance?
a) A listing of all the balances in the ledger ❏
b) A particular type of account ❏
c) Another name for the profit and loss account ❏
d) Another name for the balance sheet ❏

9. Which of the following mistakes will *not* be disclosed by a trial balance?
a) One side of an entry not posted (double entry not complete) ❏
b) A mistake in writing out the brought forward balances ❏
c) The right amount posted to the wrong account ❏
d) Posting of wrong amount ❏

10. What is a compensating error?
a) Posting of wrong amount ❏
b) A wrong addition on the account ❏
c) A mistake in listing or adding the trial balance ❏
d) Two mistakes for the same amount, one increasing or reducing the debits and one increasing or reducing the credits ❏

CHAPTER 11

Preparation for the accounts

Now that we have learned the basic principles of bookkeeping and discovered how to prepare accurate and complete bookkeeping records, we can turn our attention to the process involved in preparing the final accounts. However, there is more work to be done first.

Next we must look at important accounting entries which are not yet recorded in the trial balance but which are vital to the preparation of accurate accounts. We then conclude this chapter by seeing how the trial balance is adjusted to reflect these entries.

The programme is:

- accruals
- prepayments
- reserves and provisions
- depreciation
- posting final adjustments and the extended trial balance.

Accruals

We concluded the previous chapter by considering the trial balance. This should accurately reflect the position after posting all the entries. But what about charges that have not yet been put into the accounts? Sometimes a supplier may be late submitting an invoice. If you work in a large accounts office, you will know that an occasional invoice may be submitted a year or more after the event.

Furthermore, suppliers' invoices may be lost or held up pending approval. The more quickly the books are closed off after the end of the accounting period, the more numerous will be the invoices not entered.

These problems can be overcome by entering what are called accruals. Accruals are **costs incurred but not yet entered**. They are calculated in one of two ways:

1 a specific invoice received after the close off
   - If the electricity bill to 31 March is £1,507.46 and accounts are done for the year to 31 March, then you will accrue either £1,507 or £1,500.
2 an informed estimate
   - If the electricity bill averages £1,000 a quarter and the last bill is up to 15 March, it would be reasonable to accrue £170 at 31 March. It is usual for most accruals to be informed estimates.

The accounting entry is to debit the account of the expense (e.g. electricity) and to credit the accruals account. The accruals account is a liability account because it is money owing by the business.

Prepayments

A prepayment is the exact opposite of an accrual, which is a cost incurred but not yet entered. A prepayment is **a cost entered but not yet incurred**.

A prepayment may be necessary because a supplier has raised an invoice early, or because you have left the books open to catch as many invoices as possible and one from the next period has slipped through. For example, an invoice dated

3 July may slip through if you make the accounts up to 30 June but leave the books open for two weeks beyond that date.

More usually, a prepayment may be necessary because an invoice has been entered that covers a benefit to be received in the future. A common example is insurance, which may be paid a year in advance.

> ## Prepayments in practice
>
> Consider an insurance invoice for £12,000 that has been paid on 31 December for insurance cover over the following 12 months. Let us assume that the business prepared its accounts at 30 June. Obviously, unless an adjustment is made, overheads will be too large and the profit will be too small.
>
> The answer is to prepay six-twelfths of £12,000, which equals £6,000. Insurance (an overhead account) is credited with £6,000 and the prepayments account is debited £6,000.

The prepayments account is an asset account because it is money paid in advance for goods and services. It is like the deposit that you may pay in February for your summer holiday to be taken in August.

You may be asking what eventually happens to the entries for accruals and prepayments after the accounts have been prepared. The answer is that they are reversed. This is explained later.

Test your understanding

You should now take a few moments to test your understanding by writing down the entries for the following. The answers are given at the end of the chapter.

A staff restaurant prepares accounts at 31 May

- A £70 invoice for bread from the wholesalers dated 8 June has been entered into the books.
- The telephone account for the quarter to 31 March was £600. No later invoice has been received.

- Six months' water rates in advance totalling £900 were paid on 31 March.
- Food with a total value of £700 was delivered to the canteen on 29 May. No invoice has been received.
- Wages average £350 a week and are paid weekly in arrears. Payment has been made for work done up to 26 May. (A seven-day week is worked.)

Reserves

In Chapter 9 you read that reserves were part of the capital of a business and represented money belonging to the shareholders or other owners. However, the term has a very different meaning as well.

Reserves are made to cover an event that may well happen (or has actually happened) but which is not adequately recorded in the books.

Bad debt reserves

A bad debt reserve is an easily understood example. Company A made a credit sale of £100,000 to Company B. The entries in the books of Company A were:

- Sales account   £100,000 credit
- Trade debtors' account   £100,000 debit

Good news so far. The balance of the sales account will eventually be credited to the profit and loss account and will increase profit. It is expected that Company B will soon send a cheque for £100,000 to clear the trade debtors' account. But Company B's chairman is arrested and charged with fraud, the directors resign, the company goes into liquidation, and the liquidator forecasts an eventual dividend of 10p in the pound to unsecured creditors.

To put it mildly, the books of Company A do not reflect the true position. They overstate the true profit by £90,000. Company A will need the following entry in its books:

- Bad debt reserve account   £90,000 credit
- Bad debt account   £90,000 debit

The bad debts account is a charge to the profit and loss account. This reduces the £100,000 sale contribution to a realistic £10,000.

The bad debt reserve account is placed against the trade debtors' account in the balance sheet. It is thus reduced to £10,000, which is the amount expected to be paid eventually.

Bad debt reserves may be against specific debts as above, or they may be a realistic general reserve. For example, a book club sells books to the public by post and sends out the books before payment is made. At any one time it is owed money by many thousands of different customers. Each debt is individually small. Experience may show that a bad debt reserve of, say, 5 per cent of the total outstanding is necessary.

Provisions

Provisions are very similar to reserves and, in practice, the two terms are almost interchangeable. Reserves and provisions are necessary for more than just bad debts. The list is very long and you may well be able to think of some circumstances that relate to a business with which you are familiar. The following are just some of the possibilities.

● **Provision for settlement discounts payable**

Suppose that your business offers 5 per cent settlement discount to all customers who pay within 30 days of invoice date. Unless you make a provision, you will overstate the profits. Not all customers will take advantage of the settlement discount so perhaps a provision of 4 per cent of the total sum outstanding would be realistic.

● **Provision for fulfilling warranty claim obligations**

Suppose that you supply double-glazed windows and guarantee to repair faulty workmanship free of charge for up to ten years after installation. A realistic provision for the cost of future repairs would be necessary.

● **Provision for settlement of outstanding legal claims**

These could be for alleged negligence, faulty workmanship, wrongful dismissal, libel or many other matters. Again, a realistic estimate of the eventual cost should be provided.

● Provision for losses on a contract or joint venture

Perhaps one of these has gone wrong. Your organization has a legal obligation to complete the work, but it is clear that a loss will be made at the end. Provision should be made for the loss as soon as it can realistically be foreseen. You should not wait to charge the profit and loss account in future years.

In all cases the accounting entry is:

- Credit a suitably named reserve or provision account
- Debit the appropriate account in the profit and loss section.

Depreciation

Current assets are assets with a value available to the business in the short term, usually taken to mean up to a year. Examples are cash, stock, and trade debtors (money owing by customers).

Fixed assets are assets with a value available in the long term, usually taken to mean more than a year. Examples are motor vehicles, leases, plant and machinery, and computer equipment.

Some fixed assets hold their value indefinitely, but most do not. The value of most fixed assets diminishes either with time (e.g. leases), with wear and tear (e.g. plant and equipment), or with both (e.g. cars). Computer equipment frequently diminishes in value due to obsolescence.

Depreciation in action

Perhaps the simplest example of a depreciating fixed asset is a lease. Take leasehold property purchased for £300,000, and with ten years of the lease remaining. On the day that the property is purchased it is worth £300,000. Ten years later it is worth nothing. Its value falls by £30,000 each year. If the accounts do not recognize this, both the profit and the value of the assets will be overstated.

It is therefore necessary to write off most fixed assets over a period of time. A formula must be found that fairly reflects the reduction in value. In the case of the £300,000 lease described in the example the annual bookkeeping entry is:

● depreciation account   £30,000 debit
● leasehold property account   £30,000 credit.

The depreciation account is a profit and loss account item and it reduces the profit. The credit to the leasehold property account reduces the value of the asset, which you will remember is a debit balance. This is the straight-line method of depreciation, which is the most common and the simplest. It involves writing off an equal amount over a fixed number of years.

Another common method is the reducing balance method. This writes off a given percentage of the remaining balance. A feature of this method is that the value of the asset in the books can never quite reach zero. This is usually realistic; after all, even a 20-year-old car is worth something.

An example of this is an item of machinery purchased for £100,000 and written off at 25 per cent per year on the reducing balance method. The depreciation charge will be as follows:

● **Year 1**   25% × £100,000 = £25,000
● **Year 2**   25% × £75,000   = £18,750
● **Year 3**   25% × £56,250   = £14,063

There are other methods as well. Care must be taken to choose an appropriate depreciation policy and it must be applied consistently from year to year.

Posting final adjustments and the extended trial balance

In the previous chapter we saw that the production of the trial balance is a key stage in preparing accounts. We finish this chapter by considering how the trial balance is finalized for the preparation of the accounts.

If the accounts are very simple and everything is up to date, there may not be any further entries to post. In these cases the accountant can proceed directly to prepare the accounts. We will look at accounts preparation in detail in Chapters 12 and 13.

This is unusual, though, especially if there are a lot of entries. It is usually necessary to list the trial balance, open the accounts for the next period and then work through a list of adjustments to the trial balance. There are nearly always accruals and prepayments. There are often reserves and provisions to enter and mistakes to be corrected, and there may be many other adjustments as well.

There are two basic approaches for posting the adjustments – actually posting the entries or making an extended trial balance – and we will consider these in turn. It is likely that a computerized system will handle the posting of the final adjustments, but the following explains the principles.

Posting the entries

All the adjustments are posted in the ledgers and then a new trial balance is listed. This new trial balance is used to prepare the accounts. All the adjustment entries are then reverse posted into the ledgers in the next period. This reverse posting is necessary because the ledgers have to be restored to the position before the adjustments.

This may be difficult to understand, but consider an accrual of £1,000 for a late telephone bill. The accrual is a debit to the overhead account. In the next period the reverse posting puts a credit of £1,000 into the overhead account. When the actual invoice for £1,000 arrives, it is a debit and cancels out the credit, leaving a nil balance. This is correct because it was a late invoice that should affect profit only in the earlier period.

Computerized accounting systems usually operate in this way. This is because it is relatively simple for the computer to be programmed to reverse post automatically into the following period.

The extended trial balance

The second approach is to list all the adjustments into extra columns to the trial balance (one debit column and one credit column). The trial balance is then repeated, taking account of the adjustments. The whole thing is contained in one page and there are six columns in total (sometimes eight columns but we will not bother with this). It is extremely important that all the adjustments are properly cross-referenced to a full list of the changes and a narrative explanation of them.

Test your understanding

We will conclude this chapter by looking at an extended trial balance for Bridget Murphy, a public relations consultant. She commences business on 1 July and the extended trial balance is at the end of her first year in business on the following 30 June. Note that the title and date should be given at the top.

The extended trial balance is given below and you should study it carefully. It incorporates adjustments to reflect the following:

● Motor vehicle and office equipment should both be depreciated by 25 per cent.
● Bridget has not yet entered an invoice for £5,000 for work that she has done.
● Bank interest to 30 June not yet entered into the books is £2,643.
● On 21 May Bridget paid £2,400 insurance to cover a year in advance.
● Bridget has received invoices as follows but not entered them into the books:
  – Office expenses   £1,800
  – Travel expenses   £246
  – Stationery   £679.
● Her telephone account averages £1,800 a quarter and she has paid the bill up to 31 May.
● Bridget believes that £1,000 owing to her will turn out to be a bad debt.

	Opening Trial Balance		Adjustments		Closing Trial Balance	
	Debit £	Credit £	Debit £	Credit £	Debit £	Credit £
Motor vehicles	20,000.00				20,000.00	
Office equipment	15,000.00				15,000.00	
Depreciation of motor vehicles				5,000.00		5,000.00
Depreciation of office equipment				3,750.00		3,750.00
Bank account		23,185.16				23,185.16
Trade debtors	5,708.31		5,000.00		10,708.31	
Trade creditors		661.19				661.19
Reserve for bad debts				1,000.00		1,000.00
Accruals				5,968.00		5,968.00
Prepayments			2,400.00		2,400.00	
Fees invoiced		62,000.00		5,000.00		67,000.00
Salaries	12,000.00				12,000.00	
Insurance	4,600.00			2,400.00	2,200.00	
Office expenses	7,309.14		1,800.00		9,109.14	
Travel expenses	11,111.18		246.00		11,357.18	
Stationery	3,209.47		679.00		3,888.47	
Telephone	6,908.25		600.00		7,508.25	
Interest			2,643.00		2,643.00	
Bad debts			1,000.00		1,000.00	
Depreciation			8,750.00		8,750.00	
	85,846.35	85,846.35	23,118.00	23,118.00	106,564.35	106,564.35

Summary

In this chapter we have examined some of the calculations that have to be made before the final accounts are prepared, and we have seen how these are incorporated into the trial balance. Specifically we have:

- studied accruals and prepayments
- tested our understanding of accruals and prepayments
- studied reserves and provisions
- studied depreciation
- seen how the adjustments are entered into the accounts
- studied the extended trial balance.

Next we move on to a detailed examination of the profit and loss account.

Test your understanding
Answers

A staff restaurant prepares accounts at 31 May

	Debit £	Credit £
Prepayments account	70	
Food purchased account		70
Accruals account		400
Telephone account	400	
Prepayments account	600	
Water rates account		600
Accruals account		700
Food purchased account	700	
Accruals account		250
Wages account	250	

Fact-check (answers at the back)

1. What is an accrual?
   a) A cost entered but not yet incurred ❏
   b) A cost incurred but not yet entered ❏
   c) Total costs for the period ❏
   d) Cheques issued but not yet recorded on the bank statement ❏

2. If a telephone bill is normally about £3,000 per quarter and the last bill received was for the quarter to 30 September, what should be the accrual in the accounts for the year to 30 November?
   a) £1,000 ❏
   b) £2,000 ❏
   c) £3,000 ❏
   d) £12,000 ❏

3. What is a prepayment?
   a) A cost entered but not yet incurred ❏
   b) A cost incurred but not yet entered ❏
   c) Total costs for the period ❏
   d) Cheques issued but not yet recorded on the bank statement ❏

4. A supplier submits an invoice for £12,000 dated 1 October for a year's rent in advance for the period commencing 1 November. It is entered in the books for the period to 30 September. What should be the prepayment in the accounts for the year to 30 September?
   a) £13,000 ❏
   b) £1,000 ❏
   c) £12,000 ❏
   d) £6,000 ❏

5. A company is owed £10,000,000 by its customers. It offers a prompt payment discount of 3% and experience shows that about two-thirds of the customers take advantage of it. What sum should be created as a reserve?
   a) £100,000 ❏
   b) £150,000 ❏
   c) £200,000 ❏
   d) £300,000 ❏

6. A company has created a bad debt reserve of £6,000 in respect of money owing by Company X. However, Company X subsequently pays £1,500. What entry must be made in the bad debt reserve account?
   a) £6,000 debit ❏
   b) £4,500 debit ❏
   c) £4,500 credit ❏
   d) £1,500 debit ❏

7. A car costing £60,000 is written off at 25% per year using the straight-line method. What is the depreciation charge in the third year?

a) £60,000 ❏
b) £45,000 ❏
c) £30,000 ❏
d) £15,000 ❏

8. A car costing £60,000 is written off at 25% per year using the reducing balance method. What is the depreciation charge in the third year?

a) £15,000 ❏
b) £11,250 ❏
c) £8,437 ❏
d) £6,328 ❏

9. Given the facts in Question 8, when will the car be written down to nil value?

a) After four years ❏
b) After six years ❏
c) After eight years ❏
d) Never ❏

10. On 1 July a company purchases leasehold property for £500,000. The lease has 20 years left to run. What should be the depreciation charge in the year to 31 December?

a) £12,500 ❏
b) £25,000 ❏
c) £50,000 ❏
d) £500,000 ❏

CHAPTER 12

The profit and loss account

During the first four chapters of this Part we have worked through the principles of bookkeeping up to the extended trial balance. We are now ready to see the accounts resulting from this work. This chapter will look at the internal profit and loss account that is produced for the benefit of managers, and Chapter 13 will study the other main part of the accounts, the balance sheet.

Once again, the steps are explained in detail to help your understanding, even though in most offices computers will of course do much of the work. Now you will learn exactly what a profit and loss account is, and how it works.

This programme also covers examples of:

- a straightforward profit and loss account
- a trading business
- a manufacturing business.

We will also look at two further important points about profit and loss accounts.

What is the profit and loss account?

The profit and loss account is a **summary of all the revenue and expense items** occurring in a specified period of time. The profit and loss account should be properly headed and the period of time stated.

The period is usually a year, especially in the case of published accounts, but you may encounter other periods. Internal profit statements prepared for management may be done weekly, monthly, quarterly or for some other convenient period. The selection of the period does matter. Consider a typical greetings card shop preparing a profit statement for the six months to 31 August. Twenty-five per cent of a year's turnover comes in the five weeks ending on 24 December.

The bookkeeping procedure is as follows.

1 Make sure that everything posted is up to date.
2 Post all the final adjustments. This was explained in the previous chapter.
3 List the final adjusted trial balance, although a computerized system will probably make this unnecessary.
4 Extract the revenue and expense accounts and list these separately. If the credit balances exceed the debit balances, there is a profit. If the debit balances are greater, there is a loss.
5 Open the ledger for the next period. All the revenue and expense accounts will be opened with a nil balance. The net profit or net loss will be transferred to the capital account, thus increasing or decreasing the amount of capital that the proprietor has invested in the business. This ensures that the trial balance continues to balance.
6 The accruals and prepayments are reverse posted into the new period.

A straightforward profit and loss account

There are more things to learn when goods are purchased for resale and stocks are held. A step beyond that is when manufacturing takes place. We will study all this later, but first of all you need to understand a straightforward profit and loss account. The examples are well illustrated with the figures for Bridget Murphy, the public relations consultant whose extended trial balance was listed in the previous chapter.

Please refer back to that extended trial balance. You should be able to recognize which accounts are revenue and expense accounts. You should therefore be able to follow how her profit and loss account is extracted. It is given below.

Bridget Murphy	Profit and loss account for year to 30 June	
	£	£
Fees invoiced		67,000
Less expenses:		
Salaries	12,000	
Insurance	2,200	
Office expenses	9,109	
Travel expenses	11,357	
Stationery	3,888	
Telephone	7,508	
Interest	2,643	
Bad debts	1,000	
Depreciation	8,750	
		58,455
Net Profit		8,545

Test your understanding

Now test your knowledge of the profit and loss account by preparing one yourself, using the following example. The answer is given at the end of the chapter, but prepare the account before looking at it.

Bernard Smith starts work as a painter and decorator on 1 June

He does not hold stocks of materials as he buys just enough for each job. At the following 31 May his trial balance is as follows:

	Debit	Credit
	£	£
Motor van	6,000.00	
Ladder and tools	1,000.00	
Bank account	300.00	
Trade debtors	700.00	
Trade creditors		400.00
Invoiced sales		15,000.00
Materials used	2,000.00	
Motor expenses	1,400.00	
Other overhead costs	4,000.00	
	15,400.00	15,400.00

Bernard is advised that he should depreciate the motor van by 25 per cent, and the ladder and tools by 10 per cent.

He believes that half the trade debtors are an irrecoverable bad debt. He holds an invoice for materials for £600 and an overheads invoice for £200. Neither has been entered into the books. He has paid £500 for a year's insurance in advance.

A customer has complained about bad workmanship. Bernard has agreed to spend £200 on putting it right.

A trading business

So far we have only considered businesses that do not hold stock. It is now time to see how the accounts deal with this problem.

You will, I hope, quickly see that the profit and loss account must only show the cost of the goods sold in the period. You will obtain a wrong figure, perhaps a ridiculous figure, if the cost of goods purchased in the period is used.

The cost of goods sold in the period is obtained in the following way:

1 Take the value of stock at the beginning of the period.
2 Add purchases during the period.
3 Subtract the value of stock at the end of the period.

The value of stock at the beginning and end of the period may be established by stocktaking. If financial controls are extremely good, they may be calculated figures, with occasional stock checks to prove the system and the figures. If there has been any theft or other form of stock shrinkage, stock will be reduced and consequently the cost of sales will be increased.

The principle is illustrated by the following profit and loss account of a school tuck shop. In this simple example there are no costs other than the cost of the food sold.

● Sales in the month of February total £430.
● Stock at 31 January was £100.
● Stock at 28 February was £120.
● Purchases in February were £380.

School tuck shop
Profit and loss account for February month

	£	£
Sales		430
Stock at 31 January	100	
Add purchases in February	380	
	480	
Less stock at 28 February	120	
		360
Net profit		70

Exactly the same principles apply in the profit and loss accounts of big stores and supermarkets – although, of course, the figures are considerably bigger! These companies buy food and other products from their suppliers, they have stock checks at the beginning and end of each trading period (or they calculate the stock) and they sell to the public.

A manufacturing business

You have already seen that the profit and loss account of a trading company must contain only the cost of the goods actually sold. The cost of goods purchased and held in stock must be excluded. For the same reason the profit and loss account of a manufacturing company must contain only the manufacturing costs of the goods actually sold in the period. The manufacturing costs of goods not sold must be excluded.

As with a trading company, it will probably be necessary for a manufacturing business to stocktake at the beginning and end of the period, but if controls are very good it may not always be necessary.

Sometimes the manufacturing costs are shown in a separate manufacturing account. This leads to a manufacturing profit that is carried forward to the profit and loss account. Other costs are deducted in the main profit and loss account to give the overall profit or loss. Similarly, trading activities are sometimes shown in a separate trading account. This method of presentation is optional and not followed here. We will show everything in the main profit and loss account.

These are the key points to remember:

● There are definite starting and finishing dates.
● Total sales appear at the top.
● The net profit or loss is at the bottom.
● All revenue and expense accounts are included.
● Only expenditure on goods actually sold is included.

The following example shows the principles for a manufacturing business.

Bognor Cases Ltd manufactures and sells suitcases

● Sales in the year to 30 June 2017 were £1,000,000.
● Purchases of raw materials and components in the year totalled £400,000.
● Stock at 30 June 2016 was £320,000 and at 30 June 2017 it was £365,000.
● Wages of production staff were £216,000.
● Factory rent was £110,000 and power costs were £40,000.

- Other production costs were £40,000.
- Salaries totalled £82,000. Other overheads were £66,000.

Bognor Cases Ltd
Profit and loss account for year to 30 June 2017

	£	£
Sales		1,000,000
Stock at 30.6.16	320,000	
Add purchases	400,000	
	720,000	
Less stock at 30.6.17	365,000	
	355,000	
Production wages	216,000	
Factory rent	110,000	
Power costs	40,000	
Other production costs	40,000	
Cost of manufacturing		761,000
		239,000
Less overheads		
Salaries	82,000	
Other overheads	66,000	
		148,000
Net profit		91,000

Note that the costs are split into two sections. All costs relating to the product and manufacturing go into the top part. These contribute to the cost of manufacturing and to the subtotal, which is the manufacturing profit. Overhead costs go below this subtotal.

Test your understanding

You should find the following exercise quite easy. The answer is given at the end of the chapter, but set it out before looking.

North West Garden Novelties Ltd manufactures and sells garden gnomes

- Sales in the year to 30 April 2015 were £600,000.
- Purchases of materials totalled £200,000. Stock at 30 April 2014 was £50,000 and stock at 30 April 2015 was £40,000.
- Production wages in the year were £280,000 and other production costs were £90,000. Total overheads were £60,000.

Two key concepts

To complete our study of the profit and loss account, we will consider two further important concepts.

Match cost to income

When we studied trading companies and manufacturing companies, we saw that the cost of goods sold, and not of any other goods, should be brought into the account.

The same applies to all the costs, and an example of where it is particularly relevant is a long-term construction contract, such as building London's Olympic Stadium. When 30 per cent of a project is included in income, it is vital that costs exactly relating to this 30 per cent are included.

Prepare accounts on a prudent basis

Again, construction projects are a good example. Profits should not be taken before they have been earned. A loss should be taken when it can be realistically foreseen, but a profit should only be taken after it has been earned.

Summary

In this chapter we have learned about the profit and loss account, the summary of all the revenue and expense items in a business that occur over a specified period of time. We have also tested our understanding with some practical exercises. We should now have:

- understood exactly what a profit and loss account is
- studied a simple example
- looked at trading businesses
- looked at manufacturing businesses
- briefly looked at two important concepts.

Now we progress to the other main part of the accounts, the balance sheet.

Test your understanding

Answers

Bernard Smith

Bernard Smith
Profit and loss account for year to 31 May

	£	£
Invoiced sales		15,000
Less costs:		
Materials used	2,200	
Motor expenses	1,400	
Other overhead costs	3,700	
Depreciation	1,600	
Bad debt	350	
Remedial work	200	
		9,450
Net profit		**5,550**

North West Garden Novelties

North West Novelties Ltd
Profit and loss account for year to 30 April 2015

	£	£
Sales		600,000
Stock at 30.4.14	50,000	
Add purchases	200,000	
	250,000	
Less stock at 30.4.15	40,000	
	210,000	
Production wages	280,000	
Other production costs	90,000	
Cost of manufacturing		580,000
		20,000
Less total overheads		60,000
Net loss for year		**(40,000)**

This is the first time that we have encountered a loss. Note that it is shown by means of a bracketed figure.

Fact-check (answers at the back)

1. Where do the figures in the profit and loss account come from?
   - a) The balance sheet ❑
   - b) The cash book ❑
   - c) The trial balance ❑
   - d) The sales ledger and the purchase ledger ❑

2. What happens to the net profit or loss?
   - a) It stays where it is ❑
   - b) It is transferred to the capital account ❑
   - c) It is paid out as a dividend (if it is a profit) ❑
   - d) It is invested ❑

3. Which accounts go into the profit and loss account?
   - a) The revenue and expense accounts ❑
   - b) The asset and liability accounts ❑
   - c) The capital accounts ❑
   - d) All of them ❑

4. What must happen in the profit and loss account if the business buys and sells goods?
   - a) The cost of goods purchased in the period must be included ❑
   - b) Stock at the beginning of the period must be included ❑
   - c) Stock at the end of the period must be included ❑
   - d) The cost of goods sold in the period must be included ❑

5. How do you ascertain the cost of goods sold in the period?
   - a) Closing stock plus purchases less opening stock ❑
   - b) Opening stock plus purchases less closing stock ❑
   - c) An informed estimate by a trained person ❑
   - d) Opening stock less closing stock ❑

6. What is the effect in the profit and loss account of the theft of stock?
   - a) Stock is reduced ❑
   - b) Overheads are increased ❑
   - c) Sales are reduced ❑
   - d) The cost of sales is increased ❑

7. Where does factory rent appear in the profit and loss account of a manufacturing company?
   - a) In the overheads ❑
   - b) In the cost of manufacturing ❑
   - c) Added to the purchases of materials and components ❑
   - d) As a deduction from net profit ❑

8. It is expected that a long-term project will make a loss. When should the loss be brought into the profit and loss account?
   - a) In equal instalments over the life of the project ❑
   - b) On completion of the project ❑
   - c) As soon as it can realistically be foreseen ❑
   - d) One year after completion of the project ❑

9. Where do assets appear in the profit and loss account?

a) As part of sales ❏
b) As a reduction in overheads ❏
c) As an addition to the net profit ❏
d) Assets do not appear in the profit and loss account ❏

10. Which of the following statements about the profit and loss account is true?

a) It covers the period of time stated in the heading ❏
b) It is at the fixed date stated in the heading ❏
c) It must cover a period of a year ❏
d) It must cover a period of at least a month ❏

CHAPTER 13

The balance sheet

The two main constituent parts of a set of accounts are the profit and loss account and the balance sheet. Now that you are familiar with the principles of the profit and loss account, we can progress to the balance sheet. In this chapter you will learn exactly what a balance sheet is, and the programme also covers:

- the concept of ownership (the capital accounts)
- the layout of the balance sheet
- how to prepare your own balance sheet
- the main balance sheet headings: fixed assets, current assets, current liabilities, net current assets and long-term liabilities.

These are the concepts you will need to know about before you can gain a full understanding of published accounts.

What is a balance sheet?

You can help yourself remember the answer to this question by thinking of the literal meaning of the two words 'balance' and 'sheet'.

Balance This means that the balance sheet must balance. There are two sides to it and they must total to the same figure. Put another way, the sum of the debit balances must equal the sum of the credit balances; all the figures come from the extended trial balance.

Sheet This means literally a sheet of paper on which the figures are listed.

Earlier we saw that there are five different types of account. In the previous chapter we saw that the revenue and expense accounts are extracted from the extended trial balance and that these accounts make up the profit and loss account. The balance sheet is made up from everything that is left. These are the three remaining types of account:

- asset accounts (debit balances)
- liability accounts (credit balances)
- capital accounts (normally credit balances)

The profit or loss at the bottom of the profit and loss account is added to, or subtracted from, the capital accounts. The result is that the balance sheet balances, which is essential. We have seen that the profit and loss account covers a given period of time. If trading is continuing, the profit or loss would be different if the period were to be one day shorter or longer. The balance sheet is not like that. It is a listing of the balances on just one fixed date, almost always the date at the end of the trading period.

The concept of ownership

Asset and liability accounts are relatively easy to comprehend, but you may have a problem understanding the capital accounts. Sometimes there is just one account called the capital account. In other cases, there may be several accounts: share capital account, revenue reserves account and so on.

What are the capital accounts?

The capital accounts represent the money invested in the business by the owners. If the company is wound up, and if the assets and liabilities are worth exactly book value, the owners will be paid out exactly the value of the capital accounts.

The owners of a business are a different entity from the business itself. This is easy to understand in the case of a listed public company. If you own shares in Barclays Bank plc, you are not the same as the bank. The capital accounts in the books of Barclays Bank plc represent the debt owing to you and to the other shareholders.

The principle is exactly the same in the accounts of a one-man or one-woman business. Let us return to Bridget Murphy, the public relations consultant. Bridget Murphy the person is separate from Bridget Murphy the business. If she is efficient, she will have two bank accounts, one for her business and one for her personal affairs. She may even pay herself a 'salary' from one bank account to the other.

If Bridget Murphy's business is wound up, what is left after everything has been collected in and paid out belongs to her. The final cheque in the cheque book pays her the value of the capital accounts.

This is the reason that the capital accounts are listed with the liabilities.

The layout of the balance sheet

Until the 1950s, it was the practice to set out the figures on a balance sheet side by side. The liabilities (credit balances) were listed in the left-hand column, and the assets (debit balances) were listed in the right-hand column. The two columns, of course, added up to the same figure.

You will almost certainly never see a balance sheet set out like this as it is now just about universally the practice to set out balance sheets in a vertical format. The examples in this chapter are set out in this way.

A vertical balance sheet shows liabilities deducted from assets in a logical manner. The whole thing adds down to the net worth of the business, which is shown at the bottom. This 'net worth' is represented by the capital accounts.

This is best illustrated with an example. The balance sheet of a partnership where the two partners participate 50/50 in the profits is shown below.

Smith and Jones
Balance sheet at 30 April 2015

	£	£
Fixed assets		
Freehold property	200,000	
Plant and machinery	120,000	
Motor vehicles	40,000	
		360,000
Current assets		
Stock	170,000	
Trade debtors	130,000	
	300,000	
Less current liabilities		
Bank overdraft	60,000	
Trade creditors	120,000	
	180,000	
Net current assets		120,000
		480,000
Capital accounts		
Smith		240,000
Jones		240,000
		480,000

This is, of course, a simple balance sheet. In practice, there would be several notes giving relevant details of how the figures are made up. Note that the net worth of the partnership is £480,000. If the partnership were to be wound up, if the assets and liabilities achieved exactly book value, and if there were no winding-up expenses, Smith and Jones would get £240,000 each.

Test your understanding

Now prepare a balance sheet from the trial balance given below. The answer is given at the end of the chapter, but prepare your answer before checking. The accounts are given in alphabetical order, not the order in which they appear in the balance sheet.

John Cohen
Trial balance at 30 April 2015

	Debit £	Credit £
Bank account	10,000	
Capital reserve		70,000
Depreciation on motor vehicle		30,000
Depreciation on plant and machinery		140,000
Leasehold property	100,000	
Motor vehicles	60,000	
Plant and machinery	280,000	
Revenue reserves		240,000
Stock	150,000	
Taxation		80,000
Trade creditors		200,000
Trade debtors	160,000	
	760,000	760,000

Taxation is money owing to the government by the business. Depreciation must be netted off against the relevant asset accounts. This means that the difference between the two figures is shown in the balance sheet.

The main balance sheet headings

Of course, not every individual account in the trial balance appears individually in the balance sheet. If it did, the balance sheet of a major company would have to be hundreds of pages long. The need for this is overcome by grouping accounts of a similar type. For example, there may be several bank accounts but they will appear in the balance sheet as just one total figure.

The following explanations will help you understand the headings commonly used in balance sheets.

Fixed assets

These are assets whose use generates benefit to the business in the long term. This is usually taken to mean a year or more. Because of their fixed and long-term nature, they are grouped separately from current assets, whose value can be expected to be realized in the short term.

It is normally necessary to depreciate fixed assets – this was studied in detail earlier. In practice, it is rare for fixed assets to be actually worth exactly their written down value in the books, for several reasons:

● the arbitrary nature of the depreciation rules
● individual circumstances
● inflation.

Examples of fixed assets are:

● freehold property
● leasehold property
● plant and equipment
● computers
● fixtures and fittings
● motor vehicles.

Asset strippers specialize in finding companies where the fixed assets are actually worth more than the book value. They then purchase the company and unlock the value by selling some or all of the assets and realizing the profit.

Current assets

These are assets whose value is available to the business immediately (such as cash) or in the short term. This is either because they are part of the trading cycle (such as stock and trade debtors) or because they are short-term investments (such as a 90-day bank deposit account). The definition of 'short term' is usually taken to be less than a year.

Debtors are usually current assets. The definition of a debtor is a person owing money to the business, such as a customer for goods sold. Examples of current assets are:

● stock
● trade debtors
● bank accounts
● short-term investments.

Current liabilities

These are liabilities that the business could be called upon to pay off in the short term. Examples are:

● trade creditors
● bank overdrafts
● taxation payable within one year
● hire purchase payable within one year.

The definition of a creditor is a person to whom the business owes money, such as a supplier.

Net current assets

This is also known as **working capital** and it is extremely important. It is the difference between current assets and current liabilities, and it can be a negative figure if the liabilities are greater.

It is extremely important because net current assets are what are available to finance the day-to-day running of the business. If net current assets are insufficient for this purpose, the business may have to close or seek some other form of finance. It is possible for a business to be profitable but have to close due to a shortage of working capital. It is relatively common for a business to be profitable but nonetheless embarrassed by a shortage of working capital.

Long-term liabilities

The John Cohen example above did not include one, but long-term liabilities are liabilities that are payable after more than a year. An example is a **fixed-term bank loan**. A business may be able to solve the problem of a shortage of working capital by obtaining a long-term liability in place of a bank overdraft.

Bank overdrafts are invariably legally repayable on demand. This means in theory, and very occasionally in practice, that the bank manager can demand repayment at 3 p.m. and, if payment has not been received, take steps to appoint an administrator or receiver at 4 p.m. On the other hand, a long-term fixed loan is repayable only when stipulated by the agreement and according to the conditions in the agreement.

Let us consider a ten-year loan of £1,000,000, repayable by ten equal annual instalments of £100,000. The balance sheet would show £900,000 under long-term liabilities and £100,000 under current liabilities. After a year, and one repayment, the balance sheet would show £800,000 under long-term liabilities and £100,000 under current liabilities. Hire purchase contract balances are split in the same way. The part repayable after a year is shown in long-term liabilities.

Solving a shortage of working capital

A business has an obvious incentive to make as many as possible of its liabilities long-term liabilities. This eases the pressure on working capital.

Summary

In this chapter we have studied the remaining concepts you will need to know about before you can gain an understanding of published accounts. You have seen how accounts are prepared from basic bookkeeping records. You have learned:

- exactly what a balance sheet is
- how ownership is shown in the accounts
- how balance sheets are laid out
- how to prepare a balance sheet
- the meaning of the main balance sheet headings.

Test your understanding

Answers

John Cohen

John Cohen

Balance sheet at 30 April 2015

	£	£
Fixed assets		
Leasehold property	100,000	
Plant and machinery	140,000	
Motor vehicles	30,000	
		270,000
Current assets		
Stock	150,000	
Trade debtors	160,000	
Bank	10,000	
	320,000	
Less current liabilities		
Trade creditors	200,000	
Taxation	80,000	
	280,000	
Net current assets		40,000
		310,000
Capital		
Capital reserve	70,000	
Revenue reserve	240,000	
		310,000

Fact-check (answers at the back)

1. Why does the balance sheet balance, even though not all the balances in the trial balance are included?
   a) It is not always the case that the balance sheet must balance ❑
   b) It is because the balancing figure is included with the assets ❑
   c) It is because the balancing figure is included with the liabilities ❑
   d) It is because the net profit or loss is added to (or subtracted from) the capital accounts ❑

2. What is the state of the capital accounts?
   a) Always credit ❑
   b) Usually credit ❑
   c) Usually debit ❑
   d) Always debit ❑

3. What does it mean if the capital accounts of a company add up to a net debit balance?
   a) The business is insolvent and needs an injection of capital ❑
   b) The shareholders are required by law to buy more shares ❑
   c) The shareholders are required by law to loan money to the company ❑
   d) Shareholders are required to repay past dividends ❑

4. Total assets less total liabilities equals what?
   a) The working capital ❑
   b) The share capital ❑
   c) The net worth of the business ❑
   d) The non-current liabilities ❑

5. What is normally first shown in a balance sheet?
   a) Capital ❑
   b) Current assets ❑
   c) Fixed assets ❑
   d) Working capital ❑

6. Where does stock go in a balance sheet?
   a) In fixed assets ❑
   b) In current assets ❑
   c) In current liabilities ❑
   d) In long-term liabilities ❑

7. How short term must a liability be in order for it to be classed as a current liability?
   a) Payable within a month ❑
   b) Payable within six months ❑
   c) Payable within a year ❑
   d) Payable within two years ❑

8. Debtors are usually what?
   a) Current assets ❑
   b) Current liabilities ❑
   c) Long-term liabilities ❑
   d) Capital ❑

9. Is it possible for a business to be profitable but to be short of working capital?

a) Yes, and it is relatively common ❏

b) Yes, but it is very unlikely ❏

c) No, it is not possible ❏

d) The question is self-evidently absurd ❏

10. A company borrows £300,000 from a bank. It is a long-term loan repayable in equal monthly instalments over five years. How much of this will be classed as a current liability in a balance sheet three years later?

a) £300,000 ❏

b) Nothing ❏

c) £120,000 ❏

d) £60,000 ❏

7 × 7

1 Seven things to do regularly

- Do the bank reconciliation and investigate any discrepancies.
- Do other relevant reconciliations and take any necessary action.
- Consider the adequacy of the bad debt reserve. If it is too big or too small, it will affect the profit.
- If relevant, consider the stock reserve (for lost, damaged, obsolete stock etc.). If it is too big or too small, the profit will be affected.
- Remind yourself of the significance of GIGO, which stands for 'garbage in equals garbage out'. Your computer does not have a brain and any mistakes in the input will affect the information produced.
- Sort out any suspense accounts in the accounting system.
- Check the petty cash.

2 Seven things to remember

- A profit and loss account summarizes activity over a period of time. The period must be stated.
- A balance sheet summarizes assets and liabilities as at a specified date. The date must be stated.
- There are only self-imposed rules for unpublished accounts prepared for management purposes. Published accounts must conform with the law and applicable accounting standards.
- A change in accounting policies (the rules for depreciation, for example) will result in a change in the accounts figures. Details of any such change should be stated.
- The net worth of a business is shown as a liability in the balance sheet. This is because it is owing to the owners, who are separate from the business.

- Profits should be recognized when they have been earned. Losses should be recognized when they can be realistically foreseen.
- Despite the rather cruel jokes, accountants are generally very nice people.

3 Seven golden rules

- Double-entry bookkeeping is superior to single-entry bookkeeping.
- If you keep manual records (which is probably unlikely), it is debit on the left and credit on the right.
- For every debit there must be a credit.
- The sum of all the credits must equal the sum of all the debits.
- The principles of bookkeeping are timeless. Computers do exactly what can be done manually, but they do it more quickly and efficiently, and they probably present the end results in a different way.
- You very probably will not get accurate accounts unless you have accurate accruals and prepayments.
- The profit and loss account is a summary of all the revenue and expense balances. The balance sheet is a summary of all the assets and liabilities.

4 Seven things to avoid

- Putting income accounts and expenditure accounts in the balance sheet.
- Putting asset and liability accounts in the profit and loss account.
- Not having a logical numbering system for the individual accounts.
- Not keeping the bank reconciliation and other reconciliations up to date.

- Not taking sufficient care with the accruals and prepayments. This may result in the profit being overstated or understated.
- Not taking sufficient care with the reserves and provisions. An inadequate reserve (for bad debts, for example) will cause the profit to be overstated.
- Forgetting that the period of the profit and loss account must be stated and that the chosen period can make a difference. This is particularly the case if seasonal goods are sold.

5 Seven trends for tomorrow

The following trends are all discernible now. They are likely to continue.

- People will continue to question the value of the statutory audit.
- Basic bookkeeping will continue to be subcontracted to countries that pay low wages.
- There will continue to be accounting scandals.
- Accounting standards will continue to develop.
- Accounting software will become even more sophisticated.
- Suppliers, customers, the government and others will increasingly demand that businesses communicate with them electronically. This affects tax returns, payment procedures, etc.
- Managers and employees will increasingly be expected to have some knowledge of the principles of bookkeeping and accounts.

6 Seven great quotes

- 'The lack of money is the root of all evil.' Mark Twain (1835–1920), American writer
- 'When I was young I thought that money was the most important thing in life; now that I am old I know that it is.' Oscar Wilde (1854–1900), Irish writer

- 'Few have heard of Fra Luca Pacioli, the inventor of double-entry bookkeeping, but he has probably had more influence on human life than has Dante or Michelangelo.' Herbert J. Muller (1905–80), American historian

- 'Accountants are the witch-doctors of the modern world and willing to turn their hands to any kind of magic.' Charles Eustace Harman (1894–1970), British judge

- 'Civilization and profits go hand in hand.' Calvin Coolidge (1872–1933), American president

- 'Lenin was right. There is no subtler, no surer means of overturning the existing basis of society than to debauch the currency.' John Maynard Keynes (1883–1946), English economist

- 'No one would remember the Good Samaritan if he'd only had good intentions. He had money as well.' Margaret Thatcher (1925–2013), British prime minister

7 Seven great jokes*

- If an accountant's wife cannot sleep, what does she say? 'Darling, could you tell me about your work?'

- When does a person decide to become an accountant? When he realizes he doesn't have the charisma to succeed as an undertaker.

- There are three types of accountant – those who can count and those who can't.

- Why don't old accountants ever die? They just lose their balance.

- How do you know when you've found a good accountant? She has a tax loophole named after her.

- What's the definition of an auditor? Someone who goes on to the battlefield after the battle and bayonets the survivors.

- What's the definition of an accountant? Someone who solves a problem you didn't know you had in a way that you don't understand.

* The writer is an accountant.

PART 3
Your Understanding and Interpreting Accounts Masterclass

Introduction

There has never been a time when managers, and indeed people in general, were more exposed to a multitude of financial statements than they are today. To take just one example, millions of people are investors, perhaps indirectly, and are sent accounts and financial information relating to the companies in which they invest. Even non-financial managers are often involved in budgeting and regular financial reporting. They are expected to understand the accounts put in front of them and to contribute to the analysis and interpretation of the figures.

This Part of the book has been written with reference to the law of the United Kingdom, and with reference to UK accounting standards and international accounting standards. Laws vary from country to country. Most but not all of the world uses international accounting standards.

CHAPTER 14

The right approach

In this Part of the book we will be examining in detail various aspects of accounts. We will see how everything fits together and hopefully understand the bigger picture. We will aim to know what everything means and how to interpret the information. It is quite a challenge and we will get the best results if we approach it in the right way. Furthermore, we need to know about the many problems and traps that await us. So we will spend the first chapter preparing for what lies ahead. Our time will not be wasted.

The various aspects that we examine comprise:

- The approaches most likely to get the best results
  1 Look for trends
  2 Look for reasons
  3 Be open-minded
  4 Make comparisons
  5 Do not neglect the notes and the accounting policies
  6 Sometimes be suspicious.

- Traps to avoid
  1 Applying percentages to small base figures
  2 Failure to take account of a change in accounting policy
  3 Not always comparing like with like
  4 Forgetting that some things can only be known by insiders
  5 Not taking account of different lengths in the trading period
  6 Forgetting the effects of inflation
  7 Not taking account of seasonal factors
  8 Being misled by averages
  9 Not realizing that the figures have been manipulated
  10 Failure to take full account of the notes and other information.

The approaches most likely to get the best results

The right attitudes are some of those most likely to be displayed by a successful businessman or businesswoman, or indeed by persons successful in many other fields. You are advised to prepare yourself and give the job the necessary time and resources. You should be knowledgeable and cool, calm and collected. It is necessary to be determined and sometimes to be sceptical. At times you must be relentless. The following techniques and attitudes may be particularly helpful.

Look for trends

It is often very useful to examine trends because they may be much more revealing than a single figure or comparison. If you only have one year's accounts or accounts for some other single period, this will not be possible. However, at least for an established business, you will often have the figures for several periods. In the UK, companies are required to publish the figures for the previous period alongside the figures for the current period, so you will always have at least two figures or ratios to compare. The published accounts of UK listed companies are required to give key data over the previous five years.

A deteriorating payment performance, for example, often indicates liquidity problems, although it can also mean that selfish managers are hoarding cash at the expense of suppliers. If a company has gone from paying in 30 days to paying in 90 days, it may be more worrying than if it has consistently taken 90 days to pay.

Look for reasons

There may be special reasons that should be taken into account when the significance of a ratio is assessed. For example, very high expenditure on advertising right at the end of the financial period may reduce profits for the period, but hold out the promise of higher sales and profits in the next period. Of course, the extra sales and profits might not actually happen. Lord Leverhulme, the founder of Unilever, famously remarked that he knew that half of his company's massive expenditure on advertising was wasted, but he did not know which half.

Be open-minded

You will often approach the task of interpreting accounts with some preconceived ideas about what you will find and what your conclusions will be. This is inevitable and often your preconceived ideas will be correct, but you should never close your mind to the possibility that you will be wrong. Always look at the evidence and make up your mind accordingly.

Make comparisons

A close examination of a set of accounts will give you much information and it might tell you what you want to know. For example, you may be particularly interested in the ratio between net profit and turnover, which is one of the easier calculations to make. If this really is all that you want you can stop at this point, but it will very probably be revealing to compare the ratio that you have obtained with such things as:

● Last year's results
● The budget
● The industry or sector average
● The accounts of a competitor.

An apparently successful result might not look so good if it lags behind the competition, the budget and last year's figures. The opposite of course also applies.

Do not neglect the notes and the accounting policies

The figures in the financial statements are the starting point, but only the starting point. A full understanding requires a close study of the notes and the accounting policies. This really does matter.

You may be familiar with the saying 'The large print giveth and the small print taketh away'. Professional analysts always spend time studying the notes to published accounts and the accounting policies. You should do the same and you should pay particular attention to any change in accounting policies. Laws and accounting standards govern certain information that must be disclosed in the notes to published accounts of companies and also in the directors' report.

Sometimes be suspicious

Most (but not all) directors, accountants and business people are reasonably honest, which is just as well, and most of them try to present a good set of accounts that comply with the law, accounting standards and the underlying facts. Furthermore, the tax authorities and in some cases auditors are on hand to fortify their resolve. Many people are of the view that standards are higher in the UK than in many other countries. Nevertheless, a few are dishonest and some others try to show a particular result, so long as a case can be made within the rules for doing so. Still more make honest mistakes.

You can usually trust the integrity of those presenting the accounts, but not always. Perhaps the best approach is that of an old-fashioned bank manager, a species sadly now not often encountered. Ask searching questions of the figures and perhaps of the people who produced them. Do not be easily fooled. If something seems not to be right, perhaps it is not right, even if you are not an expert. Do not give up, and get to the bottom of whatever it is that concerns you.

Traps to avoid

Even experienced financial analysts can make mistakes and fall into one of the many traps that may be encountered, and it is more likely that someone not financially sophisticated will do so. To be forewarned is to be forearmed. The following are some of the more common mistakes.

Applying percentages to small base figures

David Lloyd George, a former British prime minister, once asked a civil servant to produce some statistics. The civil servant replied 'Certainly – what would you like me to prove?'. Statistics and ratios can be misleading, especially when small base figures are used. This is best illustrated with an example.

	Turnover £	Profit Before Tax £
Company A		
Year 1	1,000,000	100
Year 2	1,000,000	200
Company B		
Year 1	1,000,000	100,000
Year 2	1,000,000	101,000

Hasn't Company A done well? It has doubled its profit. Poor old Company B, on the other hand, has only managed a miserable 1 per cent increase, but of course this is a ludicrous conclusion to draw. On an identical turnover, Company B has increased its profit by £1,000, whereas Company A has only done so by £100. What is more, Company A is still virtually breaking even, but Company B is making a healthy profit.

Failure to take account of a change in accounting policy

A change in accounting policy may affect the figures and ratios, without there being any change in the underlying reality. The result will be the same in the long run but, as the great economist John Maynard Keynes once said 'In the long run we are all dead'. You will most likely be looking at the figures in the short run, probably a period of a year.

Examples include changes in depreciation policy and changes in the way that stock is valued. The profit is the same in the long term, but the declared profit will be different in the year that the change is made. Fortunately, notes to the published accounts of companies must disclose significant changes in accounting policies and spell out the consequences.

Consider a company that two years ago purchased a piece of machinery for £500,000 and in the first year depreciated it by 25 per cent. In the second year the company changed its policy and depreciated it by 20 per cent. Clearly, the declared net profit before tax will be £25,000 higher than if the change had not been made.

Not always comparing like with like

The recent accounts of a major listed company disclose the following:

Sales for year (in £ million)	9,934.3
Trade receivables (in £ million)	114.6

You can easily work out that customers take an average of 4.2 days to pay for their purchases. The calculation is:

$$\frac{114.6}{9,934.3} \times 365 = 4.2 \text{ days}$$

You may think that this is stunningly good, and that the company must employ the world's best credit controllers. This may or may not be true, but it should not be deduced from these figures. The reason for this is that the company is in the retail sector and the great majority of its sales are made for cash. Trade receivables should really be compared with just the part of sales that are made on credit.

Now consider a hypothetical widget manufacturer whose accounts disclose the following:

Sales for the year	£900,000
Trade debtors at the balance sheet date	£100,000

This appears to show that customers take an average of 40.6 days to pay. The calculation is:

$$\frac{100,000}{900,000} \times 365 = 40.6 \text{ days}$$

This too is probably wrong because sales will almost certainly exclude VAT, and trade debtors will probably include it. If trade debtors all include 20 per cent VAT, the correct calculation is:

$$\frac{83,333}{900,000} \times 365 = 33.8 \text{ days}$$

83,333 is 100,000 with the 20 per cent VAT removed.

Forgetting that some things can only be known by insiders

Published financial statements reveal a great deal, but there are some details that can really only be known by those with inside information. Consider two companies that manufacture and sell screws:

	Company A	Company B
Sales	£3,900,000	£3,700,000
Cost of sales	£2,184,000	£2,146,000
Gross margin	44%	42%

Company A appears to be slightly more efficient, but the figures could be affected by the different accounting treatment of certain factory costs, such as power and property costs. Company A might treat these costs as general overheads, whereas Company B might allocate them to production costs. Overall net profit for the whole company would of course be unaffected.

If you are an insider yourself, you may have all the information that you need, or at least be in a position to get it. If, on the other hand, you are not able to do this, a touch of caution should not come amiss. The problem is much smaller than in the past because accounting standards and more prescriptive laws have reduced the uncertainty, but there are still some things that only an insider can know.

Not taking account of different lengths in the trading period

Consider the following:

	10 months to 31 October	14 months to 31 December in the following year
Sales in period	£6,000,000	£8,400,000
Net profit before tax	£720,000	£1,008,000

Although the second period seems better, if you allow for the different lengths, the results are identical, with the profit percentage being 12 per cent in each case.

This is so conspicuous that you would have to be asleep on the job to miss the significance of the different lengths in the trading period, but the difference might not be so obvious. Most companies prepare annual accounts for an exact calendar year of 52 weeks and 1 day (52 weeks and 2 days in a leap year) but a few make it exactly 52 weeks with an occasional 53-week year to come back into line. This is disclosed, but it does make a difference and its significance can easily be missed. The following are the turnover figures for a very well-known company for three successive years.

	£m
Year 1 (52 weeks)	9,062.1
Year 2 (53 weeks)	9,536.6
Year 3 (52 weeks)	9,740.3

Turnover increased by 5.23 per cent in year 2, but a 53-week year is 1.92 per cent longer than a 52-week year, so more than a third of the increase was down to it being a longer year. It works the other way in year 3. Turnover is up by 2.13 per cent, but if we add the effect of the shorter year it is just over 4 per cent.

Forgetting the effects of inflation

It is sometimes said that carbon monoxide is the silent killer, which is why I have a carbon monoxide alarm in my house. In the same way, inflation is the silent destroyer of value. There have only been two years since 1945 when there has been nil inflation in Britain. Sometimes it is high, as when it peaked at 27.9 per cent in the 1970s, and in many years it is relatively low, but it is almost always there.

The significance of inflation should not be overlooked especially when comparing figures from different periods. The effects are cumulative and it does many things. These include devaluing savings and favouring borrowing. This is because repayments are made in less valuable money. It is a main reason why the baby boomer generation did so well by borrowing to buy property that increased in value in most years.

For a minor example of the effects of inflation you might like to look back to the previous section of this chapter. You will see that the adjusted increase in turnover between years 2 and 3 was just over 4 per cent. The figures are real and inflation was around 4 per cent at that time. After allowing for inflation there was really no increase at all.

Not taking account of seasonal factors

This is a common mistake. Consider Mr Khan who starts selling ice cream from a van on 1 October. Information from his first two six-monthly profit statements is shown below.

	6 months to 31 March	6 months to 30 September
Sales in period	£12,400	£37,200
Net profit before tax	£4,216	£12,276
Profit as a percentage of sales	34%	33%

At first glance this shows that the second period is much better than the first, but this might not be the case, although further investigation may show that there was some improvement. The reason for this conclusion is that the sale of ice cream from vans in Britain is heavily affected by the weather and the amount of daylight. Sales should be much higher in the summer months.

Being misled by averages

A man stood with one leg in a bucket of ice and the other in a bucket of boiling water, so on average he was comfortable. It is a good joke, at least in my opinion, and it is relevant here. Averages can be misleading and you may need to get behind the figures that contribute to them.

A holding company had two subsidiaries. The first one made a million pound profit and the second one made a million pound loss. So on average they broke even and this is the result shown in the holding company's group accounts. You obviously need to get behind the group accounts (which are correct) in order to understand what has happened.

Not realizing that the figures have been manipulated

This may have been done within the rules. Consider a company that usually operates with a bank overdraft. However, the managers do not pay suppliers in the last three weeks of the trading period in order to show no bank borrowings in the balance sheet. This is unfair to suppliers, but a common practice. The balance sheet will of course show trade creditors being higher than usual. The opposite practice may also be encountered. This is paying suppliers just before the balance sheet date in order to establish a false, or at least untypical, record for paying suppliers promptly. An even more dubious practice is to draw the cheques just before the balance sheet date but not release them for some time.

Failure to take full account of the notes and other information

It is sometimes said that professional analysts spend more time studying the notes to the accounts than they spend studying the actual accounts. This could be wise of them because the accounts are often just the starting point. As already mentioned, in the UK (as in nearly all other countries) the law and various accounting standards specify a great deal of information that must be disclosed in the notes to the published accounts.

Summary

In this chapter we have:

● Seen how we are most likely to get good results and the best rewards for our time and effort if we proceed in the right way. To this end we have looked at a number of attitudes and mindsets that should be brought to bear on the tasks ahead.

● Understood that our work might not be straightforward and that there are traps that could stop us getting the best results. We have studied ten of these traps and resolved to avoid them.

Next we will learn about accounting standards and see how accounts can be obtained. We will then have a first look at the different types of account and how they are made up.

Fact-check (answers at the back)

1. For how many years must the accounts of UK listed companies reveal key data?
   a) Three years ☐
   b) Four years ☐
   c) Five years ☐
   d) Six years ☐

2. With what might it be revealing to compare a company's accounts?
   a) Last year's results ☐
   b) The industry or sector average ☐
   c) The accounts of a competitor ☐
   d) All of the above ☐

3. Who said 'In the long run we are all dead'?
   a) Milton Friedman ☐
   b) Milton Keynes ☐
   c) Maynard Keynes ☐
   d) Bill Maynard ☐

4. Sales for the year are £4,021,626. Amount owing by customers at the year end is £469,318. What is the average period of credit taken by customers?
   a) 37.3 days ☐
   b) 42.6 days ☐
   c) 48.1 days ☐
   d) 55.0 days ☐

5. Which is the factor in Question 4 that might invalidate the answer?
   a) VAT may be in the sales figure but not the amount owing by customers ☐
   b) VAT may be in the amount owing by customers but not in the sales figure ☐
   c) The business might not be registered for VAT ☐
   d) The VAT return is overdue ☐

6. The previous year's profit was £100,000. This year's profit was £102,000. Inflation in the last year was 2 per cent. How have we done in real terms?
   a) Better ☐
   b) Worse ☐
   c) The same ☐
   d) There is not enough information to answer the question ☐

7. A company that has an overdraft does not pay its suppliers in the month before the financial year end. What effect will this have in the balance sheet?
   a) There will be no change ☐
   b) It will increase both creditors and debtors ☐
   c) It will increase the overdraft and the amount owing to creditors ☐
   d) It will reduce the overdraft and increase the amount owing to creditors ☐

8. Does a deteriorating payment performance always indicate that a customer has liquidity problems?

a) Yes, always ❏
b) No, never ❏
c) No, but it often does ❏
d) Only if it is around the Christmas period ❏

9. Is it a good idea to examine trends in the accounts?

a) Yes ❏
b) No ❏
c) Only if you are not busy ❏
d) It is positively harmful ❏

10. Who said that he knew that half of his company's massive expenditure on advertising was wasted, but he did not know which half?

a) Robert Maxwell ❏
b) Lord Leverhulme ❏
c) Lord Sugar ❏
d) Sir Richard Branson ❏

CHAPTER 15

An introduction to accounts

It is now time to get started. An introduction to accounts means first of all knowing how to get hold of accounts and, although you may well already know what they look like, you need to know something about accounting standards and what exactly comprises a package of financial statements and reports. We will then be able to set about examining, interpreting and understanding them, but first of all you will be introduced to them.

The topics covered in this chapter comprise:

- an example of unpublished accounts
- how to obtain copies of published accounts
- accounting standards
- accounts prepared in accordance with UK accounting standards
- accounts prepared in accordance with international accounting standards
- abbreviated accounts of small and medium-sized companies
- audit.

An example of unpublished accounts

Unpublished accounts do not have to comply with laws and accounting standards, and they are not audited. You should bear this in mind. They are usually prepared by managers for managers and can be laid out in the way that they think most suits their purposes. They are often prepared monthly or quarterly so that managers can monitor progress. There will be a profit and loss account and perhaps a balance sheet. The profit and loss account is likely to be accompanied by a listing of the expenses and a comparison with the budget. A typical profit and loss account might be as follows.

XYZ Ltd

Profit and Loss Account for the 3 Months to 31 March

	£	£
Sales		1,021,429
Stock at 31 December	326,491	
Add purchases	489,617	
	816,108	
Less stock at 31 March	299,998	
		516,110
		505,319
Less overheads		
Sales department	84,116	
Finance department	96,238	
Administration department	187,205	
		367,559
Net profit before tax		137,760

The same company's balance sheet at 31 March could be as follows

XYZ Ltd

Balance Sheet at 31 March

	£	£
Fixed assets		
Freehold property	590,000	
Computers	32,191	
Motor vehicles	22,478	
		644,669
Current assets		
Stock	299,998	
Trade debtors	87,172	
Cash in bank	63,491	
	450,661	
Less current liabilities		
Trade creditors	102,345	
Other creditors	58,991	
	161,336	
Net current assets		289,325
		933,994
Capital		
Share capital		500,000
Revenue reserve		433,994
		933,994

At this point would you please look at the accounts and draw some conclusions, bearing in mind of course the possible traps mentioned in the previous chapter, and that they are unpublished and unaudited. Having said that, I would be disappointed if you did not spot at least the following two things:

1 The direct cost of goods sold is 50.5 per cent, which may or may not be good according to circumstances. The calculation is:

$$\frac{516,110}{1,021,429} \times 100 = 50.5 \text{ per cent}$$

2 The company appears to be profitable and well financed. On this information at least, the risk of it failing would appear to be small.

How to obtain copies of published accounts

You may already have the accounts that you want. Furthermore, you may have the right to be sent copies for a particular company or other body. For example, in the UK all shareholders can require (request would be more polite) that a copy of the latest accounts be sent to them without charge. Members of building societies and other bodies have rights too. However, this section of the chapter explains how you can get copies of accounts and limited liability partnerships from Companies House.

There are more than 3,750,000 companies listed at Companies House and more than 50,000 limited liability partnerships (LLPs). All but a tiny number of unlimited companies are required to file accounts. They must also file certain other information. The accounts and other information are placed on public record and anyone can obtain a copy. You can also get accounts and other documents for previous years. You have this right and you do not have to give a reason.

The most convenient method is likely to be by using the Companies House website www.gov.uk/ch, or alternatively you can ring 0303 1234 500. You will need the company's exact registered name, its registered number, or preferably both. There is a charge of £3 per document (a set of accounts counts as a document) if it is sent by post. Contact details for Companies House are as follows.

Offices in England and Wales	Office in Scotland	Office in Northern Ireland
Crown Way Maindy Cardiff CF14 3UZ Tel 0303 1234 500	4th Floor Edinburgh Quay 2 139 Fountainbridge Edinburgh EH3 9FF Tel 0303 1234 500	Second Floor The Linenhall 32-38 Linenhall Street Belfast BT2 8BG Tel 0303 1234 500
21 Bloomsbury Street London WC1B 3XD Tel 0303 1234 500		
Website (all offices)	www.gov.uk/government/organisations/companies-house	

Accounting standards

Accounting standards were introduced in the early 1970s in response to a number of scandals (Pergamon Press was a notable example) and complaints that different companies were (perhaps quite legitimately) using different rules and getting different results. From small beginnings UK standards have grown into a comprehensive body of rules. International accounting standards also comprise a comprehensive body of rules.

Directors have an overall responsibility to ensure that the accounts give a 'true and fair view'. It is not a specific legal requirement that accounts conform with accounting standards. However, accounts almost always do conform with accounting standards. This is partly because accounting standards are generally respected, partly because failure to comply would generate suspicious questions and partly because it would result in a qualified audit report. Very occasionally directors do deviate from accounting standards and give their reasons for doing so, which is permitted.

It is a requirement that a statement be given in the notes to the accounts as to whether the accounts have been prepared in accordance with applicable accounting standards. It requires particulars of any material departure from the standards and the reasons for the departure to be given.

International accounting standards are issued by the International Accounting Standards Board and, as the name implies, are intended to be used internationally. Listed companies within the European Union are required to comply with international accounting standards, though UK listed companies may use UK standards for their subsidiary companies if they wish. Alternative Investment Market (AIM) listed companies count as listed companies for this purpose. Other UK companies can decide to use international standards if they wish, but having done so they can never return to UK standards unless their circumstances change.

Accounts prepared in accordance with UK accounting standards

The following are required if UK GAAP (generally accepted accounting principles) are used:

- A balance sheet
- A profit and loss account
- A statement of total recognized gains and losses (STRGL).

If a company revalues its assets, a note of historical cost profits and losses may follow the profit and loss account or the STRGL.

Most companies also include a cash flow statement in their financial statements.

Notes to the financial statements are also required.

Comparable figures for the previous period must in all cases be stated.

The financial statements must be accompanied by a directors' report and, for all but small companies, a business review. A chairman's report is optional.

Space does not permit extensive examples, but the following is a real example of a profit and loss account prepared in accordance with UK GAAP.

	Note	Current Year £	Previous Year £
TURNOVER	2	5,712,480	5,455,154
Cost of sales		905,147	1,331,433
GROSS PROFIT		4,807,333	4,123,721
Distribution costs		144,191	320,025
Administrative expenses		4,302,709	3,543,711
OPERATING PROFIT	3	360,433	259,985
Interest payable and similar charges	5	23,779	15,159
PROFIT ON ORDINARY ACTIVITIES BEFORE TAXATION		336,654	244,826
Tax on profit on ordinary activities		–	–
PROFIT ON ORDINARY ACTIVITIES AFTER TAXATION		336,654	244,826
Extraordinary items	6	–	462,291
PROFIT/LOSS FOR THE FINANCIAL YEAR		336,654	(217,465)
Balance brought forward		(1,801,285)	(1,583,820)
Balance carried forward		(1,464,631)	(1,801,285)

All of the activities of the company are classed as continuing.

The company has no recognized gains or losses other than the results for the year as set out above.

Accounts prepared in accordance with international accounting standards

The following are required if international accounting standards are used:

● An income statement immediately followed by a statement of comprehensive income (SORIE) or a single statement

of comprehensive income which combines the income statement and the SORIE
- A statement of financial position (this is the revised name for the balance sheet and it is still permitted to use the term balance sheet instead)
- A statement of changes in equity
- A statement of cash flows
- Notes to the financial statements.

Comparable figures for the previous period must in all cases be stated.

The financial statements must be accompanied by a directors' report and for all but small companies a business review. In the case of a listed company a chairman's report and a directors' remuneration report are required.

Abbreviated accounts of small and medium-sized companies

In the UK, small and medium-sized companies may prepare abbreviated accounts for Companies House, though they must send full accounts to their members (this usually means their shareholders). There are a few exceptions but otherwise the definitions are:

Small company

For accounts periods commencing 1 January 2016 (earlier at directors' discretion) a company that on a group basis satisfies any two of the following three conditions for both the current financial year and previous financial year.

- Turnover not more than £10,200,000
- Balance sheet total not more than £5,100,000
- Average number of employees not more than 50.

Less information still may be supplied to Companies House by Micro-entities, though they must provide more information to their members. Subject to conditions a micro-entity has a turnover of less than £632,000.

Medium-sized company

For accounts periods commencing 1 January 2016 (earlier at directors' discretion) a company that on a group basis satisfies any two of the following three conditions for both the current financial year and the previous financial year:

● Turnover not more than £36,000,000
● Balance sheet total not more than £18,000,000
● Average number of employees not more than 250.

The privilege of abbreviated accounts relates to accounts sent to the Registrar of Companies, and are thus placed on public record. It does not apply to the accounts that must be sent to company members. A company need not take advantage of any or all of the privileges of abbreviated accounts.

The privileges of small and medium-sized accounts are as follows:

Small company

● No profit and loss account is necessary
● No directors' report is necessary
● The balance sheet and notes may be in summarized form.

Medium-sized company

Certain information relating to the profit and loss account need not be disclosed. In particular, it is not necessary to show other operating income and cost of sales. The balance sheet and notes must be shown in full. Medium-sized companies are required to disclose their turnover.

Small and medium-sized companies do not have to take advantage of any or all of these privileges but most of them do. Analysing small and medium-sized companies' abbreviated accounts is frustrating because of the lack of information. This is particularly true of small companies.

Audit

Subject to complicated rules and exceptions a company may be exempted from the audit requirement if it is dormant or if it is a subsidiary company. Under the small company regime an audit is not required if the following conditions apply:

- It is a private company
- It is a small company as defined in this chapter
- It is not part of a group that is required to prepare audited accounts.

There are one or two exceptions such as banking companies.

The auditor has a number of responsibilities, including stating in the audit report an opinion as to whether or not the financial statements give a 'true and fair view'. The auditor does not certify the figures, a point which is frequently misunderstood.

Summary

We have done a lot in this chapter. We have:

● seen an example of unpublished accounts, the sort that you might see during the year in the course of your employment.

● noted how to obtain copies of the published accounts of registered companies and limited liability partnerships.

● discovered why accounting standards are so important in understanding and interpreting accounts.

● found out more about accounts prepared in accordance with both UK accounting standards and international accounting standards.

● looked at the definitions of small and medium-sized companies for accounting purposes and seen how their accounts need to provide less information.

● had a brief introduction to the subject of audit.

Now we start examining the accounts in detail starting with the one that many people turn to first. This is the profit and loss account, which will be called the income statement if international accounting standards have been used.

Fact-check (answers at the back)

1. Must unpublished accounts comply with accounting standards?
   a) Yes ❏
   b) No ❏
   c) Only if the accounts are for a company that is insolvent ❏
   d) Only if it is a listed company ❏

2. Which of general partnerships and limited liability partnerships are required to file accounts at Companies House?
   a) Both general partnerships and limited liability partnerships ❏
   b) Neither general partnerships nor limited liability partnerships ❏
   c) Just general partnerships ❏
   d) Just limited liability partnerships ❏

3. Can you get copies of accounts for previous years from Companies House?
   a) Yes ❏
   b) No ❏
   c) Only if you pay more ❏
   d) Only for the previous three years ❏

4. What is the charge for obtaining a set of accounts by post from Companies House?
   a) £10 ❏
   b) £1 ❏
   c) £2 ❏
   d) £3 ❏

5. Must AIM listed companies use international accounting standards?
   a) Yes ❏
   b) No ❏
   c) Only if they have never used UK standards ❏
   d) Only if the company is less than five years old ❏

6. Must the accounts of public companies be audited?
   a) Yes ❏
   b) No ❏
   c) Only if turnover is more than £6,500,000 ❏
   d) Only if they are listed on a stock exchange ❏

7. What name is used for the profit and loss account if international accounting standards are used?
   a) Profit statement ❏
   b) Profit or loss statement ❏
   c) Income statement ❏
   d) Statement of surplus or deficit ❏

8. Using either UK accounting standards or international accounting standards, for how many previous periods must comparable figures be stated?
   a) One previous period ❏
   b) Two previous periods ❏
   c) Three previous periods ❏
   d) Four previous periods ❏

9. For whom or what must small companies provide a profit and loss account?

a) Just Companies House ❏
b) Just their members (this usually means shareholders) ❏
c) Both Companies House and their members ❏
d) Neither Companies House nor their members ❏

10. Does an auditor certify the accuracy of the financial statements?

a) Yes ❏
b) No ❏
c) Only if it is a public company ❏
d) Only if it is for the first accounting period of a newly registered company ❏

CHAPTER 16

The profit and loss account or income statement

If you studied the previous chapter carefully you will know why what most people instinctively call the profit and loss account is sometimes called the income statement. Why did they have to change the term? In the words of the hymn 'Change and decay in all around I see'.

The first financial statement that we study in detail is the one that most people turn to first. Many consider it to be the most important. We will see what the profit and loss account is and what it does, and we will see how it is laid out, conforming with each of the two sets of accounting standards. We will look at the long list of information that must be disclosed in the notes and, finally and very importantly, we will do some relevant analysis work.

The topics covered in this chapter comprise:

- what is a profit and loss account or income statement?
- extra factors for trading and manufacturing businesses
- income statement prepared in accordance with international accounting standards (IFRS)
- profit and loss account prepared in accordance with UK accounting standards (UK GAAP)
- SORIE and STRGL
- information that must be given
- some useful analysis.

What is a profit and loss account or income statement?

A profit and loss account or income statement is a summary of the accounts of an income and expense nature in the bookkeeping system. Invoiced sales and rental income are examples of accounts of an income nature, and salaries and advertising costs are examples of accounts of an expenditure nature. The difference between the total of the income accounts and the total of the expenditure accounts is the profit or loss for the period.

The heading of the profit and loss account or income statement must state the period of time that it covers. This is often a year, but could be some other period. It is important to understand that it is a summary of activity over a period of time. So, for example, if in the course of a year 10,000 invoices to customers have been issued and they total 6 million pounds, it is 6 million pounds that will appear in the profit and loss account. This is fundamentally different from a balance sheet which lists assets and liabilities as at a stated date, not activity over a period of time.

It is obviously important that accounts be properly classified, as a mistake can distort the figures. For example, if an account of an expenditure nature (such as the costs of running company cars) is classed as an asset (such as the purchase of company cars) both the profit and the fixed assets in the balance sheet will be overstated.

In published accounts at least, revenue should be sales made outside the group. Whether or not revenue is recognized for the period is a big and contentious subject, with individual decisions being a matter for accounting standards and individual judgement. This can be a factor in such things as major construction projects lasting several years. Whether payment has been received for the sales is not material.

There are only common sense considerations if the profit and loss account is unpublished and for internal use only, but a published profit and loss account must be laid out in a certain way with required supporting information given in the notes. Specified headings must be used, but they may be omitted if not relevant to a particular profit and loss account or income statement.

Extra factors for trading and manufacturing businesses

If a company sells goods rather than provides services, it is important that its profit and loss account or income statement only includes the cost of goods sold in the period, rather than the cost of goods purchased. The following shows how it is done.

	£	£
Sales		10,000,000
Stock at the beginning of the period	3,000,000	
Add purchases during the period	8,000,000	
	11,000,000	
Less stock at the end of the period	5,000,000	
Cost of goods sold		6,000,000
		4,000,000

It would obviously be a dreadful mistake to say that the cost of goods sold was £8,000,000, being the cost of goods purchased in the period.

The same principle applies in the accounts of a business that manufactures goods. The total manufacturing cost of goods sold in the period must be brought into the profit and loss account or income statement, not the amount spent on manufacturing. The cost of raw materials, bought in components and manufacturing costs for just the goods sold is what is wanted.

Income statement prepared in accordance with international accounting standards (IFRS)

The following is an actual example of an income statement prepared in accordance with international accounting standards. It is for a subsidiary company within a group and it is a very simple and straightforward example. Income statements can be and often are much longer and much more complicated. It is the real income statement of a real company, but we will call it Company A.

Company A

Income Statement for the Year to.....

	Note	Current Year £000	Previous Year £000
Revenue	3	1,604	1,243
Selling and distribution expenses		(52)	(41)
Administrative expenses		(1,386)	(1,134)
Operating profit	4	166	68
Profit before taxation		166	68
Tax expense	7	(46)	(22)
Profit for the year		120	46

Revenue and operating profit is derived entirely from continuing operations.

All profits are attributable to the owners of the company, as there is no non-controlling interest.

The company has no recognized gains or losses for the current or prior year other than those recognized in the company's income statement, hence no statement of comprehensive income is prepared.

Note 3 explains the source of the company's revenue and states how much of it was earned outside the United Kingdom.

Note 4 gives details of certain expenses deducted in arriving at the operating profit.

Note 7 explains in detail the calculation of the taxation charge.

Profit and loss account prepared in accordance with UK accounting standards (UK GAAP)

The following is an actual example of a profit and loss account prepared in accordance with UK accounting standards. It is the real profit and loss account of a real company, but we will call it Company B.

Company B

Profit and Loss Account for the Year to.....

	Note	Current Year £	Previous Year £
Turnover	1	22,680,815	25,792,130
Cost of sales		(12,076,105)	(15,154,851)
Gross profit		10,604,710	10,637,279
		46.8%	41.2%
Distribution costs		(387,026)	(422,807)
Administrative expenses		(11,434,707)	(11,379,665)
Other operating income	3	657,110	334,760
		(11,164,623)	(11,467,712)
Operating loss before amortization of goodwill		(559,913)	(830,433)
Goodwill amortization	8	(267,017)	(298,250)
Operating loss		(826,930)	(1,128,683)
Interest receivable and similar income	4	164,819	156,890

		£	£
Loss on ordinary activities before taxation		(662,111)	(971,793)
Tax on loss on ordinary activities	5	457,126	169,894
Loss on ordinary activities after taxation	19	(204,985)	(801,899)

CONSOLIDATED STATEMENT OF TOTAL RECOGNIZED GAINS AND LOSSES

	£	£
Loss attributable to shareholders	(204,985)	(726,899)
Unrealized deficit on revaluation of investment properties	–	(75,000)
Total recognized losses since last financial statements	(204,985)	(801,899)

Note 1 is 'turnover and loss on ordinary activities before taxation'. It splits the turnover between sales in the UK and sales overseas, and it details expenditure on:

● audit services
● depreciation of tangible fixed assets
● amortization of intangibles
● operating lease rentals
● profit or loss on sale of fixed assets
● loss on foreign exchange.

Note 3 gives details of operating income from sources other than the main business. This includes income from leasing premises.

Note 8 gives further details of goodwill amortization. Goodwill is the amount paid for a business in excess of its book value and it must be amortized (written off) over a number of years.

Note 4 splits the interest receivable between bank interest and other interest.

Note 5 gives details of the tax charge or tax credit. It is a credit in this case because the company has made a significant loss.

Note 19 is headed 'reconciliation of movements in total equity shareholders' funds'. This note relates to the balance sheet as well as the profit and loss account and it shows how the value of the share capital and reserves is affected by the after-tax loss and the payment of dividends.

SORIE and STRGL

We had better start by stating what these acronyms stand for.

SORIE stands for 'statement of recognized income and expense' and this is required if an income statement is prepared using international accounting standards. It must appear under the income statement or be incorporated in a single statement of comprehensive income.

STRGL sounds rather like struggle and it might be a struggle to prepare, but this is not correct. It stands for 'statement of total recognized gains and losses'. It must appear under the profit and loss account if it is prepared using UK accounting standards.

SORIE and STRGL fulfil essentially the same purpose. As already stated in this chapter an income statement and a profit and loss account summarize the accounts in the bookkeeping system of an income and expense nature. The difference between the two totals is the profit or loss for the period. However, under accounting rules some gains and losses go straight to the balance sheet without first passing through the income statement or profit and loss account. In the balance sheet they increase or decrease the value of the business according to whether they are gains or losses.

This is done because the gains or losses are not realized gains or losses. They might not actually happen or, if they do, the realized gains or losses might be for different amounts. Despite this it is considered right to show them in the accounts, which is what SORIE and STRGL do. An example of such an unrealized gain or loss is a revaluation of some of the fixed assets at an amount different from the book value.

The foot of the income statement of Company A, which is shown in this chapter, states that there is nothing to report in a statement of comprehensive income. Company B, whose profit and loss account is also shown in this chapter, had one thing to report in the previous year. Investment properties were valued at £75,000 less than the book value. This shortfall is reflected in the balance sheet but has not passed through the profit and loss account.

The list of factors can be long and technical. The consolidated statement of comprehensive income in a recent set of accounts of Marks and Spencer Group plc lists the following:

- foreign currency translation differences
- actuarial (losses)/gains on retirement benefit schemes
- tax on retirement benefit schemes
- cash flow and net investment hedges
- fair value movements in equity
- reclassified and reported in net profit
- amount recognized in inventories
- tax on cash flow hedges and net investment hedges.

It sounds complicated and troublesome and it probably is.

Information that must be given

In the case of a company, the Companies Act and accounting standards require extensive information to be given in the notes. If there is nothing to report under a particular heading, it is not necessary to have that heading in the notes. The following are many of the requirements:

The amount of the company's profit or loss on ordinary activities before taxation

This is 'profit before tax' which is obviously a key figure and probably familiar to you. It is often the first figure in the entire accounts package that users of accounts turn to. Ordinary activities exclude extraordinary income and expenditure, and they also exclude exceptional income and expenditure. These are explained next.

Extraordinary income and expenditure

These are separate from the ordinary activities of the company and must be identified as such. An extreme and unrealistic example is a mining company opening a massage parlour.

Exceptional income and expenditure

These are derived from ordinary activities, but are exceptional because of their size or some other factor. A possible example is significant redundancy and other costs incurred when closing a division or activities at a particular location. It is sometimes said that directors have an incentive to class costs as exceptional in order to make the result of ordinary activities look better. This would be both wrong and hopefully very unusual.

Prior year adjustments

These may be necessitated by the discovery of a fundamental error in previous accounts or by a change in accounting policy. The policy on valuing stocks is a possible example as this affects reported profits.

Interest payable and receivable and similar

Interest payable must be analysed between the following categories:

- amounts payable on bank loans and overdrafts
- loans of any other kind made to the company
- lease finance charges allocated for the year.

Gains and losses on the repurchase or early settlement of debt should be separately disclosed as should the unwinding of any discount on provisions.

Income from listed investments
Rent receivable in connection with land
Payments for the hire of plant and machinery
Details of auditors' remuneration

This must be split as follows:

- remuneration (inclusive of sums paid in respect of expenses)
- the aggregate of other fees paid to the auditors and their associates, with a split showing the categories of services provided
- the nature of any benefit in kind provided to the auditors.

Details of turnover

The requirements are quite detailed but, as a minimum, a note must show the breakdown by geographical region and by class of business. The note for Company B, whose profit and loss account was shown earlier in this chapter, states that there was only one class of business. It then gives the following information.

	Current Year £	Previous Year £
Existing operations		
United Kingdom	20,715,244	23,951,158
Overseas	1,965,571	1,840,972
	22,680,815	25,792,130

Employees

The average number of persons employed by the company in the year, determined on a monthly basis, must be shown. There must be an analysis between appropriate categories, as determined by the directors, of the monthly number of employees.

The aggregate amounts for the period must be shown for:

● wages and salaries
● social security costs
● other pension costs.

The basis of any foreign currency translation

Details of any transfers to and from reserves

Appropriations (including dividends)

Details must be given of:

● the aggregate amount of dividends paid and proposed
● the amount set aside or proposed to be set aside to, or withdrawn or proposed to be withdrawn, from reserves
● the amounts set aside for redemption of share capital or for redemption of loans
● the aggregate of dividends for each class of share
● the amount of any appropriation of profits in respect of non-equity shares other than dividends.

Government grants

The effect of government grants on the results for the period must be shown.

Capitalization, depreciation, amortization and impairment

The requirements are quite lengthy and detailed.

Directors' remuneration

There are separate and much greater requirements for quoted companies, but the following must be given for other companies:

- amounts paid to or receivable by directors in respect of qualifying services
- amounts paid to or receivable by directors in respect of long-term incentive schemes
- any company contributions paid to pension schemes.

The following must be disclosed if the aggregate directors' emoluments are £200,000 or higher:

- the emoluments of the highest paid director
- the value of the company contributions paid, or treated as paid, to a money purchase pension scheme in respect of the highest paid director
- where the highest paid director is a member of a defined benefit pension scheme, and has performed pensionable qualifying services in the year
  - a) the amount at the end of the year of his/her accrued pension
  - b) the amount at the end of the year of his/her accrued lump sum
- if the highest paid director exercised any share options in the year, then a statement of this fact
- if the highest paid director received, or became entitled to receive, any shares under a long-term incentive scheme, then a statement of that fact.

Pension costs

Taxation

An analysis of tax payable must be given. There are lengthy detailed requirements.

Some useful analysis

Following are three very common and useful examples of ratio analysis that can be applied to a profit and loss account and supporting notes:

Profit to turnover

This is possibly the simplest of the ratios and one of the most commonly used. It is profit expressed as a percentage of turnover in the year. Sometimes profit before interest payable is used. Sometimes it is profit before tax and sometimes it is profit after tax. As with all the ratios you are free to use the definition that best suits your purposes. The turnover figure does not change of course.

Company A did not pay any interest in the year so interest is not relevant in this case. Using profit before tax the percentage is:

$$\frac{166}{1,604} \times 100 = 10.3 \text{ per cent.}$$

Is this good or not? It sounds all right and it probably is all right, but we do not really know. We need to ask questions such as:

- what was expected?
- what was the budget?
- how did the competition do?
- are there any special factors that should be taken into account?
- what sort of business is the company in?

Company B made a loss both before and after tax. The tax figure is actually a credit because of the loss. Despite this, the company is well funded and because of excellent profits in earlier years it has a secure balance sheet, as we will see when we look at it in the next chapter. It had no need to borrow and in fact there was interest receivable. Using the figure for the operating loss, the loss to turnover percentage is:

$$\frac{826,930}{22,680,815} \times 100 = 3.6 \text{ per cent.}$$

At least it was better than in the previous year.

This accounting ratio is often quoted by people who say 'Look after the top line and the bottom line will look after itself'. There can be an element of truth in this but there are inherent flaws, as you will find if you consistently sell goods at below cost price. Buying turnover at the expense of margins might not be a good idea.

Gross profit margin

In a manufacturing or trading business, gross profit (or gross loss) is the difference between sales and the cost of manufacturing or buying the products sold. In a service business it is the difference between sales and the direct cost of providing the service. In both cases overheads are excluded from the calculation.

Gross margin is particularly important in many businesses because cost of sales is usually by far the biggest cost. If the cost of sales can be reduced by a few percentage points, it can have a big impact on net profit on the bottom line. British supermarkets are just one example of businesses that work hard, and often successfully, to hold down the cost of sales and maintain a satisfactory gross profit margin.

It is not a legal requirement that the gross profit percentage be stated in the accounts, but Company B very helpfully states on the face of the profit and loss account that it is 46.8 per cent. This means that the cost of sales is 53.2 per cent. Is this good? Once again it all depends. Some businesses have a policy of seeking high margins, even at the expense of turnover. Other businesses do the opposite. To use the well-known phrase, they 'pile it high and sell it cheap'. What is best depends on many factors, including the policy of the competition.

Interest cover

This is an important and much-studied ratio, especially when borrowing is high relative to shareholders' funds. This situation, known as being highly geared, is explained later in this Part. It is also particularly significant when the interest charge is high relative to profits. Obviously a company that cannot pay its interest charge has severe problems and might not be able to carry on, at least not without a fresh injection of funds.

Interest cover is profit before interest and tax divided by the interest charge. The higher the resulting number the more easily the business is managing to pay the interest charge. The following is an example of the calculation:

	£000
Interest	814
Operating profit	8,698
Interest cover	10.7 times

This is obviously not a problem, and companies A and B, whose details were given earlier, are still better placed because they have no interest charge at all. But what about this?

	£000
Interest	719
Operating profit	790
Interest cover	1.1 times

This is worrying and there are questions to be answered.

Summary

In this chapter we have had a close look at the profit and loss account (or income statement). In particular we have:

- Seen the purpose of the profit and loss account and seen examples of how it is laid out, using both international and UK standards. We have also seen what supporting information must be provided in the notes.
- Looked at the statement of recognized income and expense (SORIE) and the statement of total recognized gains and losses (STRGL). We have seen how they record unrealized gains and losses not recorded in the profit and loss account.
- Been introduced to three regularly used accounting ratios that are used in connection with profit and loss accounts.

Next we will move on to the balance sheet (which might be called the statement of financial position). This is usually regarded as the second main component of the financial statements and it is fundamentally different from the profit and loss account.

Fact-check (answers at the back)

1. What must be stated in the heading of a profit and loss account?
- **a)** Whether it complies with the law ❑
- **b)** Whether it complies with accounting standards ❑
- **c)** The period of time that it covers ❑
- **d)** Whether it has been audited ❑

2. What is the consequence if an account of an expenditure nature is wrongly classed as a fixed asset?
- **a)** Both the profit and the fixed assets in the balance sheet will be overstated ❑
- **b)** Both the profit and the fixed assets in the balance sheet will be understated ❑
- **c)** Both income and expenditure in the profit and loss account will be overstated ❑
- **d)** The increase in the fixed assets will be compensated by an increase in the depreciation charge ❑

3. Stock at 31 December is £400,000. Purchases in the six months to 30 June are £1,600,000. Stock at 30 June is £600,000. What is the cost of sales for the six months to 30 June?
- **a)** £1,600,000 ❑
- **b)** £1,400,000 ❑
- **c)** £400,000 ❑
- **d)** £600,000 ❑

4. Which phrase best sums up the purpose of the statement of recognized income and expense (SORIE)?
- **a)** It is an essential step in making the balance sheet balance ❑
- **b)** It repeats the most important elements of the income statement ❑
- **c)** It summarizes the income and expenditure ❑
- **d)** It states unrealized gains and losses that have passed to the balance sheet without affecting the income statement ❑

5. Which phrase best sums up 'exceptional income and expenditure'?
- **a)** They are separate from the ordinary activities of the company ❑
- **b)** They are derived from ordinary activities, but are exceptional because of their size or some other factor ❑
- **c)** They are exceptionally large ❑
- **d)** They are exceptionally important ❑

6. Where must the breakdown of turnover by geographical region be shown?
- **a)** In the balance sheet ❑
- **b)** In the profit and loss account ❑
- **c)** In the directors' report ❑
- **d)** In the notes ❑

7. When must the term 'income statement' be used?

a) When international accounting standards are used ❑

b) When UK accounting standards are used ❑

c) When it is a listed company ❑

d) When it is a small or medium-sized company ❑

8. Turnover is £1,000,000, profit before tax is £100,000 and profit after tax is £79,000. What is the profit after tax to turnover percentage?

a) 10.0 per cent ❑

b) 9.0 per cent ❑

c) 7.9 per cent ❑

d) 8.5 per cent ❑

9. Turnover is £10,000,000 and the gross profit margin is 36.3 per cent. Is this good?

a) Yes ❑

b) No ❑

c) Perhaps ❑

d) Only if the company is in the retail sector ❑

10. Interest payable is £1,264,000 and the operating profit is £7,388,000. What is the interest cover?

a) 4.8 times ❑

b) 5.8 times ❑

c) It is not covered ❑

d) 9.1 times ❑

CHAPTER 17

The balance sheet or statement of financial position

The balance sheet is usually regarded as one of the two main financial statements and it is our task to thoroughly understand it. We will study what it is, what it is for and how it is laid out. This will be when it is an internal document prepared for management, when it is prepared in accordance with international accounting standards and when it is prepared in accordance with UK accounting standards.

We will see what is meant by the main balance sheet headings and see what information must be disclosed in the notes to a published balance sheet.

The topics covered in this chapter comprise:

- what is a balance sheet or statement of financial position?
- the concept of ownership
- the layout of the balance sheet
- statement of financial position (or balance sheet) prepared in accordance with international financial standards (IFRS)
- balance sheet prepared in accordance with UK accounting standards
- information that must be given.

What is a balance sheet or statement of financial position?

A balance sheet or statement of financial position is very different from a profit and loss account or income statement. These summarize income and expenditure over a period, the difference between total income and total expenditure being the profit or loss. A balance sheet or statement of financial position, on the other hand, is a listing of the assets and liabilities in a logical way as at a stated date.

A balance sheet is virtually always dated the last day of the profit and loss account period. The profit from the profit and loss account is transferred to the balance sheet, which ensures that it balances. If the balance sheet (or statement of financial position) is published, the corresponding figures from the previous balance sheet (which will be dated the last day of the previous profit and loss period) must be given.

Another analogy which you might find helpful is to think of a balance sheet as a freeze-frame picture. It summarizes the assets and liabilities on a fixed date. If the date were to be one day earlier or one day later, the figures would be different.

Statement of financial position (or balance sheet) prepared in accordance with international financial standards (IFRS)

The following is the statement of financial position of Company A. It is dated at the end of the trading period covered in that income statement and the profit is incorporated in it.

Company A

Statement of Financial Position as at.....

	Notes	Current Date £000	Previous Date £000
Non-current assets			
Intangible assets – goodwill	8	162	162
Property, plant and equipment	9	83	52
Deferred tax asset	7	13	6
		258	220
Current assets			
Trade and other receivables	10	73	306
Cash and cash equivalents	11	492	344
		565	650
Total assets		823	870
Current liabilities			
Trade and other payables	12	(306)	(499)
Income tax payable		(50)	(24)
		(356)	(523)
Total liabilities		(356)	(523)
Net assets		467	347
Equity			
Equity share capital	16	250	250
Retained earnings		217	97
Total equity		467	347

As explained earlier in this chapter, the assets less the liabilities is £467,000 and this is the 'net worth' of the company. It represents the shareholders' investment in the company.

Note 8 relates to goodwill. This exists because in a previous year the company paid more than net book value for another company. This excess payment is left in its balance sheet. Note 8 explains why no impairment is necessary.

Note 9 gives details of the fixed assets, the depreciation charge in the year and net book value at the balance sheet date.

Note 11 reveals that the £492,000 is all represented by cash at the bank and cash in hand.

Note 12 gives the split of trade and other payables as:

	£000
Trade payables	156
Social security	20
Other payables	130
	306

Note 16 gives details of the authorized and issued share capital. There is only one class of share.

Balance sheet prepared in accordance with UK accounting standards

The following is the balance sheet of Company B, whose profit and loss account was shown in the previous chapter. It is dated at the end of the trading period covered in that and the loss is incorporated in it.

Company B

Balance Sheet as at.....

	Note	Current Date £	Previous Date £
Fixed assets			
Goodwill	8	1,616,743	729,345
Tangible fixed assets	9	7,101,740	7,818,028
Investments	10	12,187,649	5,445,145
		20,906,132	13,992,518
Current assets			
Stocks	12	7,167,091	6,264,078
Debtors	13	6,163,713	4,601,141

Fixed-term deposits	15	2,191,436	12,381,235
Cash at bank and in hand		3,834,521	2,875,493
		19,356,761	26,121,947
Creditors, amounts falling due within one year	16	(3,129,758)	(2,114,299)
Net current assets		16,227,003	24,007,648
Total assets less current liabilities		37,133,135	38,000,166
Provisions for liabilities and charges	17	(303,320)	(665,366)
		36,829,815	37,334,800
Capital and reserves			
Called up share capital	18	100,000	100,000
Revaluation reserve	19	142,721	142,721
Profit and loss account	19	36,587,094	37,092,079
Equity shareholders' funds	19	36,829,815	37,334,800

I said in the previous chapter that despite the loss the company was not threatened and had a secure balance sheet, and this can be readily seen. In fact it has more than six million pounds of cash and a 'net worth' of £36,829,815. Nevertheless, losses are, of course, bad news and there has been a deterioration over the year.

Company B's balance sheet has more notes than Company A's balance sheet. This is not because UK standards generate more notes than international standards. It is because the company is bigger and its structure is more complicated. As you would expect there is a mass of detail in the notes and they answer many of the questions that will occur to you.

Goodwill has increased due to acquisitions in the year but, unlike Company A, there has been amortization during the period. It is explained in note 8. You will probably notice the very big reduction in fixed-term deposits which is in current assets, and the big increase in investments which is in fixed assets. Details are contained in notes 15 and 10.

The directors' report states that business conditions were extremely challenging and that this was a main reason for the loss. In light of this it is interesting to see the increase in stocks and debtors, despite the reduction in turnover. Note 13 discloses that £954,261 of the increase in debtors was down to the increase in trade debtors. Customers were taking longer to pay.

Information that must be given

In the case of a company, the Companies Act and accounting standards require certain information to be given in the notes. If there is nothing to report under a particular heading, it is not necessary to have that heading in the notes. The following are many of the requirements.

Details of share capital and debentures

This includes separate details of authorized and issued share capital, details of any debentures and information about any redeemable preference shares. Since 1 October 2009, it has been possible to dispense with the concept of authorized share capital.

Details of tangible fixed assets and depreciation
Details of investments

Separate details for listed and unlisted investments must be given. Details of aggregate market value must be given if this differs from the balance sheet value.

Details of movements in reserves and provisions
Details of indebtedness

Convertible debt must be analysed between amounts falling due:

● In one year or less, or on demand
● Between one and two years

- Between two and five years
- In five years or more.

In respect of debt that is due for repayment wholly or partly after five years, terms of interest and repayment must be stated. So too must details of any security given.

Details of any cumulative dividends in arrears

Details of any guarantees given

Details of capital commitments and other commitments at the balance sheet date

Details of contingent liabilities at the balance sheet date

A contingent liability is one that may never be realized. An example is a pending legal case which could result in the company having to pay damages. The company might win or the action might be withdrawn, but it could result in a future payment. To the extent that a reserve for this has not been created in the accounts, details should be given in a note. It is normal for directors to state their view of the likelihood of the contingency being realized.

Debtors

The analysis given in the note must separate sums falling due within one year from sums falling due after one year.

Post-balance sheet events

For non-adjusting post-balance sheet events and the reversal of a transaction which was entered in to alter the appearance of the balance sheet it is necessary to show:

- The nature of the event
- An estimate of the financial effect, or a statement that it is not practicable to make such an estimate
- An explanation of the taxation implications, where necessary for a proper understanding of the financial position.

Summary

In this chapter we have studied in some detail the balance sheet (or statement of financial position). We have:

- seen what it is, its purpose and how it is fundamentally different from the profit and loss account
- seen how it is laid out to comply with both international and UK accounting standards
- studied the information that must be provided in accompanying notes.

Fact-check (answers at the back)

1. Which of the following statements is true about a balance sheet?
   a) It summarizes the assets and liabilities over a stated period ❏
   b) It summarizes the assets and liabilities at a stated date ❏
   c) It compares the profit with the assets ❏
   d) It is a more detailed version of the profit and loss account ❏

2. In which category in the balance sheet will plant and machinery be classed?
   a) Fixed assets ❏
   b) Current assets ❏
   c) Current liabilities ❏
   d) Capital and reserves ❏

3. During what period must liabilities be liable to be discharged in order to be classed as current liabilities?
   a) Up to three months ❏
   b) Up to six months ❏
   c) Up to one year ❏
   d) Up to two years ❏

4. Which of the following must be disclosed in notes to the accounts?
   a) Details of share capital and debentures ❏
   b) Details of any cumulative dividends in arrears ❏
   c) Details of contingent liabilities at the balance sheet date ❏
   d) All of the above ❏

5. What is represented by the total of the capital accounts?
   a) The total share capital ❏
   b) Share capital plus share premium ❏
   c) Revenue reserves ❏
   d) The net worth of the business at book value ❏

6. Does a registered company have a legal existence and personality separate from the shareholders who own it?
   a) Sometimes ❏
   b) Yes ❏
   c) No ❏
   d) Only if it is insolvent ❏

7. Does the business of a sole trader have a legal existence and personality separate from the person who owns it?
   a) Sometimes ❏
   b) Yes ❏
   c) No ❏
   d) Only if it is insolvent ❏

8. A company took a bank loan of £6,000,000 two years ago. It is repayable over five years in 60 equal monthly instalments. How will the remaining balance be shown in the balance sheet?
   a) £3,600,000 in current liabilities ❏
   b) £3,600,000 in long-term liabilities ❏
   c) £1,200,000 in current liabilities and £2,400,000 in long-term liabilities ❏
   d) £1,800,000 in current liabilities and £1,800,000 in long-term liabilities ❏

CHAPTER 18

Cash flow statement and group accounts

In this chapter we examine the two things identified in the heading to this chapter. I suspect that you
will find the cash flow statement more difficult than
group accounts.

The cash flow statement explains the movement of
cash into and out of the business during the period
covered by the accounts. It identifies the difference in
cash between the two balance sheet dates and it
reconciles this difference with the profit and loss in
the period. We will have a close look at two examples.

The final part of our work is the subject of group
accounts. We will see why they are necessary, in
what circumstances they must be prepared and
their key features.

The topics covered comprise:

- the differences between cash and profit
- the importance of cash and working capital
- the concept of the cash flow statement
- cash flow statement for company using
  UK accounting standards
- statement of cash flows for company using
  international accounting standards
- group accounts.

The differences between cash and profit

Cash is most definitely not the same as profit. Most people know this, so my apologies if I am telling you what you already know and what seems obvious, but a surprising number of people are confused on the point. You may well have heard comments such as 'Don't be silly. We can't have run out of money – we are making a profit'. Cash and profit (apart from dividends, etc.) may be the same in the very long term or when a business is wound up, but they will almost certainly be different (perhaps very different) at any given time. The following are some of the reasons:

Dividends

Dividends are a distribution of profit, not a charge against profit (in the way that salaries and other expenses are a charge against profit).

Capital expenditure and depreciation

Payment for capital expenditure is usually immediate or nearly so, but the effect on profit is spread over a number of years. Consider a motor car that is purchased for £30,000 on the first day of the accounting year. Unless it is being bought on hire purchase, £30,000 cash will go out of the business at or near the beginning of the year. On the other hand it will probably be depreciated over four years, so £7,500 will be charged to the profit and loss account in the first year. In that year the effect on cash will be £22,500 worse than the effect on profit. In the following year there will be no effect on cash but a further £7,500 depreciation charge to the profit and loss account.

Investments

The purchase of investments will take cash out of the business but will have no effect on the profit and loss account. The effect will be the opposite when the investments are sold.

Loans

A loan to the business puts cash into the business but has no effect on profit, though of course interest will probably have to be paid. A loan made by the business will have the opposite effect.

The purchase of stock for resale

This normally has to be paid for shortly after it is purchased. The goods purchased only affect the profit and loss account when they are sold, which is usually later.

Bad debt reserve and other reserves

The creation of a bad debt reserve or other reserve reduces the profit but has no effect on the cash. Time will eventually show whether the reserve was correct, too high or too low, and the difference will then be unwound.

Tax

In the UK, corporation tax (for a company) and income tax (for a sole trader or partnership) are normally paid to HMRC after the trading period to which they relate.

Timing differences relating to sales and purchases

Sales are usually credited to the profit and loss account when goods are delivered or services performed. Payment is usually received from customers later. Purchases are usually debited to the profit and loss account as they are made. Suppliers are usually paid later.

The importance of cash and working capital

It is tempting, but of course wrong, to say that cash is the notes and coins found in the petty cash box. This is part of cash, but only a very small part. Cash is the total of all the bank balances plus any notes and coins. The bank balances almost always make up virtually all the cash total. Bank overdrafts must be deducted. It is possible, and indeed very common, for total cash to be a minus figure. Cash for Company B at the balance sheet date is the apparently large sum of £6,025,957 (fixed-term deposits of £2,191,436 plus cash at the bank and in hand of £3,834,521). These figures can be seen in the balance sheet that was reproduced in Chapter 17.

Working capital is net current assets, which is the difference between current assets and current liabilities. Working capital is usually a positive figure and the bigger the figure the bigger the margin of safety. If working capital is a negative figure, it is a very worrying sign of possible trouble and at the very least a reason for asking searching questions. Working capital for Company B is the seemingly very large sum of £16,277,003.

It is possible, and indeed it is not uncommon, for a business to fail even though it is making profits at the time of its failure. This is because it does not have enough cash to pay its suppliers as the debts fall due for payment. Profits are obviously very desirable and very important, and in the long term they provide the means to pay the suppliers, but in the short term it is necessary to have cash.

It is possible, and quite common, for a very profitable, rapidly expanding business to run out of cash. This is because a rapidly expanding business usually has an increasing need for working capital. Cash goes out of the business before a greater amount of cash comes into the business. It may be necessary to take on more staff and pay them and it may be necessary to take larger premises. It may be necessary to buy more stock to meet the greater volume of orders.

This does not, of course, mean that a business should not be profitable and rapidly expanding. It means that the owners should ensure that it does have sufficient cash and working capital. Perhaps more share capital should be injected into the company. Perhaps steps should be taken to convert a short-term bank overdraft into a long-term bank loan. Perhaps the payment of dividends should be stopped for a while. There are many possibilities.

Working capital and cash are both very important. The control of working capital is a step towards the control of cash. If working capital is adequate, it is likely that cash will be adequate or at least that cash will become adequate in the near future.

It is not possible to give the 'right' figures or proportions for cash or working capital, though it is possible to state categorically that they should be sufficient. This is because businesses vary and circumstances vary. If there is a sure source of further capital or resources if needed, it may be possible to operate with smaller working capital. It is also very helpful if the suppliers value the business and are willing to be supportive.

It is possible to have too much cash and too much working capital. This is wasteful because money is tied up in working capital that could profitably be invested elsewhere. Alternatively, the surplus money could be paid out to the owners of the business. Working capital should be sufficient but not excessive.

The concept of the cash flow statement

This can be stated very simply, although it often gets complicated in practice. The difference between the cash totals in two balance sheets is identified. The two balance sheets are the ones at the beginning and end of the profit and loss period. The various factors affecting the difference are identified and listed, so that the reasons for the change in the cash totals are explained. There are usually notes to support the figures in the statement.

If UK accounting standards are used, it is called the cash flow statement. If international accounting standards are used, it is called the statement of cash flows. They do the same job but the rules about layout are different.

The information disclosed is interesting and valuable. One reason for this is that, short of fraud, it is virtually impossible to cheat. It is sometimes said that profit is partly a matter of opinion. This is inevitable for a number of reasons. For example, it is necessary to take a view on the value of stock and this in turn has an effect on profit. Cash, on the other hand, is very much a matter of fact. It is there or it is not there.

Cash flow statement for company using UK accounting standards

Following is the cash flow statement of Company B, together with notes 23, 24 and 26. All this is taken from the company's financial statements package. The profit and loss account is shown in Chapter 16 and the balance sheet is shown in Chapter 17. We will then examine the layout and what the figures reveal.

	Note	Current Year £	Previous Year £
Net cash (outflow)/inflow from operating activities	23	(817,026)	663,643
Returns on investments and servicing of finance	24	164,819	156,890
Taxation	24	(109,795)	397,568
Capital expenditure and financial investment	24	(6,864,216)	(2,424,999)
Acquisitions and disposals	24	(1,288,095)	–
Management of liquid resources	24	10,189,799	(5,253,148)
Net cash outflow before financing		1,275,486	(6,460,046)
Equity dividends paid	19	(300,000)	(300,000)
Increase/(decrease) in cash in the year	26	975,486	(6,760,046)

Note 23: Reconciliation of operating loss to operating cash flows

	Current Year £	Previous Year £
Operating loss	(826,930)	(830,433)
Depreciation	930,177	846,034
Amortization	267,017	–
Impairment of investment	–	75,000
Profit on disposal of tangible fixed assets	(54,241)	–
(Increase)/decrease in stocks	(250,043)	257,917
(Increase)/decrease in debtors	(805,506)	1,356,658
Decrease in creditors	(77,500)	(1,041,533)
Net cash (outflow)/inflow from operating activities	(817,026)	663,643

Note 24: Analysis of cash flows

	Current Year £	Previous Year £
Returns on investments and servicing of finance		
Interest received	164,819	156,890
Taxation		
UK corporation tax refunded	(109,795)	(397,568)
Capital expenditure and financial investment		
Purchase of tangible fixed assets	(468,977)	(215,526)
Sale of tangible fixed assets	347,265	9,585
Purchase of fixed asset investments	(6,750,000)	(3,778,310)
Sale of fixed asset investments	7,496	1,559,252
Net cash outflow from capital expenditure and financial investment	(6,864,216)	(2,424,999)
Acquisitions and disposals		
Net cash acquired with subsidiary	68,655	–
Cost of purchase of subsidiary	(1,356,750)	–
	(1,288,095)	–
Management of liquid resources		
Decrease/(increase) in fixed-term deposit	10,189,799	(5,253,148)

Note 26: Reconciliation of net cash flow to movement in net funds

	Current Year £	Previous Year £
Increase/(decrease) in cash	975,486	(6,760,046)
Cash flow from changes in debt	(10,189,799)	5,253,148
Net debt acquired with subsidiary	(2,093)	–
Change in net funds raising from cash flows	(9,216,406)	(1,506,898)
Net funds at beginning of year	15,240,270	16,747,168
Net funds at end of year	6,023,864	15,240,270

The operating loss, shown in the profit and loss account, was £826,930, but despite this the cash flow statement shows an increase in cash during the year of £975,486. This rather conveniently illustrates the point that cash and profit are not the same thing. It is one of the jobs of the cash flow statement and relevant notes to identify the factors that caused the difference.

The increase of cash of £975,486 is calculated as follows:

	£
Cash at bank and in hand – current year	3,834,521
Cash at bank and in hand – previous year	2,875,493
	959,028
Add previous year overdraft eliminated in current year	16,458
	975,486

The first two figures are taken directly from the balance sheet. The separate overdraft of £16,458 is disclosed in a note that is not reproduced in this chapter.

The statement shows that a dividend of £300,000 was paid during the year and this, of course, is a cash distribution and does not affect the profit. After adding this back the figure to be explained is £1,275,486.

The operating loss in the profit and loss account is £826,930. Note 23 lists the various factors that moved this figure to a net cash outflow of £817,026, which is the first figure in the cash flow statement. Hopefully everything in note 23 will be understood. To take just one item, the figure of £930,177 for depreciation is favourable for cash. This is because it is a non-cash charge to the profit and loss account and must therefore be added back.

Explanations for the remaining items in the cash flow statement are given in note 24. Once again, hopefully it will all be understood. To explain just one figure, cash outflow of £1,288,095 related to the purchase of a subsidiary company.

It all comes together, though I realize that understanding it all will be challenging. Note 26 shows how the company gets from £975,486 to net funds at the end of the year. Net funds is not quite the same thing as the definition of cash. The figure of £6,023,864 is made up as follows:

	£
Fixed-term deposits	2,191,436
Cash at bank and in hand	3,834,521
	6,025,957
Less net debt acquired with subsidiary	2,093
	£6,023,864

The first two figures come from the balance sheet and the last figure comes from note 26.

Statement of cash flows for company using international accounting standards

The concept is of course the same and the details have a lot of similarities, but there are some differences. The cash flow statement is divided into three sections, but companies may decide which section is most appropriate for a particular heading in light of their individual circumstances. The three headings are:

- Operating activities
- Investing activities
- Financing activities.

The following is the statement of cash flows for Company A and, you may be relieved to know, it is an extremely simple example. They can be much longer and much more complicated. The income statement for Company A was included in Chapter 16 and its statement of financial position was included in Chapter 17.

	Note	Current Year £000	Previous Year £000
Operating activities			
Profit for the year		120	46
Adjustments			
Tax on continuing operations		46	22
Depreciation and impairment of property, plant and equipment		36	35
Decrease/(increase) in trade and other receivables		233	(183)
(Decrease)/increase in trade and other payables		(194)	129
Cash generated from operations		241	49
Income taxes paid		(26)	(9)
Net cash flow from operating activities		215	40
Investing activities			
Payments to acquire property, plant and equipment		(67)	(20)
Net cash flows from investing activities		(67)	(20)
Increase in cash and cash equivalents		148	20
Cash and cash equivalents at the beginning of the year	11	344	324
Cash and cash equivalents at the year end	11	492	344

The profit for the year of £120,000 is after tax and is taken from the income statement. The figure of £492,000 for cash and cash equivalents is taken from the statement of financial position. Only two of the three required headings are used. This is because there is nothing to report under the heading of 'financing activities'.

It is possible that you might be puzzled by the cash inflow of £233,000 caused by the decrease in trade and other receivables. The calculation is:

	£
Trade and other receivables at beginning of period	306,000
Less trade and other receivables at end of period	73,000
	233,000

Less is owing to the company, which means that payments have come in, which in turn means that there has been a cash inflow. Like so many things in accounts the figures need interpreting. Perhaps customers have paid more quickly and the credit controllers have done a good job, but there could be other reasons. Perhaps there was very little invoicing at the end part of the year and consequently there was less money to collect at the balance sheet date.

Group accounts

Why are group accounts necessary? Please consider the following group structure and the following circumstances.

Devonshire Widgets Ltd owns 100 per cent of the shares in the three other companies. Devonshire Widgets Ltd pays

£50,000 for a consignment of widgets and sells them to Plymouth Widgets Ltd for £100,000. This company sells them to Torquay Widgets Ltd for £200,000 and they are in stock at the balance sheet date. The accounts of Devonshire Widgets Ltd show a profit of £50,000 and the accounts of Plymouth Widgets Ltd show a profit of £100,000. The accounts of Torquay Widgets Ltd show stock of £200,000 and no profit or loss effect. Furthermore and as a separate matter, the four balance sheets (all with the same date) disclose the following.

- Devonshire Widgets Ltd owes £600,000 to Plymouth Widgets Ltd
- Plymouth Widgets Ltd owes £600,000 to Torquay Widgets Ltd
- Torquay Widgets Ltd owes £600,000 to Exeter Widgets Ltd
- Exeter Widgets Ltd owes £600,000 to Devonshire Widgets Ltd.

Without group accounts the accounts of each company would be misleading. The consequences of group accounts mean that the effect of inter-group trading is eliminated. Revenue is only recognized when sales outside the group are made. In the example, if and when Torquay Widgets Ltd sells the widgets outside the group for £330,000 it will recognize a profit of £130,000. The group profit and loss account will then show sales of £330,000, cost of sales of £50,000 and a profit contribution of £280,000. Until that happy day there will be no effect on the group profit and loss account, and the group balance sheet will include the widgets with a stock value of £50,000. Furthermore, the group balance sheet will net off all the intercompany debts of £600,000 and it will show nothing payable or receivable in respect of them.

Each company in a group is required to prepare and file at Companies House its own individual accounts, even though they contribute to group accounts.

A parent company/subsidiary company relationship exists when the parent company is in one of the following positions:

- Holds a majority of the voting rights
- Is a member and has the right to appoint or remove directors holding a majority of the voting rights at meetings of the board

- Has the right to exercise a dominant influence over the other company:
  - a) by virtue of provisions contained in the undertaking's articles; or
  - b) by virtue of a control contract
- Is a member and controls alone, pursuant to an agreement with other shareholders or members, a majority of the voting rights in the undertaking
- Has a participating interest and:
  - a) it actually exercises a dominant influence over it; or
  - b) it and the subsidiary undertaking are managed on a unified basis.

A participating interest is an interest held on a *long-term basis* for the purpose of securing a contribution to its activities by the exercise of control or influence. A holding of 20 per cent of the shares is a participating interest, unless it is shown not to be so.

Group accounts need not be presented where one of the following applies:

- The company is not listed on the stock exchange of an EU member state and is more than 50 per cent owned by a parent undertaking established in an EU member state, and is included in its group accounts drawn up in accordance with the seventh directive
- No member of the group is a public company and the group qualifies as a small or medium-sized group
- The subsidiary companies are not material
- The rights of the parent company are subject to long-term restrictions
- Inclusion would cause disproportionate expense or delay
- The parent company's interest is held with a view to resale
- The activities are so different that inclusion would be incompatible with a true and fair view.

Summary

We have covered a lot of ground in this chapter and some of it has been quite challenging. Well done if you have grasped all the points. We have:

● noted that profit is most definitely not the same thing as cash, and we have seen some of the reasons why this is not the case

● seen why cash and working capital is so important

● discovered the purpose of a cash flow statement (statement of cash flows if international accounting standards are used)

● studied in detail real-life examples of a cash flow statement and a statement of cash flows

● seen why group accounts may be necessary, some key principles of group accounts and in what circumstances group accounts are required.

Next we will move on to the reports.

Fact-check (answers at the back)

1. It is called the cash flow statement if UK accounting standards are used. What is it called if international accounting standards are used?
   a) Cash movement statement ❏
   b) Cash statement ❏
   c) Cash variation statement ❏
   d) Statement of cash flows ❏

2. What are dividends?
   a) A distribution of profit ❏
   b) A charge against profit ❏
   c) Net profit after tax ❏
   d) A bookkeeping entry that does not affect cash ❏

3. Ignoring interest, what does a loan to the business affect?
   a) Profit ❏
   b) Cash ❏
   c) Both profit and cash ❏
   d) Neither profit nor cash ❏

4. Cash in the petty cash box is £200 and the bank overdraft is £100,000. What is the cash figure for most purposes?
   a) £200 positive ❏
   b) £100,000 negative ❏
   c) £99,800 negative ❏
   d) £100,200 negative ❏

5. What does a cash flow statement link?
   a) The cash position in two balance sheets ❏
   b) Two profit and loss accounts ❏
   c) The profit and loss account and the balance sheet ❏
   d) Net assets in two balance sheets ❏

6. Trade and other receivables in the previous balance sheet was £80,000. Trade and other receivables in the current balance sheet is £230,000. What is the effect on the cash flow statement?
   a) £150,000 outflow ❏
   b) £150,000 inflow ❏
   c) £230,000 outflow ❏
   d) £230,000 inflow ❏

7. A company sells goods to its subsidiary company for £60,000. The subsidiary company sells half the goods outside the group for £50,000 and has the remainder in stock at the balance sheet date. What amount must be shown in sales in the group profit and loss account?
   a) £60,000 ❏
   b) £50,000 ❏
   c) £30,000 ❏
   d) £100,000 ❏

8. The directors believe that the accounts of a small subsidiary company are not material. Must group accounts be prepared?
   a) Yes, always ❏
   b) Usually ❏
   c) Not usually ❏
   d) No ❏

9. What does depreciation affect?
   a) Both cash and profit ❏
   b) Neither cash nor profit ❏
   c) Profit ❏
   d) Cash ❏

10. Is it difficult to manipulate the figures in the cash flow statement?

a) Yes – short of fraud it is virtually impossible ❑

b) It is fairly difficult ❑

c) It is fairly easy ❑

d) It is very easy ❑

CHAPTER 19

The reports

During the last five chapters we have tried to understand and interpret accounts, which are very much a matter of figures. Now we round off by looking at the reports, which are largely a matter of words. Directors of registered companies have a legal obligation to accompany the accounts with certain reports. These give factual information beyond what is in the accounts and help the reader understand and interpret the figures and the company's strategy and position.

This chapter relates to UK companies. It may be different in other countries and it is different for other types of organization. There is a lot to get through and it might be hard going, but it will hopefully be worth the effort.

The topics covered comprise:

- directors' report
- directors' report in a publicly traded company
- directors' report in a small company
- business review
- remuneration report
- other reports and information
- audit report.

Directors' report

The Companies Act and regulations made under its authority require directors to provide a directors' report with the statutory accounts. Its contents are prescribed by law, although if there is nothing to report under a particular heading it may be omitted. The required disclosures are as follows:

Directors' names

The report must give the names of all persons who were directors for any part of the year, with dates of becoming a director and ceasing to be a director if applicable.

Principal activities

This shows the principal activities of the company in the course of the year. There may be more than one.

Proposed dividend

The amount (if any) of a dividend that the directors propose should be paid.

Disclosure to auditors

Unless the company is claiming exemption from audit, the directors' report must state that:

- So far as the directors are aware, there is no relevant audit information of which the company's auditor is unaware
- All directors have taken all the steps that they ought to have taken as directors in order to make themselves aware of any relevant audit information and to establish that the company's auditor is aware of that information.

It is a criminal offence to make this statement without the belief that it is true, and it is binding on the directors individually as well as collectively.

Any difference in market value of land

If, in the opinion of the directors, the market value of land owned by the company differs from its book value, the report must disclose this fact. This is only if the directors are of the opinion that the members' (this usually means the shareholders) attention should be drawn to it.

Political donations

Details must be given if political donations exceed £2,000 in total.

Charitable donations

Details must be given if charitable donations exceed £2,000 in total. Wholly owned subsidiary companies incorporated in the UK are excluded from this requirement.

Financial instruments

Details of the use of financial instruments must be given if this is material for an assessment of the company's financial position. This sounds rather boring but it can be vastly important. Significant companies have collapsed due to problems with financial instruments.

Post-balance sheet events

Details must be given of any important events that have taken place since the date of the balance sheet. This could be very significant indeed. Public companies have six months to publish their accounts and private companies have nine months, but even if the directors do it quickly the accounts are out of date by the time they are read.

An indication of likely future development of the business

This could be very significant.

An indication of the activities in research and development

Many companies will have nothing to report but, for example, a major drugs company will probably have a lot to report and it could be of critical importance.

An indication of the existence of branches outside the United Kingdom

This is only necessary for limited companies, but all but about 4,000 companies are limited companies.

Details concerning any acquisitions of its own shares by the company or its nominees

This is rare but it is legal in some circumstances.

Disabled employees

The following is only required if the average weekly number of employees is greater than 250, excluding employees who work wholly or mainly outside the UK:

There must be a statement describing the policy which the company has applied during the year for:

- Giving full and fair consideration to applications for employment from disabled persons
- Continuing the employment of, and training of, employees who have become disabled whilst employed by the company
- The training, career development and promotion of disabled persons employed by the company.

I ask your indulgence for a personal question and a personal point of view. Have you ever seen a directors' report that does not describe the company's policy in generous and compassionate terms? No – neither have I, even though some companies do not in practice live up to what they say are their policies. I rather doubt the value of the requirement, but perhaps I am rather cynical.

Information for employees

The following is only required if the average weekly number of employees is greater than 250, excluding employees who work wholly or mainly outside the UK.

There must be a statement describing the action taken during the year to introduce, maintain or develop arrangements intended to:

- Provide employees systematically with information on matters of concern to them as employees
- Consult employees or their representatives on a regular basis so that their views can be taken into account in making decisions likely to affect their interests
- Encourage the involvement of employees in the company's performance through an employee share scheme or other means
- Achieve a common awareness on the part of all employees of the financial and economic factors affecting the performance of the company.

In practice a rather bland statement is often given. My personal views are the same as set out in the part about disabled employees. I have never seen a directors' report that says company policy is to only give employees the minimum possible information.

Payment of suppliers

The following must be given for public companies and for large private companies that are subsidiaries of public companies:

- A statement of policy on the payment of suppliers
- If the company subscribes to a code on payment practices, such as the CBI code, this must be stated, and it must also be stated how details of the code may be obtained
- A statement of the average number of days' credit outstanding at the balance sheet date.

It is not unknown for companies to 'window dress' the average number of days' credit outstanding by making extensive payments just before the balance sheet date. Sadly, it is also by no means unknown for companies to actually pay suppliers in a way completely different from the stated policy. Some powerful and well-known companies do it. You can probably name some of them.

Directors' report in a publicly traded company

A publicly traded company is one which at the end of the relevant period has securities traded on a regulated market. This does not include AIM. Such companies must provide the information previously listed in this chapter. The lengthy list of additional information includes:

- The structure of the company's capital
- In the case of each person with a significant direct or indirect holding of securities in the company, such details as are known to the company of:

  a) The identity of the person
  b) The size of the holding
  c) The nature of the holding.

Directors' report in a small company

The definition of a small company was given in Chapter 15. If you have a good memory, you will recall that it is that in two successive years, and counted on a group basis, the company satisfied two out of three conditions. One of these was that turnover did not exceed £10,200,000.

The directors' report with the accounts sent to the members (this usually means the shareholders) must disclose:

- The names of the persons who were directors at any time during the year
- The principal activities of the company during the year
- Political donations exceeding £2,000 in aggregate
- Charitable donations exceeding £2,000 in aggregate
- If the average number of employees exceeds 250, a statement describing the company's policy towards the employment, training and career development of disabled persons
- Disclosures concerning acquisition by the company of its own shares during the period.

This relates to the accounts sent to the members and nothing need be included if there is nothing to report under the heading. No directors' report is required for the abbreviated accounts that small companies may send to Companies House.

Business review

Unless the company is a small company, the directors' report must include or be accompanied by a business review. Its purpose is to inform the members (this usually means the shareholders) and help them assess how the directors have performed their duty to promote the success of the company. The business review must contain:

- A fair review of the company's business
- A description of the principal risks and uncertainties facing the company
- A balanced and comprehensive analysis of the development and performance of the company's business during the financial year
- A balanced and comprehensive analysis of the position of the company's business at the end of the year, consistent with the size and complexity of the business.

This is for all companies that are required to have a business review. More information is required if the company is a quoted company. This includes (but is not limited to):

- The main trends and factors likely to affect the future development, performance and position of the company's business
- Information about environmental matters (including the impact of the company's business on the environment, the company's employees and social and community issues)
- To the extent necessary for an understanding of the development, performance or position of the company's business an analysis using key performance indicators.

The business review can be fascinating and valuable. This is more likely when directors approach it in the right spirit and aim to increase the reader's understanding. The opposite approach is a box-ticking exercise intended merely to comply with their legal obligations.

Remuneration report

The remuneration report is only a requirement for quoted companies. The remuneration in question is that of directors and there is a legal requirement that a mass of information be given. The reports are frequently 15 or more pages long. If you read everything thoroughly, it will probably take quite a while and it will probably be very interesting, especially as much of the disclosure is for each director by name.

Some of the information is subject to audit and some is not. The part that is not subject to audit includes the following:

- Information regarding the members of and advisers to the remuneration committee
- A statement of the company's policy on directors' remuneration for the following financial year including details on performance conditions
- A performance graph that sets out the total shareholder return on the class of equity share capital that caused the company to fall within the definition of 'quoted company'
- Information regarding directors' contracts of service.

The part that is subject to audit includes considerable detail concerning salaries and fees, bonuses, expenses, compensation for loss of office, non-cash benefits, share options, long-term incentive schemes, pensions, excess retirement benefits of directors and past directors, compensation paid to past directors and sums paid to third parties in respect of a director's services.

There must be a separate vote of the shareholders on the remuneration report at the meeting at which the accounts are laid, which is usually the annual general meeting. A vote to reject the remuneration report is a serious matter and can lead to resignations of directors, changes in the composition of the remuneration committee and better explanations. In practice votes to reject the remuneration report are rare.

Shareholders have a binding vote on a resolution to approve the directors' remuneration policy, and this is required every three years. Payments outside the terms of approved policy are not permitted.

Other reports and information

The law prescribes information that must be included in the reports and most companies comply with the law, provide the information and leave it at that. However, some companies choose to go beyond this minimum, even though it is quite an extensive minimum. They may, for example, provide a chairman's report or extend the directors' report beyond the statutory requirement. It is not unknown for the directors (and the chairman in particular) to give their views on such matters as bureaucracy, interest rates and the government of the day.

Listed companies are required by the Listing rules to give more information than other companies and may choose to give more still. For example, the recent reports and accounts of a major listed company consist of 112 pages. They contain, among other things, a chairman's statement, a chief executive's review, a section on 'performance and marketplace', and a section on governance. Some of the material in these sections provides information required by the directors' report and the business review, and these documents refer the reader to the appropriate section. The reports and accounts of some listed companies are considerably longer.

Audit report

Chapter 15 gives details of when an audit report is required. The auditor gives an opinion but does not certify the accuracy of the figures, a point which auditors are keen to stress but which is often misunderstood.

The first duty of the auditor is to give an opinion as to whether the accounts give a 'true and fair view' and whether or not the information in the directors' report is consistent with the accounts. They must also give an opinion as to whether the part of the remuneration report that is subject to audit has been properly prepared. There is more, but that will do for the purposes of this chapter.

The audit report almost always gives a favourable opinion on these matters. This is partly because of the integrity and professionalism of most directors, but also because of their fear of the consequences of a qualified audit report. If the auditor threatens to qualify the report, most directors will, with greater or lesser grace, agree to the necessary changes. Some audit qualifications may be technical and not too worrying, but you should certainly take a qualified audit report seriously. Normally a quick glance for assurance is all that is necessary.

Summary

In this chapter we have looked at the reports which must accompany the financial statements of a company registered in the UK. If you are a person who thrives on mastering a lot of information, you will have coped admirably and probably enjoyed it. If you are not a detail person, it will have been more difficult, but well done for persevering. We have:

- Studied a list of the detailed information that must, by law, be included in the directors' report. This has included the special provisions for publicly traded companies and small companies.
- Looked at the business review, which gives extra information and helps us understand the company's position, key indicators and strategy.
- Seen the remuneration report which, for understandable reasons, is often the part of the accounts package that gets most media attention and sometimes provokes indignation. If you are a highly paid director, you might think that this is unfair and disproportionate. If the company is a bank and you are one of its shareholders or customers, you might (or might not) think that this is very understandable.
- Examined the contents of the audit report.

Fact-check (answers at the back)

1. What is the basis for the information that must be provided in the directors' report of a registered UK company?
   a) The law ☐
   b) Accounting standards ☐
   c) The wishes of the directors ☐
   d) Common sense ☐

2. Ruth Cohen became a director on 8 February and resigned with effect from 12 June in the same year. What (if any) details must be included in the directors' report for the year to 31 December?
   a) Nothing must be included ☐
   b) The name and the starting and finishing dates must be given ☐
   c) Just the name must be given ☐
   d) The name and the starting date must be given ☐

3. The directors' report must include a statement that relevant information has been disclosed to the auditor. On which directors is this binding?
   a) The directors as a group ☐
   b) Just on directors who have held office for the whole year ☐
   c) The directors as a group and each director individually ☐
   d) Only on directors who wish to be associated with the statement ☐

4. A company has given £6,100 to the Labour party. Must this be disclosed in the directors' report?
   a) No ☐
   b) Only if it is a listed company ☐
   c) Only if the amount is significant in relation to the company's turnover ☐
   d) Yes ☐

5. A UK company has given £7,103 to a US charity that helps homeless people in the state of Arizona. Must this be disclosed in the directors' report?
   a) Yes ☐
   b) Only if the company has business in the United States ☐
   c) Only if the company does not have business in the United States ☐
   d) No ☐

6. The directors' report must contain a statement about the company's policy on the payment of suppliers. To which companies does this apply?
   a) All companies ☐
   b) Public companies and large private companies that are subsidiaries of public companies ☐
   c) All companies except small companies ☐
   d) Public companies ☐

7. A company has a turnover of £4,101,000 and a balance sheet total of £2,044,000. It has employed an average of 317 people. Does it qualify as a small company for the purposes of the directors' report?
   a) No ❏
   b) Yes ❏
   c) Yes – unless it is a public company or part of a larger group ❏
   d) Yes – unless it is regulated by the Financial Conduct Authority ❏

8. Must a large private company include in its business review information about environmental matters?
   a) Yes ❏
   b) Only if the company produces hazardous waste ❏
   c) Only if a trade union requests it to do so ❏
   d) No ❏

9. Must a remuneration report include a statement of the company's policy on directors' remuneration for the following financial year?
   a) Yes – but this part of the remuneration report is not subject to audit ❏
   b) Yes – and this part of the directors' remuneration report is subject to audit ❏
   c) Only if the policy has changed ❏
   d) No ❏

10. For whom is the audit report primarily intended?
    a) The directors ❏
    b) The members (this usually means the shareholders) ❏
    c) The government ❏
    d) The European Union ❏

NB The information needed to answer question 10 is not given in the chapter so if you have got 57 questions out of 57 in Part 3 correct, you should look on it as a tiebreaker. Congratulations if you get it right.

7 × 7

1 Seven things to remember

- Figures in the accounts are probably more meaningful if they are compared with something. Possibilities include last year's figures, the budget and figures in the accounts of competitors.
- A profit and loss account summarizes activity during a stated period. A balance sheet summarizes assets and liabilities at a stated date.
- Cool, calm deliberation untangles every knot.
- Group accounts eliminate the effects of inter-group trading and inter-group indebtedness.
- Cash flow statements summarize cash movements between two balance sheet dates.
- In a balance sheet assets are normally listed in order from the most fixed to the most fluid.
- The bottom section of a balance sheet represents the 'net worth' of the business.

2 Seven more things to remember

- When it comes to accounting ratios you can decide what should be compared with what.
- Listed companies are required to show key figures for five accounting periods.
- In a balance sheet it is rarely the case that the assets are actually worth exactly the stated amounts.
- 'Net current assets' means the same as 'working capital'.
- There are some things that only an insider can know. The total purchases made in a period is an example.
- The accounts are a matter of figures, whereas the reports are a matter of words.
- The directors' report is required by law to include certain specified information.

3 Seven things to avoid

- Failing to give sufficient attention to the notes in the accounts.
- Giving too much credence to percentages applied to small base figures.
- Overlooking the effects of inflation – particularly when comparing figures over a period of several years.
- Overlooking the fact that unpublished accounts do not have to conform with the law and accounting standards, and will probably not be audited.
- Not comparing like with like. This can happen in many ways, but comparing accounts that cover different lengths of time is an obvious example. Comparisons are possible so long as suitable adjustments are made.
- Overlooking the significance of tax on profits. Some very large and important companies (apparently legally) pay very little tax. Other companies pay much more.
- Forgetting that there are two ways to increase the return on capital employed. One is to increase the profit and the other is to reduce the capital employed.

4 Seven more things to avoid

- Failing to note the significance of changes in accounting policy.
- Forgetting that high gearing increases both the potential rewards and potential risks. Low gearing is less adventurous but you might sleep more soundly.
- Forgetting that cash and profit (after allowing for dividends etc.) may be the same in the long run, but as Keynes wrote 'in the long run we are all dead'. They will probably be different, perhaps very different, in the short term.
- Forgetting that examining trends may be as important (or more important) than examining a single set of figures.
- Overlooking the fact that seasonal factors may be very significant.

- Not realizing that directors may have 'window-dressed' the balance sheet. A possible example is paying suppliers just before the balance sheet date. This can make it appear that the business has a better payment record than is normally the case.
- Not giving sufficient credence to the importance of cash and working capital.

5 Seven plausible predictions

- Directors of listed companies will continue to try and justify ever increasing remuneration for themselves.
- The population at large will not believe these attempted justifications.
- The accounts packages of listed companies will continue to get bigger.
- There will still be frauds and scandals.
- Businesses will continue to try and minimize their tax payments. Despite governments' best endeavours many of them will succeed.
- The dragon of inflation has (at the time of writing) been subdued, but it has not been slain. Inflation will return.
- Laws and accounting standards will continue to get more prescriptive. The scope for judgment will accordingly be reduced.

6 Seven accounting definitions

- **Fixed assets** Tangible assets that are held for the long term. Examples are freehold land and buildings, leasehold land and buildings, plant and machinery, computers and motor vehicles.
- **Current assets** Cash and other resources that are expected to turn to cash or be used up within one year of the balance sheet date.
- **Current liabilities** Obligations due within one year of the balance sheet date.

- **Net current assets** The amount by which current assets exceed current liabilities. If the figure for current liabilities is greater, it is **net current liabilities**.
- **Depreciation** The systematic allocation of the cost of an asset from the balance sheet to an expense in the profit and loss account. It is charged over the useful life of the asset.
- **Accruals** Adjustments for expenses that have been incurred but not yet recorded in the accounts.
- **Prepayments** Adjustments for expenses that have been recorded in the accounts but not yet incurred.

7 Seven great quotes

- 'An investment said to have an 80 per cent chance of success sounds far more attractive than one with a 20 per cent chance of failure. The mind can't easily recognize that they are the same.' *Daniel Kahneman (1934–) Israeli-American psychologist*
- 'Goodness is the only investment that never fails.' *Henry David Thoreau (1817–62) American author*
- 'Life is like accounting - everything must be balanced' *Anon*
- 'If investing is entertaining, if you're having fun, you're probably not making any money. Good investing is boring.' *George Soros (1930–) American business magnate and investor*
- 'Successful investing takes time, discipline and patience. No matter how great the talent or effort, some things just take time: You can't produce a baby in one month by getting nine women pregnant.' *Warren Buffett (1930–) American business magnate and investor*
- 'It sounds extraordinary but it's a fact that balance sheets can make fascinating reading.' *Mary Archer (1944–) British scientist*
- 'Balance sheets and income statements are fiction, cash flow is reality.' *Chris Chocola (1962–) American businessman*

PART 4

Your Successful Budgeting and Forecasting Masterclass

Introduction

The precise number depends on the definition used, but there are millions of managers in Britain and countless others around the world. In both the public sector and the private sector many of them are involved in budgeting and forecasting. It is probably true to say that a significant number of them – by no means all, of course – do not particularly enjoy this aspect of their job, resent the time commitment and sometimes doubt the value of the end product. This is a shame because budgets and forecasts are important, to their companies or other employers and to them personally.

A mastery of budgeting and forecasting will help managers do their job more effectively and it will help with their career development too. It is important at any time, but especially so in times of recession and economic difficulty. The section at the back about surviving in tough times may be particularly important and should not be neglected.

The following chapters should help managers understand the basic principles and it should help many of them progress further. This has to be good news – for their employers and for them too. They will then be more likely to value their work and the resulting budgets and forecasts, and they might even enjoy doing them.

CHAPTER 20

Budgeting and forecasting fundamentals

It is a sound military principle that time spent reconnoitring is not wasted. From Chapter 22 through to Chapter 25 we will be examining and reviewing the different budgets and forecasts and how they are prepared. In Chapter 26 we will look at how the budgets and forecasts should be used after they have been approved. However, we start by reconnoitring the subject, establishing some important principles and answering some key questions.

The topics covered comprise:

- the differences between plans, forecasts and budgets
- are budgets and forecasts important?
- the value and purposes of budgets and forecasts
- should budgets and forecasts be left to the accountants?
- should budgets and forecasts be only for large organizations?
- the right period for budgets and forecasts
- are budgets and forecasts only relevant for an organization that has an income?
- should budgets and forecasts be optimistic or realistic?
- top-down or bottom-up?
- budget assumptions
- limiting factors
- seasonal factors.

The differences between plans, forecasts and budgets

The three terms are often confused and used in an interchangeable way. This is understandable but wrong. They are different and the differences should be understood.

Plan

This is a set of approved policies and targets for the future, and they need not be expressed in financial terms. For example, there may be a plan to achieve a position where 50 per cent of a country's population recognize a company's name. Of course, plans normally have financial implications. If only 30 per cent of a country's population currently recognize a company's name and it is intended that in three years' time this should increase to 50 per cent, it is probable that money must be spent. This expenditure will in the short term reduce both profits and cash, though in time the increased expenditure will, presumably and hopefully, have the opposite effect and increase sales (and therefore profits) and also cash.

Forecast

This is a prediction of what will happen and it is often expressed in financial terms. A forecast differs from a budget in that it is not a target. Forecasts are usually prepared and laid out in the same way as budgets, but the difference is a belief that they state what will actually happen. A budget, on the other hand, is a target and represents an aim that it is hoped (with greater or lesser confidence) will be achieved. Of course, a realistic budget is close to being a forecast.

Budget

This is a plan expressed in financial terms. There may be a single budget, which will probably be a profit budget, or a series of linked budgets. This is desirable because the linked budgets will all be useful and because they will each contribute to the realism and value of the others. For example a financial change in any budget must have an effect on the budgeted balance sheet. A budget is a target rather than a forecast and subsequent results can be monitored against it. This is to see if the budget is being achieved and, if it is not, exactly what has gone wrong and where remedial action needs to be taken. Whether budget targets should be achievable easily or only with great effort is examined later.

Are budgets and forecasts important?

Not everyone thinks that businesses should bother with budgets and forecasts, and not all businesses have them. Some managers dislike preparing them and resent their performance being monitored against them afterwards. Furthermore, they may take up a considerable amount of managers' time and, as we all know, managers' time is valuable and often in short supply. Nevertheless, budgets and forecasts are important, and if well done should be worth the time and effort put into them. The value and purposes of budgets and forecasts are reviewed next, but for now consider your answers to the following seven questions. If the answer to any of them is no, you should see why budgets and forecasts are important.

1 Do you know if the business is going to run out of cash?
2 Is your business going to make a satisfactory profit in the next year?
3 Is your company at risk of going out of business and, if so, what needs to be done to stop it happening?
4 Is your business making the maximum possible profit?
5 Is there any waste that could be cut out?
6 Do you know which departments and sections are performing efficiently and which ones are not?
7 Have you got the information to make improvements in the way that your business is run?

The value and purposes of budgets and forecasts

Budgets and forecasts enable, or perhaps force, managers to plan ahead logically and constructively, and they enable, or perhaps force, top managers to study how different parts of the business interact. They enable managers to anticipate any limiting factors and plan how they can be overcome. For example, a business may be steadily expanding in a profitable and satisfactory manner, but budgeting may reveal an impending shortage of working capital or storage facilities.

'Give us the tools and we will finish the job.' This unforgettable phrase was addressed to President Roosevelt by the Prime Minister, Winston Churchill, in a broadcast on 9 February 1941. In a completely different context it could well be adopted for budgets and forecasts. Information can be a vital tool for both senior and junior managers. Using it well should help them finish the job, which is to operate effectively and plan ahead to achieve the best possible results.

In the unlikely event that nothing whatsoever is done with the completed budgets, the discipline of preparing them has still forced managers to plan the future logically. This means considering such things as:

- Where do we intend to be at the end of the budget period?
- How a department and budget interacts with other departments and other budgets.
- Are there any limiting factors and what are they?
- Should we be aware of any particular dangers and, if so, what should be done about them?
- What actions must be taken to achieve the budgeted results?
- What are realistic, achievable targets to set ourselves?

Of course, it is highly desirable that the budgets are afterwards used as a control tool and most organizations do use them in this way. Regular reports should enable managers to see departures from the budgeted figures and take correcting action. This is covered in detail in Chapter 26.

Should budgets and forecasts be left to the accountants?

Most thoughtful people answer 'no' to this question; this is also my strong opinion, and I am an accountant. Nevertheless, there are arguments that can be made for making budgets and forecasts the responsibility of only the accountants. They include:

- The job will probably be done more quickly.
- There will be no encroachment on the valuable time of the other managers, who will be left free to do whatever it is that they do. For example, sales managers will spend more time selling and production managers will spend more time producing.
- Many non-financial managers do not like working on budgets and forecasts and, strange as it might seem, many financial managers do enjoy it. Perhaps the best results may be obtained from people who enjoy what they are doing.

The probably more compelling arguments for involving the non-financial managers include:

- The resulting budget or forecast is more likely to be realistic. The non-financial managers may well have information not known to the accountants, and they will probably have a good idea about what can and cannot be achieved.
- The non-financial managers will hopefully be able to suggest sensible changes and efficiency savings.
- The budget or forecast is likely to be better and, which is extremely important, it is much more likely that all managers will feel committed to it afterwards. If they have contributed to it, they should feel a sense of ownership. Of course the budget may not be exactly what they want but it might be,

and at the very least they should feel that their points of view have had a fair hearing and been taken into account.

Whether or not non-financial managers have contributed, it is almost certainly best that the accountants should co-ordinate the budgets and forecasts. They are best placed to see that the final budgets are complete and without inconsistencies. Regardless of how they are prepared and reviewed, final approval should be given at a very high level.

Budgets and forecasts is a rather serious subject, so perhaps a little humour might help us concentrate. It is often said that many accountants are introverts, which helps us know if a person is an accountant. An accountant will look at your shoes rather than look you in the eye. The only people more introverted than accountants are actuaries. An actuary will look at their own shoes rather than your shoes.

Should budgets and forecasts only be for large organizations?

The answer to this question is no. Small organizations and even one-person businesses potentially have all the issues and needs of large businesses. The figures will be smaller, but the need for good budgets and good forecasts is just as compelling.

The right period for budgets and forecasts

Budgets and forecasts most often cover a period of a year. This is because most companies prepare their statutory accounts for this length of time and many other organizations do the same. There are obvious advantages in having the budget or forecast period correspond with the financial reporting period. 'What's the profit going to be for this year?' is a frequently asked question. Having budgets and forecasts for the same period makes it easier to give an informed answer.

Having said that, there is no law or rule that makes this compulsory. Unlike most accounts, budgets and forecasts do not have to be published. You can have whatever period you like for whatever reason you like.

The divisions within a budget period of a year are often monthly, but they do not have to be. Perhaps weekly or some other period would be more appropriate. An obvious problem is that the length of a calendar month varies between 28 days and 31 days. Many budgets and forecasts are based on 13 four-week periods in order to make each period comparable with the others. This leaves just one spare day (two in a leap year) to add in somewhere. There are no rules, so do what is best in your individual circumstances.

Are budgets and forecasts only relevant for an organization that has an income?

The answer to this question is no, of course not. Organizations and departments that just spend money should strive to do so effectively and efficiently, and good expenditure budgets should be useful tools in achieving these desirable ends. Sections of central and local government come into this category. In the UK, Her Majesty's Revenue & Customs (HMRC) is an obvious example, even though it will insist on calling taxpayers its customers. As taxpayers we all wish it well in its efforts to control costs and perform efficiently.

If your direct interest is only in expenditure budgets and forecasts, some of Part 4 will not be immediately relevant to you. On the other hand, perhaps your next job will be managing director of a large company and with a salary to match, so perhaps you had better pay attention to the whole section.

Should budgets and forecasts be optimistic or realistic?

For forecasts the answer to this question should be self-evident. They should be neither optimistic nor pessimistic, and if they are one or the other they should not really be called forecasts. They should of course be realistic. This does not mean that they will be exactly achieved, but it does mean that at the time of preparation they represent what is considered to be the midpoint of likely outcomes. Forecasts should not necessarily be the figures first submitted. They should be these numbers adjusted to reflect changes and improvements that can confidently be predicted.

There are different opinions concerning the degree of optimism that should be incorporated into budgets. The following is a review of some of the options.

Easily achievable

Very few advocate this, though it does have the advantage that nasty surprises are unlikely. The big disadvantage is that it will provide no motivation for managers to innovate, work hard and generally strive to reach their targets. They will be able to do so in 'cruise mode' and will have no budgetary incentive to do better.

The midpoint of the likely outcomes

The difference between a budget and a forecast can be a very narrow distinction, so a realistic budget would perhaps be better called a forecast. Indeed, budgets are sometimes called budgetary forecasts. A good forecast has many virtues, but a disadvantage is that it does not set managers achievable targets beyond the middle range of likely outcomes.

Ambitious but definitely achievable

Managers are set budgetary targets that cannot easily be attained. They will have to work hard in order to do so. Nevertheless, the targets are definitely achievable. They are not so ambitious that managers will give up because they can see no prospect of success.

Extremely difficult to achieve

Managers are set budgetary targets that are so difficult that there is a high risk that they will fail to achieve them. Only with skill, exceptional effort and perhaps luck will they do so. An advantage is that it might get exceptional results from exceptional people, but a disadvantage is the high risk of failure and demotivation. If this approach is adopted, the result must clearly be regarded as a budget and not a forecast. There may be unfortunate consequences, perhaps including running out of money, if the business is over-dependent on such a budget being achieved.

Most people think that *Ambitious but definitely achievable* is the best, and this is my opinion.

Top-down or bottom-up?

There are many different approaches to budgeting but two in particular should be mentioned:

Bottom-up method

Each manager and department is required to submit budget proposals. They are given few, if any, targets and are simply encouraged to submit good proposals in the interests of the organization. When all the budget proposals have been received, they are collated into the master budgets, which may or may not be acceptable. If they are not acceptable, then top management calls for revisions.

Top-down method

Top management issues budget targets. Lower levels of management must then submit proposals that achieve these targets.

Each method has advantages and disadvantages. The bottom-up method may encourage managers to be innovative and realistic, and they may later feel more committed to the budgets that they have shaped. On the other hand, they may be lazy and make unrealistic submissions. When using the bottom-up method, managers will still need to be informed of limiting factors in other departments, and it may be helpful for them to be informed of significant parameters.

In practice there is often less difference between the two methods than might be supposed. It is important that at some stage there be a full and frank exchange of views. Everyone should be encouraged to put forward any constructive point of view and everyone should commit themselves to listening with an open mind. Needless to say, top management will and should have the final decisions.

Budget assumptions

Whether the adopted philosophy is top-down or bottom-up, or indeed some variation or other method, it is usually sensible for top management to issue some budget assumptions that should be used. Examples could be:

- An average 5 per cent wage increase on 1 April
- Interest rates to be unchanged
- Necessary funds will be provided by the parent company
- The main government contract will be renewed on the same terms
- No competitor will enter or leave the market
- Rent payable will increase by 10 per cent on 1 April
- General inflation in the economy will be 4 per cent.

Without assumptions such as these, managers may make uninformed and conflicting proposals.

Please list six sensible budget assumptions besides those above.

Limiting factors

Many budgets amount to a plan for expansion, and it is sometimes the case that one or more limiting factors must be taken into account. These may be obvious before budgeting work starts or they may become apparent while the budget is being prepared. It is important that limiting factors be recognized. It will then be necessary to incorporate into the budget some action to remove them, and this usually involves spending money. Alternatively it may be decided that, in this budget period at least, expansion will take place only up to the point of the limiting factor and not beyond.

An example of a limiting factor is a vital warehouse that is continually 85 per cent full, and at certain times of the year is 90 per cent full. This could be a limiting factor if planned expansion is more than 15 per cent and perhaps if the planned expansion is more than 10 per cent. It might be possible to move goods through the warehouse more quickly, but it may be necessary to buy or rent additional or replacement premises. Please think of three other possible limiting factors and write them down.

Seasonal factors

Seasonal factors are not relevant in all budgets, but they are in many and it can be a bad mistake to ignore them. This is best illustrated with an example.

In the UK it is likely that a greetings card shop will achieve 25 per cent of its annual sales in the three weeks leading up to Christmas. Sales will also be above average in the months of February through to June. This is because of the so-called Spring Seasons ranges for Valentine's Day, Easter, Mother's Day and Father's Day. This will obviously affect the sales budget, but there will be other implications too. Perhaps staff costs will be higher in certain months and it will affect stock purchases, borrowing and bank interest.

Summary

In this chapter we have:

● looked at the differences between plans, budgets and forecasts and why the differences are important
● seen why budgets and forecasts are important
● considered whether budgets and forecasts should be easily achievable or prepared on an optimistic basis
● looked at the different approaches to preparing budgets and forecasts
● examined the importance of limiting factors, budget assumptions and other factors that must be taken into account
● answered some key questions.

In the next chapter we will examine different budgeting techniques. We will also look in detail at the programme for planning the budgets and forecasts, and how they are reviewed and approved.

Fact-check (answers at the back)

1. Must a budget always be expressed in financial terms?
a) Yes, always ❏
b) No, never ❏
c) It is optional ❏
d) Almost always ❏

2. Which of the following are advantages of preparing budgets and forecasts?
a) It enables the organization to comply with the law ❏
b) It gives managers information that will help them manage ❏
c) It proves that the accounting records balance ❏
d) All of the above ❏

3. Which of the following statements is true if completed and approved budgets are subsequently ignored?
a) The whole exercise has been a complete waste of time ❏
b) The budgets should be done again ❏
c) The discipline of preparing the budgets has been of some value ❏
d) Nothing has been lost because the whole value lies in the preparation ❏

4. Which of the following are advantages of leaving budgets to the accountants?
a) They have got the time to do it ❏
b) They always know a lot about budgets ❏
c) Other managers can go home early ❏
d) There will be no encroachment on the valuable time of the other managers ❏

5. Must budgets and forecasts always cover a period of a year?
a) Yes ❏
b) No and they never do ❏
c) No – because they must cover a period of six months ❏
d) No – but they often do ❏

6. In most people's opinion, which of the following statements are true?
a) Budgets should be easily achievable ❏
b) Budgets should be the midpoint of likely outcomes ❏
c) Budgets should be ambitious but definitely achievable ❏
d) Budgets should be extremely difficult to achieve ❏

324

7. Which of the following statements are suitable for inclusion in a list of budget assumptions?

a) The business will have a good year ❏

b) The business will have a disappointing year ❏

c) Customers will take an average of 60 days to pay ❏

d) All managers will be happy ❏

8. Which of the following is a limiting factor?

a) New staff are essential and they take six months to train properly ❏

b) Traffic congestion near the office is bad ❏

c) The bank manager does not like us ❏

d) The coffee machine does not work properly ❏

9. 'It is hoped that 90 per cent of our waste is recycled'. Is this:

a) a plan ❏

b) a forecast ❏

c) a budget ❏

d) none of the above? ❏

10. Should departments that have no revenue prepare expenditure budgets?

a) Definitely not ❏

b) Probably not ❏

c) Probably yes ❏

d) It's a silly question ❏

CHAPTER 21

More budgeting and forecasting fundamentals

We start by looking at different budgeting and forecasting methods and seeing the advantages and disadvantages of each. This should help you prepare your budgets and help you decide which methods are most appropriate for your organization. We then move on to the mechanics of budget preparation, which is a big section of this chapter and covers several aspects of the subject. Finally, there is something about the way that budgets are approved. If you are a very senior manager this is intended for you, and if you are not it may help you make a sensible case to the bosses.

The topics covered comprise:

- incremental budgets and forecasts
- zero-based budgets
- flexible budgets
- rolling budgets
- the mechanics of budget preparation
- the budget or forecast plan and timetable
- budget approval.

Incremental budgets and forecasts

Incremental budgets and forecasts use the previous year's actual figures as a basis, and then increase them or decrease them by an appropriate amount or (more usually) an appropriate percentage. At its worst this might be a single percentage applied across the board, but this would be very unsatisfactory. The variance percentage should be carefully thought out and driven by significant factors. At its very simplest, if there is going to be a rent increase of 3 per cent on the first day of the budget year, the rent budget will be increased by 3 per cent. This does not, of course, mean that all the budget figures should be increased by 3 per cent. Each item in the budget should be looked at individually. Even the rent budget might need a second look. It could be that extra premises will be rented part way through the year. Incremental budgets and forecasts have the merit of probably taking less time to prepare than some other methods.

An obvious objection to this approach is that it does not compel a thorough analysis of costs and revenue. Zero-based budgets do that and these are examined next in this chapter. On the other hand, *and with the important proviso that there is a proper review*, incremental budgeting may well be sensible. It is most likely to be useful in well-established organizations where past activity is likely to be a good starting point when forecasting the future. The approach is widely practised and likely to be used for at least part of the budgeting process.

Zero-based budgets

The philosophy of zero-based budgeting is that every part of the budget must be formulated on its merits and without reference to what has happened in the past. This differs from the more usual baseline budgeting, in which the budget may largely be based on adapting what has previously happened.

It is worth illustrating this with a very simple example. Let us suppose that last year's wage bill was £1 million. Baseline budgeting might take last year's figure plus a wage rise of 5 per cent, giving a total of £1,050,000. Zero-based budgeting, on the other hand, would mean that the justification for each employee must be examined and the expected wages of each employee must be examined. This might give a result of £1,050,000, but it might give a very different figure.

Zero-based budgeting has definite advantages. It should help identify and eliminate waste. It encourages managers to find cost-effective ways to improve operations and it may motivate them towards being innovative and more efficient. It should also encourage the efficient allocation of resources and detect inflated budgets.

Despite all this, there are major disadvantages to zero-based methods. The most obvious is the amount of time and complexity involved in the process. Without the benefit of historical or budgeted data on which to base their assumptions, managers may unnecessarily be forced to justify routine operations. Some businesses have predictable operations that vary little over time. It is neither efficient nor effective for a manager to spend a great deal of effort developing data that could be obtained quickly and accurately by extrapolating historical data.

Flexible budgets

Consider the following:

	Budget	Actual
Units sold	10,000	6,349
Units produced	10,100	6,567
Factory wages	$1,000,000	$936,117

At first glance, factory wages are $63,883 below budget, which is cause for satisfaction. However, a second and more thoughtful examination will reveal that sales and production are both massively under budget. After taking this into account, it is probably correct to conclude that factory wages were, in fact, very unsatisfactory. This illustrates an advantage of flexible budgets. In such budgets, related costs are budgeted at different levels to accommodate a range of possible outcomes. Meaningful budgets are then available to compare with actual figures, even though events may not turn out as predicted.

A flexible budget may be defined in one of two ways:

● A budget which allows for variations in cost for each selected level of output over a range of possible outputs
● A budget which is added to and adjusted each quarter (or other period) so that there is no artificial break-off period. The cumulative results and their effect on future planning can be seen quite readily.

Rolling budgets

In the case of a fixed-period budget or forecast, a budget or forecast is, not surprisingly, prepared for a fixed period, which is often a year. Actual results are then monitored against the budget or forecast and towards the end of the period a further budget or forecast is made for the following period. This is what happens in most cases.

The principle of a rolling budget or forecast is that periodically, say quarterly, what has actually happened is consigned to history and a new budget for this period of time is added to the end of the budget. This is illustrated with the following, which shows just sales.

	Budget	Actual
January to March	£1,900,000	£2,040,000
April to June	£2,000,000	
July to September	£2,100,000	
October to December	£2,200,000	
	£8,200,000	

After or just before the end of the first quarter a sales budget for the following January to March is prepared, and the budget is then as follows:

	Budget
April to June	£2,000,000
July to September	£2,100,000
October to December	£2,200,000
January to March	£2,090,000
	£8,390,000

The mechanics of budget preparation

It is a very obvious point to make, but it is essential that everyone working on a budget or forecast is operating the same system. To use a colloquial phrase, everyone must be singing from the same hymn sheet. It would be a nonsense if some managers were using spreadsheets, some using paper forms and some using another system, though having said that it perhaps would not matter if they did their calculations in different ways and then entered the results into the same unified system.

It is usual for the accountants to decide and issue the budget forms and budgeting system that will be used. It is very desirable and perhaps even essential that the budget headings are the same as the headings that are used in the accounting system. Thus, stationery in a department's overhead budget will have the same meaning as stationery in the accounting system. Furthermore, the relationships between figures in the budget should be the same as in the accounting system. So, for example, invoiced sales will probably increase the total sales, increase the profit before tax, increase the tax charge, increase the profit after tax, affect the cash total and affect the balance sheet.

Spreadsheets do not contribute wisdom, but they are of enormous help in budget preparation. They greatly speed up the arithmetic aspects and enable 'what if?' questions to be answered almost instantly. When using spreadsheets figures are inserted into cells. Columns and formulae relationships must be carefully designed. Then a figure entered into a cell will affect other relevant figures throughout the budget or budgets.

For example, a figure entered into the overhead expenses of a department will consequently change:

- Total costs of the department
- Total costs of the organization
- Profit (or loss)
- Budgeted cash flow
- Budgeted balance sheet.

It is clear that spreadsheets, like many computer applications, save a vast amount of management time. So why do so many managers, in the UK and the USA at least, work longer than their parents and grandparents did and suffer more stress? It is a great mystery.

Now please test your understanding of this by writing down the effects of an increase in raw material prices in a manufacturing company. This might be very difficult if you have little or no accounting knowledge, so do not worry if you cannot do it. The answer is given after the summary at the end of this chapter.

The budget or forecast plan and timetable

These should be issued before the budgeting or forecasting work begins, and they should be issued by top management or by the accountants with the approval of top management. Managers should not be swamped with detail that is not relevant to them and it is possible that some information might be confidential and should not go to all managers. Redundancy intentions, for example, could come into this category. For these reasons some managers should perhaps not receive all the material. The following are examples of various budgets in a large organization, though there could be more or fewer depending on individual circumstances:

- Capital expenditure budget
- Sales budget
- Revenue budget
- Profit and loss budget

- Cash budget
- Budgeted balance sheet.

With the exception of the budgeted balance sheet all these budgets will be reviewed during the remaining chapters.

It should be clear which managers are responsible for which budgets. Individual managers might have responsibility for a sector of a budget and, for example, for the expenditure of a department within the profit and loss budget.

Budget targets

The differences between top-down and bottom-up were explained in the previous chapter. If a top-down approach is favoured, each manager will be given a target or targets that must be achieved in the budget. These will lead to an overall targeted profit (or loss) of a certain figure. There may be targets other than those within the profit and loss budget. There could, for example, be a target that total money owing by customers should never exceed the equivalent of 45 days' sales.

If a bottom-up approach is favoured, such targets will not be issued. Instead managers will be charged with the task of preparing to the best of their ability a responsible, constructive budget that is in the interests of their department and of the organization.

In practice the approach is likely to lie between these two extremes, and in my opinion this is sensible. Managers should be given some guideline targets but these should be short of rigid requirements. Managers should be trusted to act responsibly. If budget targets are issued, they could be along the following lines:

- The net profit will be at least 10 per cent higher than in the current year
- Each department's overall costs will not be more than 4 per cent more than in the current year
- Sales for each region will be at least 5 per cent higher than in the current year and there will be no increase in discounts allowed

- Average stock levels will be no higher than in the current year
- Suppliers will be paid after an average of 75 days
- Bad debts will not be more than 2 per cent of sales.

At this point please consider whether you prefer top-down or bottom-up and give two reasons. There are no right or wrong answers so none are given at the end of the chapter.

Budget assumptions

The desirability of top management issuing budget assumptions was explained in the previous chapter and examples of budget assumptions were listed. These should normally form part of the package given to managers.

Budget forms

This heading is perhaps a throwback to a time when budgets were done on paper and it was usual to have a budget form for each category of income and expense. Each form would have an appropriate heading and probably an identifying code number. There would be a space on each form where details of the budget calculations would be entered. These would lead to a total and there would be boxes on the form for the total to be split over months or some other appropriate period.

Perhaps the budgets will be done manually and such forms will be used, but the use of spreadsheets is much more likely. Even so, it is important that a record be kept of the calculations leading to the totals, and exactly how the totals were split into monthly divisions or divisions for some other period. These are the figures entered into the cells on the spreadsheets. Some sort of electronic record may be kept, but perhaps the forms still have their uses.

Budget timetable

The package should include a timetable for all the work to be done and the approvals given. Obviously the contents will vary from organization to organization and the number and complexity of the budgets. The following illustrates the principles for a large company and a full set of budgets.

20 March	Budget package issued
3 April	Submissions for capital expenditure budget
5 April	Submissions for sales and departmental expenditure
6 April	Board committee consideration of capital expenditure, sales and departmental expenditure submissions. Requests for revisions issued as necessary
13 April	Board committee consideration of capital expenditure budget and full profit and loss budget. Requests for revisions issued as necessary
17 April	Board committee approval of: - capital expenditure budget - profit and loss budget - cash budget - budgeted balance sheet
19 April	Full board approval of all budgets

At first sight and perhaps at second sight too, all this seems horribly bureaucratic and likely to stifle initiative. Nevertheless, a formal timetable along these lines will be necessary in a large company. There could be chaos if managers work to their own timetables without regard to the needs of other managers and the need to finish on time. Furthermore, intermediate dates are necessary because of the possible need for revisions, and because some budget calculations cannot be done until figures from other departments and budgets are available. For example, it is not possible to get the depreciation charge in the profit and loss account exactly right until details of the capital expenditure budget are known.

Having said all that, the possibilities remain that the programme and procedures may be bureaucratic and stifle initiative. Attempts should be made to minimize this. Everyone should be encouraged to talk to each other and raise problems informally, which is a good idea throughout the year anyway and does not always happen in large organizations. The whole procedure can probably be much more informal in small businesses.

Budget approval

When all the budgets are completed they should be signed off or in some way formally accepted. Perhaps this will be done by a single person such as the managing director, or perhaps by a group such as the board of directors. Hopefully the figures are satisfactory and can be readily approved, but even so the approvers should have enough knowledge to form the realistic belief that they are obtainable. If this is not the case, they should make enquiries, because they should not approve figures that they do not believe can be achieved.

This poses the question of what they should do if the figures presented to them are not satisfactory. One possibility is to order across-the-board cuts such as '10 per cent savings in all departments'. This may be tempting but in my opinion it is usually a mistake. Probably some budgets should be cut by more, and some by less or not at all. It is almost guaranteed to demotivate managers and staff, and they may decide to inflate their budget submissions next time in order to accommodate the anticipated cuts. When Ronald Reagan became Governor of California he quickly ordered such across-the-board budget cuts with some unfortunate consequences. However, the great man quickly realized that this was a mistake and adopted an individually tailored approach to achieve the necessary savings.

Summary

In this chapter we have:

- looked at different budgeting techniques and examined the advantages and disadvantages of each
- studied the mechanics of preparing budgets and seen the importance of the same systems being used by all concerned
- seen what information should be provided to get the budget work going
- looked at the elements of a budget timetable
- seen how budgets should be approved and noted a common mistake and its possible consequences.

We are now ready to start looking at the individual budgets in detail. Next we start with the capital expenditure budget, the sales budget and the revenue budget.

Answer to question in the mechanics of budget preparation section

1 Cost of sales will increase
2 Gross profit will reduce
3 Net profit will reduce

Fact-check (answers at the back)

1. On what figures are incremental budgets and forecasts based?
   a) The average of the last three years' actual figures ❏
   b) The managing director's requirements ❏
   c) Last year's budget ❏
   d) Last year's actual figures ❏

2. Which of the following is a problem with incremental budgets?
   a) They take too long to prepare ❏
   b) They do not compel a thorough analysis of costs and revenue ❏
   c) They do not involve all layers of management ❏
   d) They are inherently unreliable ❏

3. Which of the following are advantages of zero-based budgeting?
   a) It should help identify and eliminate waste ❏
   b) It encourages managers to find cost-effective ways to improve operations ❏
   c) It may motivate managers to be more efficient ❏
   d) All of the above ❏

4. Which of the following is true of flexible budgets?
   a) Related costs are budgeted at different levels to accommodate a range of possible outcomes ❏
   b) The budget timetable is flexible ❏
   c) Top managers are flexible when reviewing the results ❏
   d) Actual results are never exactly the same as the budgeted results ❏

5. Which of the following is true of rolling budgets?
   a) They are suitable for managers who cannot get it right first time ❏
   b) As a new period is added an old period is dropped off ❏
   c) You do not need to monitor the actual results against the budget ❏
   d) They have fallen out of favour and are hardly ever done ❏

6. Do spreadsheets contribute wisdom?
   a) Yes ❏
   b) No ❏
   c) Sometimes ❏
   d) It all depends ❏

7. Who should issue the budget or forecast plan and timetable?
   a) No one – it should emerge spontaneously ❏
   b) The accountants ❏
   c) Top management ❏
   d) Everyone should issue their own ❏

8. Are budget targets always provided to managers?
   a) Yes ❏
   b) No ❏
   c) Yes – but they should not be ❏
   d) No – but they should be ❏

9. Which of the following is a likely disadvantage of arbitrary, across-the-board budget cuts?
   a) They do not work ❏
   b) They demotivate managers ❏
   c) Computer systems probably cannot cope with them ❏
   d) They have been condemned by the Institute of Personnel Managers ❏

10. Which of the following budgets will be affected by an increase in revenue?
    a) The profit and loss budget ❏
    b) The cashflow budget ❏
    c) The budgeted balance sheet ❏
    d) All of the above ❏

CHAPTER 22

Capital expenditure, sales and revenue budgets

During the previous two chapters we have reconnoitred the subject of budgets and forecasts. We have explored various principles and aspects, answered some fundamental questions and looked at different budgeting and forecasting methods. It is now time to start looking at the different budgets in detail, and to do a budgeting exercise which hopefully you will not find too difficult. The three budgets that we cover next are important in their own right and are essential steps in preparing the overall profit and loss budget. They are the three headings in this chapter, namely:

- capital expenditure budget
- sales budget
- revenue budget.

Capital expenditure budget

Capital expenditure is money spent on assets that are intended to be held and which will provide continuing benefits to the business. The assets are expected to retain some or all of their value over an extended period, which is usually taken to be more than a year. This is as opposed to stock which will be resold, or raw materials or components which will be used in manufacturing. It also excludes items which will be quickly used, such as stationery. In practice there must be a minimum value before something is classed as capital expenditure. This will vary from business to business, but it could well be about £500 for an individual item. For example, a toaster for the office kitchen retains some of its value and provides benefits in the long term, but its value is too small for it to be classified as capital expenditure.

Most capital items do steadily lose their value, but over a period of more than a year. This may be as a result of wear and tear, the passage of time or obsolescence. The accounting treatment is to put capital expenditure into the balance sheet, then drip feed a depreciation charge into the profit and loss account over a suitable number of years. Budgeting should follow this accounting practice, which is one reason why a separate capital expenditure budget is needed. Commonly identified categories of capital expenditure and typical rules for their depreciation are as follows:

Category of fixed asset	Depreciation charge
Freehold land and buildings	Nil or 2 per cent per year
Leasehold land and buildings	Over the life of the lease
Plant and machinery	25 per cent per year
Computers	25 per cent per year
Motor vehicles	25 per cent per year
Fixtures and fittings	10 per cent per year

The capital expenditure budget is extremely important in some companies. The big oil companies such as Shell and BP come to mind, and also big manufacturing companies such as Rolls Royce. In their cases the capital expenditure budget could total billions. It is much less important in many other companies and may be virtually non-existent in small service companies, though any company cars should not be overlooked.

It is important to get the timing right. Expenditure on a big project may be over a number of months or an even longer period. Cash will be affected as money is spent, but depreciation usually only starts when the project is completed. If plant and machinery is depreciated over four years, a new machine costing $400,000 will result in a charge of $100,000 to the revenue expenditure budget if it is budgeted for day one of the annual budget. If, on the other hand, it is budgeted for the first day of the tenth month, the depreciation charge will be only $25,000.

> **TIP**
>
> *If the figures in the capital expenditure budget are really significant, it may be desirable to budget for known items individually and then add a contingency for each month.*

Managers should be prepared, and perhaps required, to justify their budget proposals in detail. If proposed capital expenditure is high, and especially if cash is tight, the capital expenditure budget is likely to be scrutinized very carefully by top management. This is because it may be a place where big cuts may be made. Perhaps the expenditure is not really essential or perhaps it can wait a bit longer. Must company cars really be replaced this year? I once worked for a company where capital expenditure was high and cash was always tight. To the annoyance of the managers, a very expensive item of capital expenditure had been cut from the budget in six successive years, even though it was justified by investment criteria. When I left, it was in the budget for the seventh time and it looked as though it would at last survive the cuts.

The following shows how a typical capital expenditure budget may be laid out. In practice there may well be some supporting notes to justify each item of expenditure. There may also be a separate section showing anticipated receipts from the sale of existing capital items.

Capital expenditure budget for the six months to 30 June

	Jan £000s	Feb £000s	March £000s	April £000s	May £000s	June £000s	Total £000s
Leasehold land and buildings							
New office in Windsor						900	900
						900	900
Computers							
Ref. Project Swindon	50	50	50				150
Ref. Project Reading	10	10	60	60	20		160
Contingency	5	5	5	5	5	5	30
	65	65	115	65	25	5	340
Motor cars							
Replacement cars for directors			40	70	50		160
Replacement cars for sales staff	75	75					150
New pool car						15	15
	75	75	40	70	50	15	325
Fixtures and fittings							
Contingency	4	4	4	4	4	4	24
	4	4	4	4	4	4	24
Total capital expenditure	144	144	159	139	79	924	1,589

Sales budget

It is understandable if you think that the sales budget should be the same as the revenue budget. It sometimes is, but more often it is not. This is because there is usually a period of time between taking an order and fulfilling it. In the case of a retail shop that does not give credit, the sales budget may be the same as the revenue budget, but even here there will be a timing difference if goods are out of stock and ordered for customers. The sales budget reflects expected orders taken. These orders should be reflected in the revenue budget only at the point where it is expected that deliveries will be made or services performed. The effect on cash is different again and this usually happens later still.

The sales budget should be one of the first budgets done. This is because it affects the other budgets and these cannot be finalized until the budgeted sales are known. If other budgets are prepared without this information, there is a risk that the budgets may be unbalanced. For example the budget for overheads may be expanded to cope with an additional volume of sales that will not be in the sales budget. Of course all this may be spotted and corrected when the budgets are reviewed, but it is better to get it right first time.

The sales budget is a very important one because so much else depends on it. A company that has no sales has no business, and a company that only has small sales only has a small business. The rest of the company must budget to support the level of sales that will be budgeted, with production (or purchases for resale) and perhaps overheads expanding if the sales budget indicates increased activity. The reverse is, of course, true if the sales budget indicates reduced activity.

The sales budget may be harder to do than the expenditure budgets. This is because expenditure is, or at least should be, largely within the control of the managers. The sales and marketing effort will have a big influence on the level of sales, but there will be other important factors as well. Obviously these include the sales effort of competitors, together with their pricing structure and marketing strategy. Also to be considered are the general economic climate and a host of other things, perhaps even including the weather. That is not easy to forecast a year in advance. Sir Stuart Rose, formerly of the major retail chain Marks & Spencer, once said that he did not like using the weather as an excuse, but it was hard to hit sales targets when customers had to use boats to get to the stores.

We will now see how a sales budget is laid out. It can be done in several ways but the following is a good example and covers a period of six months to 30 June. We will assume that a company's sales force is organized into two regions (southern and northern) and that it also makes exports. We will also assume that it has two products (A and B). A sells for $20 in the southern and northern regions and for $25 in the export market. B sells for $40 in the southern and northern regions and for $45 in the export market.

After a lot of work the assumptions for the sales budget have been fixed as follows:

Southern region	
Product A	1,000 units in each of the six months
Product B	1,200 units in January, then an increase of 50 units per month in each of the following months

Northern region	
Product A	1,350 units in January, February and March, then 1,160 units in each of the remaining three months
Product B	3,600 units in January, February and March, then an increase of 100 units per month in each of the following months

Exports

	Product A	Product B
January	300 units	200 units
February	300 units	200 units
March	2,000 units	200 units
April	300 units	200 units
May	600 units	200 units
June	400 units	200 units

This can be summarized in financial terms as follows:

Sales budget for six months to 30 June

	Jan $	Feb $	March $	April $	May $	June $	Total $
Southern region							
Product A	20,000	20,000	20,000	20,000	20,000	20,000	120,000
Product B	48,000	50,000	52,000	54,000	56,000	58,000	318,000
	68,000	70,000	72,000	74,000	76,000	78,000	438,000
Northern region							
Product A	27,000	27,000	27,000	23,200	23,200	23,200	150,600
Product B	144,000	144,000	144,000	148,000	152,000	156,000	888,000
	171,000	171,000	171,000	171,200	175,200	179,200	1,038,600

Sales budget for six months to 30 June

	Jan $	Feb $	March $	April $	May $	June $	Total $
Exports							
Product A	7,500	7,500	50,000	7,500	15,000	10,000	97,500
Product B	9,000	9,000	9,000	9,000	9,000	9,000	54,000
	16,500	16,500	59,000	16,500	24,000	19,000	151,500
Total sales	255,500	257,500	302,000	261,700	275,200	276,200	1,628,100

The same information can be summarized in two other ways. If it is wished to show it by product, the total split is as follows:

Product A	$368,100
Product B	$1,260,000
	$1,628,100

If it is wished to separate the home market from exports, the total split is:

Home market	$1,476,600
Exports	$151,500
	$1,628,100

Revenue budget

The revenue budget is the income that appears as the top line or top section of the profit and loss budget. It corresponds with invoiced sales to customers and invoices are usually issued when goods are delivered or services performed. However, this is not always the case. Two exceptions come to mind:

● A contract where services are performed over a period but payment is required in advance. Insurance is an example and in this case payment is often required at the beginning of the period covered by the insurance.
● Stage payments during the progress of a building contract.

The next example ignores these possible complications and you are asked to convert the sales budget in the last section

349

of this chapter into the revenue budget. You may use the blank form as a template and you can check your answer against the one at the end of this chapter.

You need to know that customers in the southern and northern regions are invoiced an average of 30 days after their orders have been placed. Export customers are invoiced an average of 60 days after their orders have been placed. Sales in the three months before the period covered by the sales budget were as follows:

	Oct $	Nov $	Dec $
Southern region			
Product A	18,107	20,134	19,726
Product B	38,111	41,296	46,344
Northern region			
Product A	26,004	26,238	26,467
Product B	145,211	99,687	151,999
Exports			
Product A	44,372	6,087	8,331
Product B	7,824	9,235	8,477

Revenue budget for six months to 30 June

	Jan $	Feb $	March $	April $	May $	June $	Total $
Southern region							
Product A							
Product B							
Northern region							
Product A							
Product B							
Exports							
Product A							
Product B							
Total sales							

Summary

In this chapter we have:

● Looked in detail at capital expenditure budgets and seen why, in some cases at least, they are very important. We have seen how a typical capital expenditure budget is prepared.

● Looked at sales budgets, which are always very important.

● Seen how a sales budget is turned into a revenue budget. Finally, you should have used information provided to set out a revenue budget.

In the next two chapters we deal with the profit and loss budget, starting with the expenditure part of it. More managers contribute to this than any of the other budgets. It is the most recognized and many consider it to be the most important.

Answer to revenue budget for six months to 30 June

	Jan $	Feb $	March $	April $	May $	June $	Total $
Southern region							
Product A	19,726	20,000	20,000	20,000	20,000	20,000	119,726
Product B	46,344	48,000	50,000	52,000	54,000	56,000	306,344
	66,070	68,000	70,000	72,000	74,000	76,000	426,070
Northern region							
Product A	26,467	27,000	27,000	27,000	23,200	23,200	153,867
Product B	151,999	144,000	144,000	144,000	148,000	152,000	883,999
	178,466	171,000	171,000	171,000	171,200	175,200	1,037,866
Exports							
Product A	6,087	8,331	7,500	7,500	50,000	7,500	86,918
Product B	9,235	8,477	9,000	9,000	9,000	9,000	53,712
	15,322	16,808	16,500	16,500	59,000	16,500	140,630
Total sales	259,858	255,808	257,500	259,500	304,200	267,700	1,604,566

Fact-check (answers at the back)

1. Which of the following is capital expenditure?
a) Purchase of goods for resale ❏
b) Bank interest ❏
c) Purchase of company cars ❏
d) Payment of wages ❏

2. £300,000 is paid to lease a building for six years. What should be the depreciation charge for the first full year?
a) £50,000 ❏
b) Nothing ❏
c) £150,000 ❏
d) £300,000 plus associated legal expenses ❏

3. Over what period is it usually considered that an asset must retain at least some of its value for it to be considered (subject to conditions) to be capital expenditure?
a) More than six months ❏
b) More than a year ❏
c) More than two years ❏
d) Indefinitely ❏

4. Can the sales budget be the same as the revenue budget?
a) Yes – and it almost always is ❏
b) Yes – but it does not often happen ❏
c) No ❏
d) Only in the engineering industry ❏

5. What goes into the revenue budget?
a) Orders already taken and orders expected to be taken, provided that they will both be invoiced in the budget period ❏
b) Orders budgeted to be taken in the budget period ❏
c) Orders taken before the start of the budget period ❏
d) Orders that will be taken in the budget period, but which will not be invoiced until after the budget period ❏

6. When should the sales budget be done?
a) It does not matter ❏
b) It should be one of the first budgets done ❏
c) It should be one of the last budgets done ❏
d) It should be done at the same time as all the other budgets ❏

7. Why may the sales budget be hard to get right?
a) Sales managers are bad at budgeting ❏
b) The assumption in the question is mistaken. Sales budgets are actually easy to get right ❏
c) A lot may depend on what competitors do ❏
d) None of the above ❏

353

8. Which of the following usually go into the capital expenditure budget?
a) Computers ❏
b) Plant and machinery ❏
c) Fixtures and fittings ❏
d) All of the above ❏

9. When should a motor car be entered into the capital expenditure budget?
a) When it is ordered ❏
b) When it is delivered and accepted ❏
c) When it is paid for ❏
d) When it is first driven ❏

10. Which of the following is not a factor in setting the sales budget?
a) The expected spend on advertising ❏
b) Competitors' pricing policy ❏
c) The depreciation charge ❏
d) Our pricing policy ❏

CHAPTER 23

Expenditure budgets

Many managers will identify most closely with the expenditure budget, perhaps together with the profit and loss budget. This is because it is the one to which they are most likely to contribute and the one against which their performance is most likely to be measured. You may therefore see this chapter as being particularly relevant. It is likely that there will be a separate expenditure mini-budget for each cost centre or department, and that these will be aggregated together to show the wider picture.

The programme is:

- the organization of the expenditure budget
- an example of an expenditure budget
- expenditure budget exercise.

The organization of the expenditure budget

In a small and uncomplicated organization the structure and layout of the expenditure budget will be straightforward. It is just a simple listing of all the categories of expenditure, with appropriate figures and the total. It will probably look like the following:

	Last year's budget £	Last year's actual £	This year's budget £
Expense category 1			
Expense category 2			
Expense category 3			
Expense category 4			
Expense category 5			
Expense category 6			
Expense category 7			
Expense category 8			
Total			

In practice there would almost certainly be more expense categories than just eight, and the budget would probably be spread over 12 monthly periods or divided in some other way. Last year's budget and last year's actual may or may not be shown. They do help when the figures are prepared and reviewed. The headings pose the obvious question of how (unless the budget is prepared after the start of the period that it covers) last year's actual can be known. Of course it cannot be known, but estimates would be inserted based on the latest available information.

This is for a small and uncomplicated organization, and the one form would possibly cover the whole business, though the expense categories might be grouped in some way. The form and headings would probably be similar in a large and complicated business, though there would be many forms and not just one. There would be a form for each cost centre or department, and the expense categories would be appropriate to that department. For example a heading for 'Advertising' would be on the form for the marketing or sales department, and a heading for 'Staff Recruitment Costs' would be on the form for the human resources department.

The budgets for the cost centres or departments might go straight into the profit and loss budget, but depending on the complexity of the organization they might be grouped in some way into functions or divisions. For example in a big company the sales department budgets might be grouped as follows:

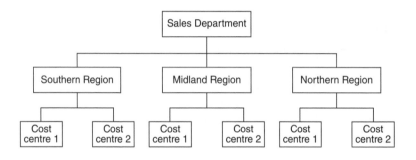

The expenditure budget for each region would be the aggregation of the expenditure budgets for the two cost centres within it. The expenditure budget for the whole sales department would be the aggregation of the expenditure budgets for the three regions. Assuming that there is an overall manager for the whole sales department, a manager for each region and a manager for each cost centre, ten different managers would have responsibility for some or all of the sales department's expenditure budget. No doubt the sales department manager and the three regional managers would review each of the budgets for which they had responsibility, and perhaps request or require that changes be made.

An example of an expenditure budget

It is now time to see an example of how an expenditure budget is prepared. The budget form contains 11 categories of expense. These have been chosen to show how a range of budget calculations might be made, not as a likely real-life department or cost centre. There are few absolutely right or wrong figures because a budget is an individual interpretation of policy and available information. You might see some of the figures differently.

The following is a list of budget assumptions issued by the managing director, together with some available and relevant information. This is followed by the completed budget form, then a note of many of the budget calculations is given.

Salaries

The current payroll (including employers' National Insurance contributions) is £1,282,441 per year. It is assumed that on 1 July there will be an average pay rise of 5 per cent. It is also assumed that redundancies on 1 October will save £80,000 per year and that one-off redundancy payments will be £23,000.

Rent

There will be a £15,000 per year increase on 1 January.

Postage

It is believed that there will be an overall 20 per cent reduction in postal use and that the reduction will gather pace during the year. It is also assumed that there will be no increase in postal charges during the year.

(Comment – in view of increases in recent years, could this last assumption perhaps be rather optimistic?)

Telephone

It is believed that a 5 per cent reduction on current costs will be achieved throughout the year.

Depreciation

The depreciation rate on company cars is 25 per cent per year, and on fixtures and fittings it is 10 per cent per year. The balance sheet position at 31 December is as follows:

	Company cars £	Fixtures and fittings £
Cost	210,000	40,000
Less depreciation to date	110,000	10,000
Net book value	100,000	30,000

The capital expenditure budget shows purchases of cars for £150,000 on 1 January and fixtures and fittings for £10,000 on 1 January. There are no plans to sell any fixed assets. All the company cars are less than three years old.

Bad debts

The managing director has instructed that an additional bad debt reserve of £7,000 per month should be budgeted.

Travel expenses

It is believed that these can be held at the level for last year.

Hotel costs

It is believed that these can be held at the level for last year.

Stationery

The managing director believes that both last year's budget and last year's actual are absurdly high. He has required a cut of 50 per cent on last year's budget.

Bank interest

It is believed that average borrowing over the coming year will be:

- Quarter 1   £850,000
- Quarter 2   £920,000

- Quarter 3   £990,000
- Quarter 4   £900,000

It is believed that the interest rate throughout the year will be 10 per cent.

Audit fee

The managing director believes that the auditors give a terrible service and charge too much, and he is annoyed that last year's actual charge is significantly over budget. He has demanded a cut of 25 per cent on last year's budget.

It is company practice to accrue the expected audit fee evenly through the year.

(Comment – the managing director is surely mistaken. All auditors give a good service and charge moderate fees.)

Expenditure budget for the year to 31 December

	Last year's budget £	Last year's actual £	Quarter 1 £	Quarter 2 £	Quarter 3 £	Quarter 4 £	Budget for total year £
Salaries	1,230,000	1,269,111	321,000	321,000	337,000	340,000	1,319,000
Rent	205,000	205,000	55,000	55,000	55,000	55,000	220,000
Postage	22,000	26,117	6,000	5,300	5,200	4,500	21,000
Telephone	34,500	39,282	9,350	9,350	9,350	9,350	37,400
Depreciation	120,000	120,000	23,750	23,750	23,750	23,750	95,000
Bad debts	60,000	76,398	21,000	21,000	21,000	21,000	84,000
Travel expenses	92,000	99,904	25,000	25,000	25,000	25,000	100,000
Hotel costs	84,000	92,317	23,000	23,000	23,000	23,000	92,000
Stationery	62,000	66,218	7,750	7,750	7,750	7,750	31,000
Bank interest	50,000	73,007	21,250	23,000	24,750	22,500	91,500
Audit fee	20,000	28,500	3,750	3,750	3,750	3,750	15,000
	1,979,500	2,095,854	516,850	517,900	535,550	535,600	2,105,900

Reasonable rounding of figures has been done throughout the calculations.

Salaries

- Quarter 1: At the current rate – £321,000
- Quarter 2: At the current rate – £321,000
- Quarter 3: At the current rate plus 5 per cent – £337,000
- Quarter 4: As per Quarter 3 less £20,000 plus £23,000 – £340,000

Postage

Eighty per cent of £26,117 is £20,893. After rounding and allowing for the reduction to be greater towards the end of the year this is split as shown.

Telephone

Ninety-five per cent of £39,282 is £37,317. This is allocated evenly throughout the budget period.

Depreciation

	Company cars £	Fixtures and fittings £
Original cost	210,000	40,000
Add budgeted purchases	150,000	10,000
	360,000	50,000

	Company cars £	Fixtures and fittings £
25 per cent depreciation on company cars		90,000
10 per cent depreciation on fixtures and fittings		5,000
		95,000

Bank interest

Quarter 1: 25 per cent × 10 per cent × £850,000 = £21,250	
Quarter 2: 25 per cent × 10 per cent × £920,000 = £23,000	
Quarter 3: 25 per cent × 10 per cent × £990,000 = £24,750	
Quarter 4: 25 per cent × 10 per cent × £900,000 = £22,500	
	£91,500

Expenditure budget exercise

It is now time for you to prepare an expenditure budget from information provided. Once again the categories of expense have been chosen to show a range of expenses and not to reflect a real-life department or cost centre. The following is a list of budget assumptions issued by the managing director, together with some available and relevant information. The completed form followed by a note of some of the calculations is given at the end of the chapter, but please fill in the blank form that follows before looking.

Overall approach

The directors are disappointed with last year's performance and the failure to achieve budget. They demand a rigorous approach to budgeting expenses and that last year's poor performance is not used as an excuse for unjustified expenditure this year.

Salaries

The payroll (including employers' National Insurance contributions) has averaged £232,000 per month in the last three months. There must be a total freeze on overtime, which will save £8,000 per month. In addition, an employee who is paid (including employers' National Insurance contributions) £60,000 a year will retire on 30 June and will not be replaced. There will be no pay increases during the year.

Computer costs

A planned project starting in March must be deferred until November and the budget must be for ongoing costs of £4,000 per month. The new project is expected to cost £35,000 spread evenly over five months and this will be additional to the ongoing work.

Property costs

The directors want a 10 per cent cut in last year's actual figures.

Office costs

The directors believe that last year's budget was realistic and note that it was achieved. They suggest that the same budget figure is used.

Bad debts

The directors recognize that it was a mistake to make no provision in last year's budget. They have asked for a budget of 1 per cent of turnover. The revenue budget is as follows:

- Quarter 1   £3,300,000
- Quarter 2   £3,800,000
- Quarter 3   £4,100,000
- Quarter 4   £3,900,000

Travel

The directors think that last year's budget was too high and that the actual expenditure was disgraceful. They have asked for a budget of £105,000.

Entertainment

The directors think that the overrun on last year's budget was not justified, even though they did quite a bit of the entertaining. They want a repeat of last year's budget.

Audit fee

The directors would like a big cut but recognize that this is not realistic. They have asked for a token cut of £2,000. The audit fee should be budgeted evenly over the whole year.

Expenditure budget for the year to 31 December

	Last year's budget £	Last year's actual £	Quarter 1 £	Quarter 2 £	Quarter 3 £	Quarter 4 £	Budget for total year £
Salaries	2,640,000	2,761,134					
Computer costs	88,000	107,922					
Property costs	107,000	121,844					
Office costs	94,000	92,316					
Bad debts	–	177,431					
Travel	136,000	162,908					
Entertainment	92,000	131,111					
Audit fee	50,000	50,000					
	3,207,000	3,604,666					

Summary

In this chapter we have:

● Looked at the structure and layout of the expenditure budget. We have seen that this may be a simple one-page document in a small organization, but more typically will be separate mini-expenditure budgets for different departments or cost centres. These are then aggregated into the whole, perhaps with intervening levels for such units as divisions or regions.

● Looked in detail at how an expenditure budget is prepared and seen an example.

Finally you will, I hope, have successfully prepared an expenditure budget from the information provided.

The expenditure budget is very important in its own right, but more than that it is an essential step towards preparing the profit and loss budget. This gives the budgeted overall profit or loss and it is what we will study next.

Answer to expenditure budget for the year to 31 December

	Last year's budget £	Last year's actual £	Quarter 1 £	Quarter 2 £	Quarter 3 £	Quarter 4 £	Budget for total year £
Salaries	2,640,000	2,761,134	672,000	672,000	657,000	657,000	2,658,000
Computer costs	88,000	107,922	12,000	12,000	12,000	26,000	62,000
Property costs	107,000	121,844	27,500	27,500	27,500	27,500	110,000
Office costs	94,000	92,316	23,500	23,500	23,500	23,500	94,000
Bad debts	–	177,431	33,000	38,000	41,000	39,000	151,000
Travel	136,000	162,908	26,250	26,250	26,250	26,250	105,000
Entertainment	92,000	131,111	23,000	23,000	23,000	23,000	92,000
Audit fee	50,000	50,000	12,000	12,000	12,000	12,000	48,000
	3,207,000	3,604,666	829,250	834,250	822,250	834,250	3,320,000

Salaries

Quarter 1: £224,000 × 3 = £672,000
Quarter 2: £224,000 × 3 = £672,000
Quarter 3: £224,000 × 3 = £672,000 less
       £15,000 = £657,000
Quarter 4: £224,000 × 3 = £672,000 less
       £15,000 = £657,000

Computer costs

Quarter 1: 3 × £4,000 = £12,000
Quarter 2: 3 × £4,000 = £12,000
Quarter 3: 3 × £4,000 = £12,000
Quarter 4: 3 × £4,000 = £12,000 plus £14,000 = £26,000

Fact-check (answers at the back)

1. What should be put into the 'Last year's actual' column when the budget is prepared before the end of last year?
   a) Last year's budget ❏
   b) Nothing ❏
   c) The best estimate of what last year's actual will be ❏
   d) Twice the actual figures for the first six months of last year ❏

2. Why will most managers identify particularly closely with the expenditure budget?
   a) It is the one to which they are most likely to contribute ❏
   b) It is the one against which they are most likely to be measured ❏
   c) It is important and probably readily understood ❏
   d) All of the above ❏

3. For what should there be a separate expenditure budget form?
   a) The whole company ❏
   b) The whole division ❏
   c) The whole department ❏
   d) For each cost centre if there is more than one cost centre in a department ❏

4. Is the capital expenditure budget a factor when the expenditure budget is prepared?
   a) Yes, always (if there is capital expenditure) ❏
   b) Sometimes ❏
   c) Not usually ❏
   d) No ❏

5. Is the amount of borrowing a factor when the expenditure budget is prepared?
   a) Yes, always (if there is borrowing) ❏
   b) Sometimes ❏
   c) Not usually ❏
   d) No ❏

6. In the UK are employers' National Insurance contributions a factor when the expenditure budget is prepared?
   a) No ❏
   b) Yes ❏
   c) Only in Scotland ❏
   d) Only if the business is making a profit ❏

7. Last year's budget for salaries was £1,000,000 and last year's actual was £1,200,000. The managing director's budget assumptions call for a 10 per cent increase in salaries from the first day of the budget year. You practise zero-based budgeting. What should the budget be?
   a) £1,000,000 ❏
   b) £1,200,000 ❏
   c) £1,320,000 ❏
   d) You should take account of the 10 per cent increase but examine if the employment of each worker is justified and budget accordingly ❏

8. The revenue budget shows a significant decrease in turnover compared with last year. Does it follow that there should be a corresponding reduction in the expenditure budget?

a) No, but the possibility should be very seriously considered ❏

b) Certainly not ❏

c) Yes ❏

d) Of course ❏

9. Why (in the writer's opinion) is an arbitrary, across-the-board 20 per cent cut in all expenditure budgets a bad idea?

a) It demotivates managers ❏

b) It makes it more likely that managers will inflate future budget submissions ❏

c) Both of the above ❏

d) Such cuts can never be achieved ❏

10. Where does the total of the expenditure budget go?

a) Nowhere ❏

b) Into the profit and loss budget ❏

c) Into the budgeted balance sheet ❏

d) Into the sales budget ❏

CHAPTER 24

The profit and loss budget

What is the most frequently asked question about budgets and forecasts? Strong contenders are 'What's the profit going to be?' or if things are not looking good 'Just how bad is it – how big is the loss?' It is the profit and loss budget or forecast that will answer these questions. They bring together into one summary all the budgeted or forecast figures of an income or expense nature (as opposed to those of an asset or liability nature). The figure at the bottom will answer these anxious questions.

The profit and loss budget therefore cannot fail to be interesting and important and this is what we study in this chapter. Taxation gets a mention for the first time and we look at break-even point and break-even charts.

The topics covered comprise:

- where do the figures come from?
- the format of the profit and loss budget
- taxation
- the profit and loss budget of a trading business
- the profit and loss budget of a manufacturing business
- break-even point and break-even charts.

Where do the figures come from?

The profit and loss account is a summary of all the accounts of an income or expense nature in the bookkeeping system. This is as opposed to assets or liabilities, which go into the balance sheet. It follows that the profit and loss budget is a summary of all budgeted income and expense.

In a very small and simple operation some of the figures might go straight into the profit and loss budget without touching a subsidiary budget, but it is very much more likely that each line is taken from the total of one of the other budgets. For example, the total of the expenditure budget may go into the profit and loss budget with a heading such as 'Expenditure'. However, it is more probable that the profit and loss budget will list several departments or cost centres. The figure for each of these departments or cost centres will be taken from the relevant sections of the expenditure budget. This is how it is done in the example that follows shortly in this chapter.

The format of the profit and loss budget

Budgets are not normally intended for publication so there is a great deal of freedom about the format. The profit and loss budget should be laid out in a way that is readily understood and most useful for managers. There are extra factors for a trading business and a manufacturing business, and there is more about them later in this chapter. There may be complications in other businesses too, but the following is an example of a profit and loss budget in a simple and straightforward company. It is a consultancy that sells its services, not a physical product.

Profit and loss budget for year to 31 December

	Last year's budget $	Last year's actual $	Quarter 1 $	Quarter 2 $	Quarter 3 $	Quarter 4 $	Total year $
Sales	7,456,000	7,184,296	1,742,000	1,800,000	1,810,000	1,860,000	7,212,000
Less direct costs	3,718,000	3,722,199	853,000	936,000	940,000	1,004,000	3,733,000
	3,738,000	3,462,097	889,000	864,000	870,000	856,000	3,479,000
Directors	422,000	461,782	115,000	115,000	118,000	119,000	467,000
Sales and Marketing Department	791,000	834,664	192,000	193,000	197,000	202,000	784,000
Finance Department	401,000	398,213	98,000	98,000	102,000	103,000	401,000
Personnel Department	266,000	279,463	65,000	65,000	65,000	65,000	260,000
Administration Department	287,000	297,185	73,000	68,000	68,000	68,000	277,000
Total other costs	2,167,000	2,271,307	543,000	539,000	550,000	557,000	2,189,000
Net profit	1,571,000	1,190,790	346,000	325,000	320,000	299,000	1,290,000

This may seem a short and simple document for a company with a turnover in excess of $7 million a year, but of course there will be other detailed budgets in support of it. The sales figures at the top of the profit and loss budget are sales that are budgeted to be invoiced to customers in the periods indicated, and not orders that are budgeted to be taken at these times. They therefore come from the revenue budget and not the sales budget. The top line is sometimes called 'Turnover', which is another name for invoiced sales.

The direct costs will be the salaries and other costs (travel, etc.) of the consultants who are providing services to the customers and generating the revenue. This will be a cost centre, or perhaps the sum of several cost centres with an expenditure budget for each one. Similarly, there will be expenditure budgets for the departments shown and perhaps more than one cost centre within each department.

Having said that, and although it is not shown in the example, one or more things do sometimes go into the budgeted profit and loss account that are not in any other budget, though they will of course always affect the budgeted balance sheet. Interest payable and investment income are two of the main ones. In the example just given they might go into Finance Department or Administration Department, but they would probably not be a good fit. Apart from anything else, they probably would not be under the control of the managers heading these departments.

Taxation

The US statesman and inventor Benjamin Franklin wrote 'In this world nothing can be said to be certain except death and taxes'. He was surely right and we have not so far mentioned taxation, so it is now time to do so.

It is almost universal practice to disregard sales tax or value added tax (VAT) in the profit and loss budget and indeed the profit and loss account. It is of course very important, and affects the cash budget and budgeted balance sheet, but any such tax collected is eventually paid over to the tax authority. It is possible to show the sales figures including tax and then deduct the tax to give the sales figures excluding tax, but it is not necessary and hardly anyone does it.

Tax on profits is another matter. In the UK this will be corporation tax for a company and income tax for a sole trader or partnership. Sometimes the view is taken that as the profit and loss budget is for the managers, and as taxation is beyond their control, it should be left out. However, it is important that at least the senior managers know the budgeted profit or loss after tax, and it is of course very important in preparing the budgeted balance sheet.

Taxation is not shown in the budgeted profit and loss account just given, but assuming corporation tax of 26 per cent the last three lines for the total year would be:

Net profit before tax	$1,290,000
Less tax	$335,400
Net profit after tax	$954,600

Before leaving the subject it is worth mentioning that Benjamin Franklin, although brilliant, was sometimes known to take risks. He invented the lightning rod and is believed to have tested it by flying a kite in a thunderstorm. Fortunately he lived to tell the tale.

The profit and loss budget of a trading business

The example earlier in this chapter was for a business that sold just its services, so we will now consider the extra factor for a business that sells goods. You already know that it is a bad mistake to put the costs of goods purchased for resale into the profit and loss budget at the time that the purchases are made. What should happen is that the costs of the goods actually invoiced to customers should go into the profit and loss budget, and they should do so in the same period that the revenue is recognized. The top section of the profit and loss budget will look like this:

Sales	£
Less cost of sales	£
Gross profit	£

The other costs will then be deducted and the final figure will be the net profit or loss.

The point about the timing is illustrated by the following example. It assumes that only one product is sold and that the selling price is always exactly twice the purchase price.

	Purchases £	Sales £	Cost of Sales £
January	2,405,000	1,020,000	510,000
February	1,996,000	1,310,000	655,000
March	1,721,000	968,000	484,000
April	234,000	2,324,000	1,162,000

Of course in real life it is not likely to be as simple as that. There will almost certainly be a range of products sold at a range of prices, and purchases will probably be from a range of suppliers at a range of prices.

The profit and loss budget of a manufacturing business

This is more complicated than the profit and loss budget of a trading company. It is similar in that physical goods are sold, but they are not purchased in a ready-to-sell condition. However, the top section of the profit and loss budget will look the same, namely:

Sales	£
Less cost of sales	£
Gross profit	£

The cost of sales will be the sum of everything spent to manufacture the goods that are sold. These costs will include direct wages, raw materials, purchased components and semi-manufactured goods, and manufacturing costs. The accounting system should be organized so that all the manufacturing costs can be identified. The profit and loss budget should follow this with various departments and cost centres that can be grouped and totalled to find the total cost of sales. It is likely that the use of standard costs will play a significant part in this. Most manufacturing businesses have a separate manufacturing budget for the total costs of manufacture.

As with the profit and loss budget of a trading business, the costs of the goods actually invoiced to customers should go into the profit and loss budget, and they should do so in the same period that the revenue is recognized.

Break-even point and break-even charts

It is extremely useful to know the budgeted level of sales at which break-even will be achieved. This is the point at which the costs exactly equal the revenues, and a break-even chart can show this. Furthermore, it can show the level of profit or loss at any particular level of sales. In order to do this, it is necessary to know:

● The amount of fixed costs
● The amount of variable costs per unit of sale
● The sales price per unit.

Fixed costs are costs that stay the same regardless of the level of sales. Office rent is a good example. In practice it may be very difficult or impossible to identify all the factors accurately. Some costs may be semi-variable and fixed costs may increase once a certain level of sales is reached. Various other problems may be encountered. Having made these qualifications, let us see how it works with a simple example.

A company imports and sells clocks. It pays $5.00 for each clock and the selling price per clock is $10.00. The company has fixed costs of $200,000.

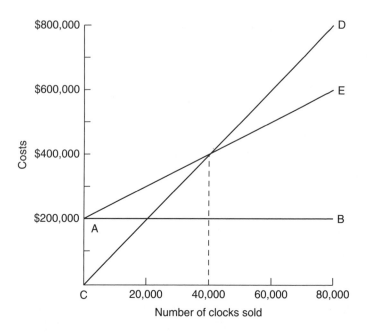

The vertical axis represents the costs.

The horizontal axis represents the number of clocks sold.

Line A–B is the fixed costs of $200,000.

Line C–D is the total sales at $10.00 per clock.

Line A–E is the total costs at $5.00 per clock plus the fixed costs.

The break-even point is the sale of 40,000 clocks. At this point sales of $400,000 are equal to fixed costs of $200,000 plus the cost of 40,000 clocks at $5.00 each. The difference between lines C–D and A–E is the profit or loss.

Summary

In this chapter we have:

- Shown why the profit and loss budget is so important and why it is often the most studied of the budgets and forecasts.
- Seen where the figures that go into this budget come from and noted that it is a summary of all the income and expenditure.
- Looked at the format of a profit and loss budget, and studied the different requirements for a trading business and a manufacturing business. We have seen that a small number of items may go straight into this budget without appearing in any other budget apart from the budgeted balance sheet.
- Seen how taxation is always a factor, though it may go into only the budgeted balance sheet.
- Had a brief look at the break-even point and break-even charts.

You probably know the importance of cash to a business and how serious it can be to run short. A good cash budget and good regular cash forecasts should make this much less likely to happen. This is the subject of our work in the next chapter and at the end you will have the opportunity to prepare a cash budget.

Fact-check (answers at the back)

1. What is often considered to be the most frequently asked question about budgets?
   a) Why is it late? ❏
   b) Who is going to be sacked? ❏
   c) What's the profit going to be? ❏
   d) Can we afford a dividend? ❏

2. Which of the following statements is true?
   a) The profit and loss budget is a summary of assets and liabilities ❏
   b) The profit and loss budget is a summary of budgeted income and expense ❏
   c) If you get the revenue right, the rest of the profit and loss budget virtually does itself ❏
   d) The layout of the profit and loss budget differs according to whether there is a profit or a loss ❏

3. Are detailed budgets normally published?
   a) Yes, always ❏
   b) Yes, usually ❏
   c) Not usually ❏
   d) Only if the tax authorities insist ❏

4. What is turnover?
   a) Orders taken ❏
   b) Invoiced sales ❏
   c) Revenue carried forward from the previous period ❏
   d) Cancelled orders ❏

5. Can the budgeted sales figure include VAT or sales tax?
   a) Yes – but only if the tax element is then deducted ❏
   b) Yes – and it is not adjusted ❏
   c) No, never ❏
   d) No, unless special permission has been given ❏

6. Only one product is sold and the selling price is always 50 per cent higher than the price paid. Purchases are:

   January £1,000,000
   February £400,000
   March £300,000

   Invoiced sales in March are budgeted to be £1,200,000. What should be the budgeted cost of sales for March?
   a) £300,000 ❏
   b) £700,000 ❏
   c) £800,000 ❏
   d) £1,200,000 ❏

7. Which of the following is likely to be a fixed cost?
   a) Bank interest ❏
   b) Insurance premiums ❏
   c) Direct wages ❏
   d) Factory rent ❏

8. Fixed costs are $1,000,000. Each unit sold is sold for $600 and the variable cost for each unit sold is $400. What is the break-even point?
   a) $3,000,000 ❏
   b) $2,000,000 ❏
   c) $2,500,000 ❏
   d) $4,000,000 ❏

9. Which of the following often goes straight into the profit and loss budget instead of another budget?

a) Depreciation ❏

b) Audit fee ❏

c) Directors' salaries ❏

d) Investment income ❏

10. What is represented by the bottom line in a profit and loss budget?

a) Total costs ❏

b) Net profit or loss ❏

c) Gross profit or loss ❏

d) Indirect costs ❏

CHAPTER 25

The cash budget

The importance of the cash budget is often underestimated and it is certainly worth a detailed study. In this chapter we do just that and then you will have a chance to prepare one from information provided. The cash budget should be one of the last to be prepared because many of its figures are taken or adapted from the contents of other budgets.

At the end of this chapter we will have studied the main budgets usually encountered. This is with the exception of the budgeted balance sheet, which comes last of all. This is important but it will almost certainly be prepared by the accountants and is beyond the terms of this book.

The topics covered comprise:

- definition of cash
- the importance of the cash budget and the cash forecast
- the distinctions between cash, profit and net worth
- the preparation of a cash budget
- cash budget exercise.

Definition of cash

Cash is the total of all the bank balances plus any notes and coins. The bank balances almost always make up virtually all the cash total. Bank borrowing must be deducted. It is possible, and indeed very common, for total cash to be a minus figure as in the following (brackets are conventionally used to indicate a negative amount):

	£
Bank balances in credit	1,000
Notes and coins	500
	1,500
Less bank overdrafts	200,000
Total cash	(198,500)

The importance of the cash budget and the cash forecast

You will probably not be surprised to be told that the cash budget and the cash forecast are extremely important. A business should aim to have the right amount of cash, not too much and not too little. Both are wrong, but not having enough is potentially much worse. Before we consider this, we will say why it is a mistake to have too much. It is because, like having too much stock, it is wasteful. Cash is tied up that could profitably be invested elsewhere or returned to the owners of the business.

Having too little cash is likely to mean that the business cannot achieve its potential. Profitable opportunities may have to be turned down. Worse, if the cash shortage is severe and unless an alternative source of finance can be obtained, the very existence of the business may be threatened. Businesses do not fold because of a lack of profits, though this of course is very unhelpful and in the long run may be fatal. Businesses fold because they cannot pay their debts as they become due. It is not uncommon for a business to fail that is making profits at the time of its failure. This is particularly true of expanding businesses.

A good cash budget and good, regular cash forecasts enable managers to manage the cash and, if problems are predicted, to take appropriate action in good time. A further reason for preparing a cash budget is that it is an essential step in preparing the budgeted balance sheet.

The distinctions between cash, profit and net worth

Cash, profit and net worth are completely different things and should not be confused, though they sometimes are, especially cash and profit. Profit is the difference between income and expenses, but not necessarily received or paid in cash. Net worth is the book value of a business as shown in a balance sheet. If the business is a company, net worth is the same as shareholders' funds. The reasons for the short-term differences between cash and profit include the following.

Timing differences

Sales are usually credited to the profit and loss account when goods are delivered or services performed. Payment is usually received from customers later. Purchases are usually debited to the profit and loss account as they are made. Suppliers are usually paid later.

Fixed assets and depreciation

Cash leaves the business when fixed assets are purchased, but in the very short term there is no effect on the profit and loss account. Depreciation is a later non-cash charge to the profit and loss account.

Loans to or from the business (including bank loans)

These affect cash but not profit, though there will very probably be an interest effect.

The purchase of investments, etc.

This affects cash but not profits.

Bad debt reserve, etc.

The creation of a reserve such as a bad debt reserve reduces profit but not cash. The later release of an over-provision increases profit but not cash.

Payment of dividends

The payment of dividends passes cash to the owners of a company. Dividends take cash out of a company and are paid out of reserves.

Taxation

Income tax and National Insurance contributions (in the UK) are payable to HMRC after they have been deducted from employees' wages and after they have affected the profit and loss account. Corporation tax (in the UK) is usually paid to HMRC after the period of the profit and loss account.

The preparation of a cash budget

The steps in doing this are as follows:

1 An appropriate form must be designed, with care being taken to ensure that the headings cover all the sources of cash coming in and all the sources of cash going out. Many different layouts are possible and a good one is shown at the end of this section of the chapter.
2 The calculated or forecast cash total at the beginning of the period covered should be entered. If it is a negative figure, which means overall net borrowing, this should be indicated

in some way. It is usual to do this with brackets or a minus sign, and this also applies to negative figures throughout the document.

3 Relevant figures and totals from other budgets should be entered. In doing this, two types of adjustment are necessary:

   a) Adjustments for non-cash items should be made. For example, the following are non-cash items that may be included in the expenses and must be added back:
   - creation of a bad debt reserve
   - depreciation of fixed assets.

   b) The figures must be adjusted for timing differences. For example, it is usually necessary to do this for the following:
   - Customers will normally pay after the sales have been recorded in the profit and loss budget
   - Suppliers will normally be paid after the purchases have been entered into the profit and loss budget or capital expenditure budget
   - Tax is normally paid to the tax authority after it has taken effect in the profit and loss budget.

4 Entries should be made for items that do not appear in the profit and loss or capital expenditure budgets. Possible examples include:
   - purchase and sale of investments
   - dividends paid.

5 The columns should be totalled and the running cash balance calculated.

Do not overlook the possibility that a cash requirement may peak between two budgeted points. It is possible for $1,000,000 to be needed on both 31 May and 30 June, but the cash requirement to be $1,100,000 on 15 June.

At this point please think about a temptation which should be resisted. What will you do if the cash budget indicates an unacceptably high or even critically high cash requirement? You might consider 'solving' the difficulty by assuming that customers will pay more quickly and suppliers will be paid more slowly. The problem is that they very understandably might not be willing to co-operate in this way. Such assumptions should be made only if it is reasonable to do so.

The following is an example of a cash budget illustrating the principles described.

Cash budget for six months to 30 June

	Jan £000	Feb £000	March £000	April £000	May £000	June £000
Receipts						
UK customers	400	400	450	450	450	500
Export customers	600	120	380	60	120	120
Government grants	10			3		
All other	4	4	4	4	4	4
	1,014	524	834	517	574	624
Payments						
Suppliers	802	407	631	506	488	482
Salaries (net)	55	55	55	59	59	59
PAYE and national insurance	18	18	18	18	20	20
Corporation tax			100			
Dividends					50	
Capital expenditure	10	10	10	75	75	10
All other	10	10	10	10	10	10
	895	500	824	668	702	581
Excess of receipts over payments	119	24	10	(151)	(128)	43
Add opening bank balance	(2,016)	(1,897)	(1,873)	(1,863)	(2,014)	(2,142)
Closing bank balance	(1,897)	(1,873)	(1,863)	(2,014)	(2,142)	(2,099)

Cash budget exercise

Hopefully this is all clear and you will now be able to complete a cash budget. The form is the same but the figures are different. A few figures have been filled in to help you. Please do the rest using the following data. The answer is at the end of the chapter.

Receipts from customers

Customers are expected to pay in an average of 60 days. Budgeted invoicing is as follows:

	UK £000	Export £000
November	905	200
December	900	200
January	905	300
February	920	300
March	920	300
April	950	350
May	950	350
June	950	350

Payments to suppliers

It is expected that suppliers will be paid in an average of 30 days. Budgeted invoices from suppliers are budgeted to be as follows:

	£000
November	820
December	810
January	800
February	850
March	900
April	900
May	900
June	950

Corporation tax

A corporation tax payment of £318,000 will be paid in May.

Dividends

A dividend of £100,000 will be paid in January.

Capital expenditure

This is budgeted to be £30,000 per month during the period of the budget.

Opening overdraft

The overdraft at 31 December is expected to be £4,320,000.

Cash budget for six months to 30 June

	Jan £000	Feb £000	March £000	April £000	May £000	June £000
Receipts						
UK customers						
Export customers						
Government grants			60			
All other	10	10	10	10	10	10
Total						
Payments						
Suppliers						
Salaries (net)	103	104	110	110	110	110
PAYE and National Insurance	34	34	34	34	34	34
Corporation tax						
Dividends						
Capital expenditure						
All other	6	6	6	6	6	6
Total						
Excess of receipts over payments						
Add opening bank balance						
Closing bank balance						

Summary

In this chapter we have:

● Established exactly what is meant by the term 'cash'. It is sometimes misunderstood and it cannot be properly budgeted if we are not absolutely sure what it is.

● Seen just why the cash budget and the cash forecast are so important. I really do hope that you never have to find this out the hard way. Perhaps budgets are not updated during the year, but it is a good idea to do regular cash forecasts.

● Established the differences between cash, profit and net worth. They are totally different and sometimes confused. It is possible to find this out the hard way, perhaps by trying to spend the profit when there is no money in the bank.

● Looked in detail at how a cash budget is prepared and seen an example.

Finally you will, I hope, have successfully prepared a cash budget.

We have now finished reviewing the budgets, which leaves what happens afterwards. We will end by looking at how budgets and forecasts should be used after completion and approval, and at periodic statements comparing actual performance with the budget or forecast.

Answer to cash budget for six months to 30 June

	Jan £000	Feb £000	March £000	April £000	May £000	June £000
Receipts						
UK customers	905	900	905	920	920	950
Export customers	200	200	300	300	300	350
Government grants			60			
All other	10	10	10	10	10	10
	1,115	1,110	1,275	1,230	1,230	1,310
Payments						
Suppliers	810	800	850	900	900	900
Salaries (net)	103	104	110	110	110	110
PAYE and National Insurance	34	34	34	34	34	34
Corporation tax					318	
Dividends	100					
Capital expenditure	30	30	30	30	30	30
All other	6	6	6	6	6	6
	1,083	974	1,030	1,080	1,398	1,080
Excess of receipts over payments	32	136	245	150	(168)	230
Add opening bank balance	(4,320)	(4,288)	(4,152)	(3,907)	(3,757)	(3,925)
Closing bank balance	(4,288)	(4,152)	(3,907)	(3,757)	(3,925)	(3,695)

Fact-check (answers at the back)

1. At what stage should the cash budget be prepared?
   - a) Normally first ❏
   - b) Normally last ❏
   - c) Normally somewhere in the middle ❏
   - d) It does not matter ❏

2. Who will normally prepare the budgeted balance sheet?
   - a) The auditor ❏
   - b) Any manager who has the time ❏
   - c) The accountants ❏
   - d) The managing director ❏

3. Does bank borrowing come within the definition of 'cash'?
   - a) Yes ❏
   - b) No ❏
   - c) It depends when the borrowing is repayable ❏
   - d) Yes in internal accounts, but not in published accounts ❏

4. Is it possible to have too much cash?
   - a) No, of course not ❏
   - b) No – and if it's a problem, it's a problem that I would like to have ❏
   - c) Yes ❏
   - d) It's a silly question ❏

5. In a company, what is a good description of 'net worth'?
   - a) The amount for which the company could be sold ❏
   - b) The value of the assets ❏
   - c) What the assets would fetch in a forced sale ❏
   - d) Shareholders' funds ❏

6. A company car is purchased for $40,000 and depreciated by 25 per cent in the first year. What is the effect on the cash budget in the first year?
   - a) $40,000 ❏
   - b) $30,000 ❏
   - c) $10,000 ❏
   - d) There is no effect ❏

7. Which budget or budgets are affected by the planned payment of a dividend?
   - a) The profit and loss budget ❏
   - b) The cash budget ❏
   - c) The budgeted balance sheet ❏
   - d) The cash budget and the budgeted balance sheet ❏

8. Payment terms for a very large customer are '30 days' but they usually pay 45 days late. When should a very large invoice dated 26 January be reflected in the cash budget?
   - a) February ❏
   - b) April ❏
   - c) May ❏
   - d) Half in April and half in May ❏

9. Which of the following should be applied to the total of the expenses in the budgeted profit and loss account when calculating the cash budget?
   - a) The creation of a bad debt reserve ❏
   - b) The depreciation charge ❏
   - c) The creation of a reserve for the settlement of a pending legal claim ❏
   - d) All of the above ❏

10. What should you **not** do if the cash budget indicates a dangerously high level of borrowing?

a) Assume (without evidence) that the customers will pay more quickly ❑

b) Discuss the problem with the bank ❑

c) Sell some investments ❑

d) Organize a new issue of shares ❑

CHAPTER 26

Monitoring progress against budgets and forecasts

After the budget or forecast has been approved comes ... possibly not much or even nothing at all. This would be unfortunate but it would not mean that the budgeting or forecasting exercise had been a complete waste of time. Those involved in the preparations will have thought logically about the organization, its finances and its future. Some at least of this will remain lodged in their minds and influence their future actions. Nevertheless, failure to monitor progress would be a great pity.

What should happen, and what usually does happen, is that regular reports giving details of budgeted and actual figures are produced. These are studied by the managers and may be reviewed at a meeting. These reports and possible meetings are important parts of this chapter. The chapter ends with some important and thought-provoking points on the need to align power and responsibility.

The topics covered comprise:

- the format of the performance reports
- variance analysis
- meetings to review the performance reports
- and finally ... some thoughts on power and responsibility.

The format of the performance reports

Regular performance reports should be issued by the accountants. These should be in the same format as the budgets and should give the figures for the actual results alongside the equivalent budget figures. Variances should also be given and it is usual to give the figures for the period (perhaps a month) and for the year to date as well. It is not normal to give all the reports to all the managers. Instead, distribution is usually done on a pyramid basis. The senior managers get most or all of the reports – perhaps in summarized form. The more junior managers get the reports for the departments that they manage. It sounds rigid and likely to offend the more junior managers, so perhaps some sensitivity on the point would not come amiss. The following are good examples of budget variance reports. The first is for one of the departments that make up the expenditure budget and it is followed by the profit and loss budget of one of a company's divisions. This latter one is based on the figures used in the example in Chapter 24.

	June month			June YTD		
	Budget $	Actual $	Variance $	Budget $	Actual $	Variance $
Salaries	20,000	20,006	(6)	120,000	120,400	(400)
Commission	2,000	2,600	(600)	12,000	14,000	(2,000)
Pension costs	2,000	2,000	–	12,000	12,000	–
Car expenses	6,000	5,700	300	36,000	34,200	1,800
Other travel	1,000	900	100	6,000	5,100	900
Hotel expenses	3,000	3,250	(250)	18,000	21,700	(3,700)
Meals	1,000	995	5	6,000	5,870	130
Other expenses	1,000	1,400	(400)	6,000	6,100	(100)
Postage	200	190	10	1,200	1,160	40
Stationery	200	205	(5)	1,200	1,270	(70)
Telephone	2,000	2,150	(150)	12,000	11,900	100
Miscellaneous	1,000	930	70	6,000	5,200	800
	39,400	40,326	(926)	236,400	238,900	(2,500)

	Quarter to 30 June			6 months to 30 June		
	Budget $	Actual $	Variance $	Budget $	Actual $	Variance $
Sales	1,800,000	1,809,321	9,321	3,542,000	3,627,172	85,172
Less Direct costs	936,000	961,278	(25,278)	1,789,000	1,863,222	(74,222)
	864,000	848,043	(15,957)	1,753,000	1,763,950	10,950
Directors	115,000	117,200	(2,200)	230,000	234,874	(4,874)
Sales and Marketing Department	193,000	191,662	1,338	385,000	384,119	881
Finance Department	98,000	107,311	(9,311)	196,000	212,843	(16,843)
Personnel Department	65,000	61,244	3,756	130,000	129,600	400
Administration Department	68,000	71,999	(3,999)	141,000	146,278	(5,278)
Total other costs	539,000	549,416	(10,416)	1,082,000	1,107,714	(25,714)
Net profit	325,000	298,627	(26,373)	671,000	656,236	(14,764)

In these examples the variances are expressed in monetary terms, but it is sometimes done in percentages instead of money or as well as money. If it is done in percentages, you should consider the size of the figures. An overrun of $50 on a budget of $100 is a 50 per cent adverse variance. This is a pity but in view of the small base figure it is probably insignificant. On the other hand an overrun of $50 on a budget of $10,000 is just a 0.5 per cent adverse variance.

Budget variance reports need interpreting and an initial reaction may be wrong. For example, in the variance report for the department there is a significant adverse variance for commission. A knee-jerk reaction might be to say that this is bad, but in fact it is probably very good. Businesses want sales staff to make high levels of sales and better than budgeted sales are likely to result in higher than budgeted commission. So well done the sales staff – please keep up the good work.

There are no absolute rules for the format of budget variance reports, so you should have one that suits your needs. However, there is a lot to be said for keeping it simple. Your computer system is probably capable of providing reams of analysis and some people might want you to have it, but if it is not going to be used it is of no use. In fact it is worse than that because it will take up managers' time and camouflage the information that is useful and should be used.

Variance analysis

Fairly obviously, a variance is the difference between a budgeted figure and the corresponding actual figure. Again fairly obviously, a variance can be favourable or unfavourable. The point of analysing variances is to see why the actual performance differs from the budgeted performance. With this knowledge we can use the information and understanding to try and improve unfavourable performances in the future, and to try to consolidate favourable variances so that they continue.

A variance may be measured on a very large unit, such as a whole division within a company, or even a whole company within a group of companies. It may be a complete department, such as the $16,843 unfavourable six-month variance in the Finance Department in the profit and loss example in this chapter. Breaking it down further it may be a category of expense within a department. The unfavourable variance of $3,700 for hotel expenses in the expenditure budget in this chapter is an example. Why did this happen? Perhaps more nights were spent in hotels or perhaps more expensive hotels were used. Perhaps it was a combination of the two. There is often more than one factor contributing to a variance.

This last point is well illustrated by a close look at sales variances. An overall variance may be caused by three factors:

- **Price variance.** This happens because the actual sales price differs from the budgeted sales price. The price variance is (actual price less budgeted price) × actual volume.
- **Volume variance.** This happens because the actual sales volume differs from the budgeted sales volume. The volume variance is (actual volume less budgeted volume) × budgeted price.
- **Mix variance.** This happens because the proportions of different products sold (at different prices) differs from the budgeted proportions. The mix variance is the difference between the total variance and the sum of the other two variances.

This is probably quite a bit to take in and understand, but the following practical example should help.

	Budget	Actual
Product A units sold	50,000	45,000
Product B units sold	30,000	37,000
	80,000	82,000
Product A sale price	£60	£63
Product B sale price	£40	£28
Product A sales	£3,000,000	£2,835,000
Product B sales	£1,200,000	£1,036,000
	£4,200,000	£3,871,000

Total variance	£4,200,000 – £3,871,000 = £329,000	unfavourable
Price variance	(£63 – £60) × 45,000 = £135,000	favourable
	(£40 – £28) × 30,000 = £360,000	unfavourable
	£225,000	unfavourable
Volume variance	(50,000 – 45,000) × £60 = £300,000	unfavourable
	(37,000 – 30,000) × £40 = £280,000	favourable
	£20,000	unfavourable
Mix variance	£329,000 – £225,000 – £20,000 = £84,000	unfavourable

Meetings to review the performance reports

Managers should regularly receive variance reports relevant to their area of responsibility. They should review them themselves and informally discuss them with their staff, their managers and other managers whose operations may influence their performance. In addition they should probably review them with their managers and colleagues at budget review meetings.

This suggestion may well induce groans from readers whose experience of meetings is that they are frequently an expensive waste of time. Yes, they often are, but they do not have to be and sometimes they get brilliant results. This is most likely if the meetings are:

- relatively short
- with an agenda
- well prepared
- with the right people there
- effectively chaired
- designed to end with a firm understanding about what will be done and who will do it.

It can be done and I speak from experience. More years ago than I care to remember, I regularly attended monthly meetings at Ford Motor Company's Thames Foundry in Dagenham, UK. The meetings were organized along the lines described above. The plant manager was able to run a friendly, informal and very effective meeting to pick over the budget variance reports and organize corrective action where necessary. One of my colleagues had a remarkable talent as a cartoonist and he always enlivened the cover of the pack of budget variance reports with an amusing and topical offering. After all these years, thank you, Dennis. You always got the meeting off to a good start.

And finally ... some thoughts on power and responsibility

'Power without responsibility has been the privilege of the harlot throughout the ages'. These words were spoken by the British Prime Minister Stanley Baldwin in a speech in 1931 and he was referring to Lord Beaverbrook's newspapers. He had a good point and it is certainly a memorable phrase, but in the context of budgets and forecasts it is the reverse that can be cause for concern. Responsibility without power is common. To some extent this may be inevitable, but it can be unfair and demotivating. It should be avoided where possible.

It is not realistic to expect that all the costs in managers' budgets will be entirely within their control. To take just one obvious example, salary costs will be very heavily influenced by company policy. It will probably not be possible (or desirable) to manage salaries without regard to company-wide policy, though of course company-wide policy (as far as it is known) should be reflected in the budget. Nevertheless, as far as is reasonably possible, power and responsibility should go hand in hand.

It is quite common for head office costs to be allocated to divisions or subsidiary companies, perhaps pro-rata to turnover or in some other 'fair' way. So, if it is done in this way, when a division contributes 20 per cent of turnover and head office costs are £1,000,000, the division would have to absorb costs of £200,000 into its profit and loss budget. This could be said to be right because the division receives the benefits provided by head office, perhaps including such things as the personnel department and the legal department. So the divisional profit, if there is one, would be overstated if this were not done. The problem is that divisional managers whose budget and performance are affected probably have little if any control over these head office costs. The situation is one of responsibility without power.

One solution is not to allocate head office costs in this way, but to keep all of them in an overall company-wide profit and loss budget. In a very simplified form this might look like the following:

	£
Contribution of Division 1	2,820,000
Contribution of Division 2	1,341,000
Contribution of Division 3	372,000
	4,533,000
Less Head Office costs	629,000
Overall budgeted profit before tax	3,904,000

This will overcome the problem of responsibility without power, but on no account should it be overlooked that head office costs are real and, to some extent at least, incurred for the benefit of the divisions.

Another solution is to allocate head office costs to the divisions or subsidiary companies, but to do so as the deduction of a single total below the profit or loss of the division or subsidiary. This mitigates responsibility without power, but still shows the divisions or subsidiaries that costs have been incurred for their benefit. As you perhaps know, divisional managers may still feel that head office costs are too high (why do they need all those pot plants?) and have been allocated between the divisions in an unfair way. The bottom part of a division's or subsidiary's budget might look like this:

	£
Divisional loss before head office costs	314,000
Add allocated part of head office costs	220,000
Divisional loss after allocated part of head office costs	534,000

Summary

In this chapter we have seen why it is important to monitor progress after the approval of budgets and forecasts. This process starts with the issue of the performance reports, and we have looked at two typical examples. We have also briefly reviewed meetings to monitor the progress. This should enable managers to:

- see the comparative figures
- work out the reasons for shortfalls and consider what might be done to put matters right
- see what went right and consider how the satisfactory performance can be maintained.

We have looked at variance analysis, part of which, with break-even charts, is possibly the most advanced work we have covered. So congratulations if you mastered it. Finally we considered the importance of, where possible, power and responsibility going together.

Fact-check (answers at the back)

1. What should happen after the budget has been agreed?

a) Regular reports giving budgeted and actual figures are produced ❑

b) Nothing ❑

c) A small budget cut should be implemented ❑

d) Budgeted expenditure should immediately be committed ❑

2. Who should normally issue the budget variance reports?

a) The managing director ❑

b) The internal auditor ❑

c) The accountants ❑

d) The company secretary ❑

3. Variance reports should usually give the figures for the period and...?

a) The budget for the corresponding period last year ❑

b) The actual figures for the corresponding period last year ❑

c) The figures for the year to date ❑

d) The budget for the whole year ❑

4. To what can a budget variance apply?

a) A whole company or division ❑

b) A whole department ❑

c) A category of expenditure (such as travel) ❑

d) All of the above ❑

5. How is the price variance calculated?

a) (actual price less budgeted price) × actual volume ❑

b) (budgeted price less actual price) × actual volume ❑

c) (actual price less budgeted price) × budgeted volume ❑

d) (budgeted price less actual price) × budgeted volume ❑

6. Why does the volume variance arise?

a) Because the actual sales volume differs from the budgeted sales volume ❑

b) Because the actual sales volume is greater than the budgeted sales volume ❑

c) Because the actual sales volume is less than the budgeted sales volume ❑

d) Because the actual sales volume is less than last year's actual sales volume ❑

7. Budgeted sale price is £10. Actual sale price is £13. Number sold is 32,000. What is the price variance?

a) £3 favourable ❑

b) £3 unfavourable ❑

c) £96,000 favourable ❑

d) £32,000 favourable ❑

8. Budgeted volume sold is 600. Actual volume sold is 560. The budgeted price is £1,000. What is the volume variance?

a) £40,000 favourable ❑

b) £40,000 unfavourable ❑

c) £600,000 ❑

d) £560,000 ❑

9. Is it realistic to expect that all the costs in managers' budgets will be entirely within their control?
   a) Yes, of course ❏
   b) No, of course not ❏
   c) No, but they should be as far as is reasonably possible ❏
   d) No, unless it is a finance company ❏

10. Which of the following should be avoided if possible?
   a) Responsibility without power ❏
   b) Power without responsibility ❏
   c) Both of the above ❏
   d) Neither of the above ❏

Surviving in tough times

Good budgeting and forecasting are useful management tools and they are always important, but in tough times their importance takes on an extra dimension. As it says in Chapter 20, *to fail to plan is to plan to fail*. Failure is always a bad idea, but in tough times the safety margin may well be much smaller and a failure can all too easily turn into a disaster. Effective budgeting and forecasting will help plan for this not to happen and it should give early warning of impending difficulties and disasters. Information will be at hand so that avoiding action can be taken. Here are 10 crucial tips.

1 Keep the budgets and forecasts up to date

You may be familiar with the saying that yesterday's newspaper is only good for wrapping the fish and chips. Not many people are interested in old news. It can be the same for budgets and forecasts. A typical budget covers a period of a year and a great deal can happen in that time. In tough times it is more likely that the underpinning assumptions will become out of date and perhaps seriously wrong. So keep looking at the budgets and forecasts, and bring them up to date as necessary.

2 Face facts

Ostriches are popularly supposed to deal with danger by putting their heads in the sand so that they cannot be seen, but ostriches are silly birds and this tactic will not help them. It will not help you either. Look at what the budgets and forecasts are telling you and, provided of course that they are well prepared and believable, accept their messages and respond accordingly. Optimism is usually to be welcomed, but it must be tempered with realism.

3 Respond quickly

You should actively use the budgets and forecasts to plan what you are going to do, and in tough times it is particularly important that your response is made quickly. If things are going wrong, a quick and decisive response may well be rewarded and delay may well be punished. You should look at the figures as soon as they become available, decide what needs to be done and then do it as soon as possible.

4 Do not underestimate the importance of cash and the cash forecast

The cash budget, the cash forecast and the importance of cash were explained in Chapter 25. It is possible and common to be both profitable and short of cash, a point which is frequently misunderstood, sometimes with disastrous consequences. Businesses do not fold because they are not making profits, though this is obviously very unhelpful and may be fatal in the long run. They fail because they cannot pay their bills as they fall due. The cash budget and cash forecasts are vital. In tough times cash forecasts should be done frequently, perhaps even weekly. They should be produced quickly and studied carefully, so that difficulties can be foreseen and corrective action planned.

5 Make sure that your customers pay you on time

Your cash budget and your cash forecast should tell you how badly your business needs cash. If it needs cash badly, and to a lesser extent even if it does not, it is important that your customers pay you on time. It may be tempting to 'solve' the problem by assuming that customers will pay more quickly, but unless there are grounds for this belief the temptation should be resisted. Positive action should be taken to try and make customers honour their obligations and pay within the contractual terms. Steps may include telephone calls, letters and emails, personal visits, third-party debt collectors and ultimately legal action.

6 Changes to the capital expenditure budget might help solve cash problems

Some at least of the capital expenditure is probably discretionary. It might not need to happen at all or it might be deferred until a later date. This would take some capital expenditure out of the budget or put it back to a later period. This would, in the short term at least, reduce the need for cash. Of course such steps would have consequences because the capital expenditure was probably in the budget for good reasons. Nevertheless, it could be considered. Alternatives could be to lease the capital items or buy them on hire purchase. This way the benefits of the assets would be obtained, but the cash effect would be deferred.

7 Consider zero-based budgets

Zero-based budgets were reviewed in Chapter 21. A feature of them is that everything must be examined and justified. This contrasts with incremental budgets, in which past figures are taken as the basis. In tough times all expenditure must be justified or jettisoned, and this is exactly what zero-based budgets do. They do have disadvantages as well as advantages. One of the disadvantages is the extra time needed for their preparation.

8 Go for 'tough but achievable'

How hard should it be to achieve the budget targets? In Chapter 20 we reviewed the various possibilities and the arguments for and against each one. There is no point in making the budget targets virtually impossible. They will not be achieved and everyone will be demotivated. There is also no point in making the targets too easy. They will be achieved, but so what? Remember the words of the Red Queen in *Alice in Wonderland*: 'All have won and all shall have prizes'. The right approach, especially in tough times, is 'tough but achievable'. Everyone should strive to reach attainable targets.

9 Do not leave everything to the accountants

If the budgets and forecasts are left to the accountants, you will probably get an elegant set of documents, but they are likely to be much more useful if a range of managers have been involved. When times are tough, you need all the managers on board. Their input is likely to contribute to more realistic budgets and forecasts, and this is exactly what you want. Furthermore, they are more likely to feel a personal commitment to seeing that they are achieved. This too is exactly what you want.

10 Keep it simple

Most of the value of budgets and forecasts can be obtained from straightforward documents, so this is what you should produce and use. Circumstances alter cases and there may be times when much more is required, but you should probably resist being deluged with information that you neither want nor need.

Answers

Part 1: Finance for Non-Financial Managers

Chapter 1: 1b; 2a; 3d; 4a; 5b; 6c; 7b; 8d; 9c; 10a.

Chapter 2: 1c; 2b; 3d; 4a; 5c; 6a; 7c; 8b; 9d; 10a.

Chapter 3: 1c; 2d; 3a; 4a; 5c; 6b; 7b; 8a; 9d; 10a.

Chapter 4: 1c; 2c; 3b; 4c; 5d; 6b; 7a; 8b; 9b; 10d.

Chapter 5: 1a; 2b; 3d; 4c; 5d; 6c; 7d; 8a and d; 9a and c; 10c.

Chapter 6: 1b; 2b; 3d; 4a; 5c; 6a; 7b; 8c; 9a; 10b.

Chapter 7: 1c; 2d; 3a; 4d; 5d; 6c; 7a; 8d; 9d; 10d.

Part 2: Bookkeeping and Accounting

Chapter 8: 1a; 2c; 3d; 4b; 5c; 6c; 7c; 8b; 9c; 10a.

Chapter 9: 1b; 2c; 3b and c; 4a; 5b; 6d; 7a; 8a; 9d; 10d.

Chapter 10: 1b; 2a; 3b; 4d; 5d; 6c; 7b; 8a; 9c; 10d.

Chapter 11: 1b; 2b; 3a; 4c; 5c; 6d (this is because it is necessary to reduce the bad debt reserve account which has a credit balance); 7d; 8c; 9d; 10a.

Chapter 12: 1c; 2b; 3a; 4d; 5b; 6d; 7b; 8c; 9d; 10a.

Chapter 13: 1d; 2b; 3a; 4c; 5c; 6b; 7c; 8a; 9a; 10d.

Part 3: Understanding and Interpreting Accounts

Chapter 14: 1c; 2d; 3c; 4b; 5b; 6c; 7d; 8c; 9a; 10b.

Chapter 15: 1b; 2d; 3a; 4d; 5a; 6a; 7c; 8a; 9b; 10b.

Chapter 16: 1c; 2a; 3b; 4d; 5b; 6d; 7a; 8c; 9c; 10b.

Chapter 17: 1b; 2a; 3c; 4d; 5d; 6b; 7c; 8c.

Chapter 18: 1d; 2a; 3b; 4c; 5a; 6a; 7b; 8d; 9c; 10a.

Chapter 19: 1a; 2b; 3c; 4d; 5d; 6b; 7c; 8d; 9a; 10b.

Part 4: Successful Budgeting and Forecasting

Chapter 20: 1a; 2b; 3c; 4d; 5d; 6c; 7c; 8a; 9d; 10c.

Chapter 21: 1d; 2b; 3d; 4a; 5b; 6b; 7c; 8b; 9b; 10d.

Chapter 22: 1c; 2a; 3b; 4b; 5a; 6b; 7c; 8d; 9b; 10c.

Chapter 23: 1c; 2d; 3d; 4a; 5a; 6b; 7d; 8a; 9c; 10b.

Chapter 24: 1c; 2b; 3c; 4b; 5a; 6c; 7d; 8a; 9d; 10b.

Chapter 25: 1b; 2c; 3a; 4c; 5d; 6d; 7d; 8b; 9d; 10a.

Chapter 26: 1a; 2c; 3c; 4d; 5a; 6a; 7c; 8b; 9c; 10c.

Glossary

Absorption costing A costing system that involves all indirect costs being allocated to individual products or cost centres.

Account A section of the financial records listing transactions of the same type.

Accounts A set of documents summarizing the financial transactions during a period and the position at the end of the period.

Accruals Costs for which value has been received, but which have not yet been entered into the books of account.

Asset account An account recording a particular type of asset.

Asset Something owned that has a value (e.g. a motor vehicle and money in a bank account).

Audit An inspection and review of the financial transactions and accounts.

Bad Debt A debt that cannot be recovered and has to be written off.

Balance sheet A summary of assets and liabilities at a stated date. The total of each must be the same figure.

Book value The value of an asset as recorded in the accounts. It may or may not be the same as the actual value.

Books A set of accounts.

Break-even point The level of sales at which revenue equals the sum of fixed costs plus variable costs.

Capital account An account showing the amount invested in a business by its owners (e.g. share capital, revenue reserves).

Capital expenditure Expenditure on items of a capital nature, i.e. assets that will have a long-term value.

Capital The amount by which the assets exceed the liabilities. It is the 'net worth' of the organization.

Cash book A record of money paid out and received.

Consolidated accounts A set of accounts showing the overall position of a group of companies. Inter-group trading and debts are eliminated.

Contingencies Costs that may be incurred in the future, e.g. the cost of settling a pending legal action.

Cost of sales The cost of items sold (includes purchase price and manufacturing cost, but excludes overheads).

Creditor Person or business to whom money is owed (e.g. an unpaid supplier).

Current assets Cash and assets expected to be turned into cash in the short term, usually taken to be within a year (e.g. stock).

Current liabilities Liabilities payable in the short term, usually taken to be within a year.

Debtor A person or business owing money to the business (e.g. a customer who has not paid for goods supplied).

Depreciation The reduction in the value of a fixed asset over a period of time (e.g. due to wear and tear).

Dividend per share The total dividends for the year divided by the number of shares in issue.

Double-entry bookkeeping A method of bookkeeping in which each transaction is recorded twice, once as a debit and once as a credit.

Expenditure account An account listing expenditure of a profit and loss nature.

Expenditure Amount of money paid out.

Fixed assets Assets intended to be held for the long term, usually taken to be more than a year.

Fixed costs Costs that do not vary according to the volume of activity, e.g. business rates.

Gearing The ratio between finance provided by the banks and other borrowing and the finance invested by the shareholders.

Gross profit Profit after deducting direct costs of manufacture and purchase, but without deducting overheads.

Holding company A company that owns a total or major share in at least one subsidiary company.

Income account An account showing sales credited or other income over a period.

Income Total sales and other income credited over a period.

Insolvent A situation where liabilities are greater than assets.

Invoice A demand (more politely, a request) for payment for goods or services.

Journal A posting medium that is used for transactions not recorded in any of the other books of entry.

Ledger A book or loose-leaf collection of all the accounts in the system. It is frequently held in computerized form.

Liability account An account recording a particular type of liability.

Liability Money owing by the organization (e.g. a bank overdraft or money owing to a supplier).

Long-term liability A debt due for payment after a period of a year.

Market value The realizable value of an asset. It may or may not be the same as the book value.

Net profit Profit after deducting all costs including overheads. It is sometimes expressed as 'Net Profit Before Tax' and sometimes as 'Net Profit After Tax'.

Nominal ledger The principal ledger. Other ledgers are subsidiary to it.

Opening balance The first balance in an accounting period brought forward from the closing balance in the previous period.

Overheads The costs (other than direct costs such as the cost of goods sold) of running a business.

Payback The period of time in which savings caused by capital expenditure equal the amount of the capital expenditure. No account is taken of interest.

Petty cash A small cash float that can be drawn on for small items of expenditure.

Prepayments Costs entered into the books of account for which the value has not yet been received.

Price/earnings ratio The current price per share divided by earnings per share.

Profit and loss account A summary of the income and expenditure accounts, showing income and expenditure in a stated period, and hence the profit or loss.

Profit The amount remaining when all costs have been deducted from the total of all the income.

Provisions Reserves created to cover claims that may or will definitely be made against the organization in the future (e.g. warranty claims and potential legal disputes).

Reconciliation Identification of the reasons for differences between figures (e.g. bank reconciliation). It may lead to corrections being made.

Reserves A term virtually interchangeable with 'provisions' - money set aside to settle definite or possible claims. It can also mean a section of the capital accounts reflecting the net worth of the business (e.g. revenue reserve).

Revenue The total of accounts of an income nature.

Single-entry bookkeeping A method of bookkeeping in which each item is entered only once. It is inferior to double-entry bookkeeping.

Solvent A situation where assets are greater than liabilities.

Standard costs Pre-set standard costs from which actual costs are measured.

Stock shrinkage Reduction in stock caused by theft, evaporation, or similar causes.

Stock turn The number of times that total stock is used (turned over) in the course of a year.

Stock Goods for sale held by a business.

Suspense account An account in which accounting entries are temporarily placed, before they are allocated to the correct, permanent place.

Trial balance A listing of all the balances in a double-entry bookkeeping system. The total of the debits must equal the total of the credits.

Turnover Invoiced sales and other income in a stated period.

Variable costs Costs that vary according to the volume of activity, e.g. direct wages.

Working capital The amount by which current assets exceeds current liabilities.

Notes